# L. David Mech

# THE·WAY·OF·THE
# WOLF

(Photo by Tom Brakefield)

Foreword by Robert Bateman

**Photography by**
Tom Brakefield    Diane Boyd    Todd Fuller
Fred Harrington    Karen Hollett    Layne Kennedy
Rick McIntyre    L. David Mech    Thomas Meier    Mike Nelson
Jane Packard    Bill Paul    Rolf Peterson

Voyageur Press

# ACKNOWLEDGMENTS

I thank Dr. Steve Fritts, U.S. Fish and Wildlife Service, Helena, Montana, and Dr. Robert Ream, University of Montana, Missoula, for reading an early draft of this manuscript and making helpful suggestions for improving its contents. Ms. Elizabeth Knight lent her editorial hand to the text to improve its readability, and I am also grateful for that.

Interior designed by Leslie Dimond
Cover designed by Kristy Tucker
Edited by Elizabeth Knight

Printed in China
First hardcover edition: 93  94  95  96  97  8  7  6  5  4
First softcover edition: 04  05  9  8  7

Library of Congress Cataloging-in-Publication Data
Mech, L. David
      The way of the wolf / L. David Mech.
         p.   cm.
      Includes bibliographical references and index.
      ISBN 0-89658-163-2
      ISBN 0-89658-179-9 (pbk.)
      1. Wolves.  2. Wolves—Behavior.  I. Title.
   QL737.C22M3998    1991
   599.74'442–dc20                   91-14415
                                    CIP

Distributed in Canada by Raincoast Books, 9050 Shaughnessy Street, Vancouver, B.C. V6P 6E5

Published by Voyageur Press, Inc.
P.O. Box 338
123 North Second Street
Stillwater, MN 55082 U.S.A.
651-430-2210, fax 651-430-2211

*Educators, fundraisers, premium and gift buyers, publicists, and marketing managers:* Looking for creative products and new sales ideas? Voyageur Press books are available at special discounts when purchased in quantities, and special editions can be created to your specifications. For details contact the marketing department at 800-888-9653.

The author is a wildlife research biologist for the U.S. Fish and Wildlife Service. However, he wrote this book on his personal time from published data available to anyone as public domain.

## TO WALLACE DAYTON,
## Conservationist, Philanthropist, and
## Advocate of Wild Land Preservation

Winner of numerous conservation awards, Mr. Dayton has long championed the environment. Some of the important organizations he has helped govern and support are The Nature Conservancy, the North American Wildlife Foundation, the Greater Yellowstone Coalition, the Wilderness Society, the International Wolf Center, and the World Wildlife Fund.

Through his long chairmanship of the Special Projects Foundation of the Big Game Club, Wallace Dayton has helped finance numerous graduate students in their research on a variety of species, including several studies of wolves and their prey. As an early International Wolf Center supporter, member of the advisory committee, and donor, Mr. Dayton played a significant role in the development of the center.

It is a pleasure to dedicate this wolf book to a person who has encouraged and supported so many important aspects of wolf conservation and wolf recovery.

---

## THE INTERNATIONAL WOLF CENTER

Part of the royalties from this book will be donated to the International Wolf Center, 1396 Highway 169, Ely, Minnesota 55731. Membership in this organization entitles one to an authoritative magazine of wolf news, *International Wolf*.

# • CONTENTS •

*(Photo by Tom Brakefield)*

# ◆ FOREWORD ◆

Unquestionably the summers I spent in Ontario's Algonquin Park in Canada were the most crucial for the formation of the person I am. In those days when I was in my late teens, early twenties, Algonquin Park had an even stronger mystique than it does today with the ease of travel and boom of tourism. I worked as a chore boy at a wildlife research camp. In my spare time, I explored by canoe or on foot areas where I was sure few people had ever been. One evening, darkness overtook me as I was quietly paddling on a still lake. I took pride in the way I could handle my paddle—Indian-like, so that it was totally noiseless. Such stillness gives an immense pleasure in itself. Then, almost like a ripple slicing through a dark reflection, a low, long howl of a wolf sliced through the silence. My first wolf. Of course, the hairs stood up on the back of my neck, an automatic ancestral reaction. I had joined the ranks of primeval people who undoubtedly had been moved in the same way throughout the ages.

For thousands of years, humans have felt that wolves were special creatures. They were not to be ignored. They have always been competitors with us for the same prey species. They were always rivals and sometimes enemies, perhaps because they were close to us in so many ways. Wolf society is similar to human society, with qualities of intelligence, strategy, loyalty, gregariousness, and even education and culture. For most of human history, we and wolves were worthy opponents, roaming the countryside in family bands as nomadic predators. The greatest change to the planet was the agricultural revolution in Neolithic times. Plants and animals were domesticated, settlements appeared, and nature was controlled and exploited to support an expanding human population.

There is no room for wolves in areas tamed by people. During the twentieth century, the Neolithic ideals have been

*(Photo by L. David Mech)*

carried to extremes in mega-agriculture, mega-logging, mega-mining, and mega-energy projects. In the last decade of the twentieth century, the most serious question facing the planet is: How do we cease this mega-exploitation so that the rich biodiversity will be sustained for future centuries?

The wolf is a superb symbol of the complex and wild world of ancient times. It was at the top of the food chain in many different habitats, from barren tundra, through dense forests, to arid canyons and deserts. It was found all over the world, and it is now extinct in much of its former range. We now have also to ask ourselves: Is there room on the planet for large predators such as bears, big cats, and wolves? These animals have always competed with us, and they always will. They need plenty of space.

Our generation is playing God. We have the choice to preserve land for the wolf and even to reintroduce it to its former habitats—or we can relegate it to zoos and storybooks. The work that David Mech and others are doing keeps alive the noble hope that this great symbol of wilderness will continue to call across the silence of the natural world for centuries to come.
　　　　　　　　　　　　　　　　　—ROBERT BATEMAN

7

# · INTRODUCTION ·

Ha! So that's how they do it! With jubilation, I watched the alpha male wolf leave the rest of his pack around their den and start backtracking "Mom," the pups' mother, who recently had returned from feeding on a musk-ox. Almost thirty years after I began my career of wolf study, I was about to solve a long-burning mystery: How do wolves find a kill that other pack members have made?

To answer this and many other wolf questions that puzzled and prodded me over the decades, I had come a long way. To within a few hours' flight of the North Pole, to be exact. Elsewhere, it is almost impossible to watch wolves close up for any time because most wolves have been so harassed that they are shy and secretive. Here, however, far north of the tree line in Canada, I had found a pack of white arctic wolves that actually let me befriend them.

I began my wolf-watching career in 1959 from a ski plane over heavily forested Isle Royale National Park in Lake Superior. The wolves there, looking almost like ants on the ice, had streamed over the island, chasing and sometimes killing moose. I chronicled those interactions for my Ph.D. degree.

Then moving on to nearby Minnesota, I learned radio-tracking. For twenty years, that technique has helped me find and remotely spy on wolves and deer, over four hundred of each. Information about movements, population trends, home ranges, territories, dispersal, survival, mortality, wolf-deer interactions, reproduction, scent marking, howling, food-consumption rates, and many other aspects of wolf and deer biology poured in.

Early 1985 brought an assignment in Denali National Park, Alaska, examining wolf numbers, pack spacing, productivity and survival, and predation on caribou, moose, and Dall sheep. That study, along with the Minnesota project, still occupies most of my time.

*Wolf confronts grizzly bear. While wolves and bears usually try to avoid each other, they sometimes do run into each other. Members of each species have been known to kill members of the other, and contests over prey kills are probably the most frequent occasions for their interaction. (Photo by Rick McIntyre)*

9

Meanwhile, a colony of captive wolves helped me supplement my information from the wild. For over ten years, the colony yielded valuable data linking the internal workings, or physiology, of wolves with their behavior. Briefer forays to help other biologists start projects in Italy, Portugal, Manitoba in Canada, and Alaska in the United States broadened my experience with my favorite animal.

The crown jewel of my wolf experience, however, was the discovery of this high arctic wolf pack. Discussed in detail in my 1988 book *The Arctic Wolf: Living with the Pack*, these wolves were to me the wonders of the wolf world. In all my other studies of wild wolves, I had to watch from afar, usually from a circling airplane. Little detail was available about the personalities and social interactions of pack members. Some of this type of information was gleaned from the captive wolves, but how typical was that of the wolves outside the fences?

Only the high arctic pack could tell me. Not only did those animals let me live within a few feet of them for weeks on end, but I could actually interact with them. This let me run various experiments to further my knowledge about wolves.

Now I was in the middle of one such test. A few hours earlier, about a mile and a half from the den a fresh musk-ox carcass had lain undiscovered by the wolves. I knew that if any pack member found the carcass, the animal would gorge and return to the den. By sniffing that wolf, the others would learn of the find. But how would the other pack members locate the carcass? Would they wait until the wolf returned and follow? Would they scout around and try to find the musk-ox themselves? Would they beg from their packmate so much that it would lead them to the bonanza?

To learn the answer, I had taken three of the wolves to the carcass. That's right. On my three-wheeled all-terrain vehicle, which I used to cover long distances over the barren terrain, I headed towards the carcass. By tossing the wolves tidbits now and then, I got them to follow. Within about two hundred yards of the carcass, Mom either smelled it or spotted it and broke out ahead of me. She approached the shaggy mass cautiously at first, but soon began tearing into it and feeding. After about twenty minutes, I headed back to the den so that I could observe Mom's behavior upon her return.

An hour and a half after she had started feasting, Mom burst over a hill towards the den, weaving from side to side and wagging her tail excitedly. As usual, this triggered a massive mobbing by pups and adults alike. Mom regurgitated, and the pups gobbled up the chunks of meat instantly—the standard feeding technique of these creatures.

Taking special note, however, was the "alpha" male (re-

*Black wolves are found primarily in the area between the northern contiguous United States and the Arctic Circle. This color is common throughout most of Alaska and southern Canada, and some packs consist entirely of blacks. (Photo by Tom Brakefield)*

ferred to as "alpha" because he was the "first" or top-ranking male in the pack). Several times he looked intently towards the direction from where Mom had just come. After some forty-five minutes of nosing the pups, tail wagging, playing, chasing, and general socializing, the alpha male got down to business. He headed up the track that Mom had made from the musk-ox to the den. Sniffing both the ground and the air, the great white male half ran towards the carcass. He did not follow the erratic route I had used. Instead he headed directly towards the musk-ox. No doubt he was backtracking Mom. When within a quarter mile of the carcass, he homed in directly by scenting the air. My question was answered. Here was one more little piece in the wolf puzzle, a fascinating but incomplete montage, an image we call *The Way of the Wolf.*

# ◆ THE WOLF ITSELF ◆

How would you like to have a wolf in your home? Chances are you already do. The civilized model comes as a dog. But delve deep into any dog's genes, and you will find a wolf.

This is not merely word play. The dog is, in every way, really a domesticated wolf. Just as dog breeds (over a hundred of them), as different as Chihuahuas and Saint Bernards, still are all dogs, so too are they all wolves. The wolf is merely the original version of the dog.

So what is this prototype like? In many respects you already know. Basic wolf nature is basic dog nature. However, because we force dogs to adjust to our own lifestyle, we only see the side of the wolf we allow or shape. One proud dog owner objected to this revelation that dog behavior is "humanized" wolf behavior by pointing out what she felt was an essential, and in her eyes "natural," difference between the two canines: "But wolves only eat every few days, whereas my dog eats three times a day."

"That's exactly my point," I replied. "Who feeds your dog? Who feeds the wolf? Both animals have the same digestive system specialized to use meat and fat. Both can gorge, and both can fast. Or, both can eat several times a day."

To uncivilize your "wolf," imagine taking away his regular food allotment and leaving him outside alone in the woods. Imagine your neighbors doing the same thing with their pet female. The two meet and team up. Imagine further ending all contact with this pair, and letting them travel, hunt, feed, rest, socialize, and breed without human intervention, and for generations.

This will give you some idea of what a wolf is like. But not entirely. Wolves are not just wild dogs. Rather, dogs are domesticated wolves. Wolf behavior has been shaped and molded to make an animal that is more tractable and trainable and easier for humans to live with—to make the dog. In this

*The wolf is the original dog. Although domesticated dogs come in over one hundred varieties, they all stem back to the wolf. Current thinking, based on the most up-to-date genetic work, indicates that domestication of the dog from the wolf probably took place several times. (Photo by Tom Brakefield)*

13

respect, the dog is essentially a juvenile wolf, dependent on and dominated by its owners who play the role of parents and older packmates. Nevertheless, the basics of behavior are the same for both animals.

The wild version of the wolf still lives today, even in some of the lower forty-eight states, although it is rare enough in these parts of the United States to make the federal list of endangered species. However, even if you ventured to where wild wolves live, you would not see them. The same ears, nose, and eyes that tell your own pet when someone outside is approaching alert the wild wolf to the danger of an intruder. The wolf disappears. Historically, humans have favored only the domesticated variety of wolf, so the wild wolf has responded accordingly by living as secretively and cautiously as possible. Those that did not were eliminated.

So picture the pristine wolf, shy and elusive, living only in its wilderness environment. No warm fireplace to lie down by, so its coat is long and bushy. No mushy gruel or hardened cereal blocks to be delivered by human hands, so its rarer meals of flesh and bones and hide all have to be earned, usually hard earned.

And at least partly because it is easier to hunt with help, the wolf has packmates. Together they can catch and kill larger animals to make their lives more efficient. To live together as a group, wolves have a social nature; they get along well and form strong attachments to other members of their pack. Dogs would do the same if we didn't give their puppies away and force the adults and the young alike to become members of a different pack—our human pack.

The wolf is the original dog and most resembles such races of dog as the Eskimo sled dog, husky, malamute, or German shepherd. Still, the wolf differs from them in build by being narrower, leaner, and more streamlined. And in the north of its range throughout the world, the wolf usually grows larger, and has bushy, fuzzier fur and larger feet.

Most wolves are a mottled gray, with tawny legs and flanks. However, in the far north wolves are a creamy white, sometimes with a light gray mane. In parts of Canada, Alaska, and the northern forty-eight states, some are pure black. Farther south, almost all wolves are tawny gray. In the Superior National Forest of Minnesota, however, I once saw a pack with three gray wolves, one black, and one white.

Scientists have long recognized two main types, or species, of wolves, the gray wolf (*Canis lupus*) and the red wolf (*Canis rufus*). Gray wolves originally lived throughout the northern hemisphere above about 20 degrees north latitude, which runs approximately through Mexico City and southern India. The only exception was the southeastern United

14

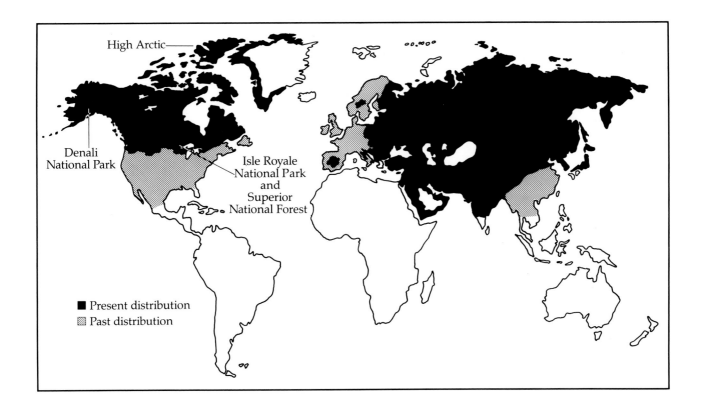

High Arctic

Denali
National Park

Isle Royale
National Park
and
Superior
National Forest

■ Present distribution
▨ Past distribution

*Past and present wolf distribution world-wide. Originally, the wolf was the most widely distributed of any wild mammal. However, as technological humans have occupied more and more of the earth, they have tended to destroy both the animal and its habitat, greatly reducing its range.*

States, where the red wolf lived. However, whether the red wolf is really distinct from the gray wolf, or whether it is really a large coyote, or a hybrid between wolves and coyotes, are still subjects of debate among biologists.

In North America, gray wolves have several common names depending on just where they live. For example, in the eastern forested areas of North America they are known as "timber wolves," in the High Arctic as "arctic wolves," on the tundra, as "tundra wolves," and in the southwestern United States and Mexico as "lobos," the Spanish name for wolf. To add to the confusion of names all designating the gray wolf is one other name that refers not to the gray, but to the wolf's smaller cousin, the coyote, which is called the "brush wolf" in many areas.

Like most other animals, gray wolves vary slightly across regions. Differences appear in size, color, and in minor skull measurements. Scientists interested in these minor geographic variations recognize different wolf races or subspecies.

However, because wolves vary in these characteristics even within one region, scientists disagree on how many races of wolves there are. In North America, for example, twenty-four subspecies were originally recognized. But individual wolves are very wide travelers, and often they cut across the arbitrary lines that the old-time scientists drew around the ranges of subspecies. Wolf biologist Dr. Steve

*Symbol of the wilderness, the wolf inhabits mostly wild and inaccessible areas. Although it can live any place where there are large prey animals it can eat, centuries of persecution by humans have exterminated wolves from all but the most remote areas. The only visible population remaining in the forty-eight contiguous states resides in northern Minnesota, so the wolf is on the U.S. endangered species list except in Alaska. Wisconsin, Michigan, Montana, Idaho, and Washington support fewer than one hundred wolves in total. (Above: Photo by Rick McIntyre. Right: Photo by Tom Brakefield)*

Fritts found one wolf that dispersed from Minnesota to Saskatchewan, passing through the supposed ranges of three subspecies. This type of information and others support a more modern view that there may be only five valid subspecies of wolves in North America.

In reality, one race of wolf is pretty much the same as any other. The behavior and natural history are similar among the various races and between North American and Eurasian wolves. In fact, any real differences seem to be more related to the precise living conditions such as food type, climate, and geographic area. Physically, too, the races are similar. Only a real expert measuring many skulls can distinguish among most races. Subspecific names, like MacKenzie Valley wolf, northern Rocky Mountain wolf, Great Plains wolf, or eastern timber wolf, are more descriptors of where a given wolf comes from than of any real differences among the animals.

Wolves do differ from coyotes, although the two can interbreed. Coyotes generally are a quarter to a half the size of wolves, and they have more sharply pointed noses, as well as proportionately larger, outward-pointing ears and smaller feet. Coyotes generally live on smaller prey such as rabbits and hares, and inhabit smaller territories, reach higher densities, breed earlier, and live in smaller groups than wolves. Usually young coyotes disperse from their parents during their first autumn, whereas wolves tend to stay longer. Thus, in winter coyotes generally travel alone or in pairs, while wolves tend to travel in packs. Nevertheless, where coyotes feed mostly on larger prey, they also live in packs. Conversely, where wolves feed mostly on garbage and smaller animals, their young tend to disperse early.

Wolves vary in size in different areas of the world. The smallest live in the southern part of the wolf's range, especially in the Middle East; there they may weigh only thirty pounds. The largest wolves inhabit midlatitude Canada, Alaska, and the Soviet Union, where they occasionally reach 175 pounds. One report that has some documentation involves a wolf from the Yukon area that supposedly weighed an unconfirmed 227 pounds! Males are usually about 20 percent larger than females.

Whatever their adult size, wolves can achieve it within their first one to two years of life. In fact, many of them reach almost adult weight by their first autumn. A medium-sized wolf, which would weigh about sixty pounds, stand thirty inches high at the shoulder, and stretch six and a half feet long, produces pups that weigh about a pound at birth. By fourteen weeks of age, the pups have gained an average of three pounds each week. From fourteen to twenty-seven weeks, they gain about 1.3 pounds per week. Finally, they reach full stature by six to twelve months.

*Large and living mostly in packs, the wolf must rely on trying to kill prey that are larger than itself: moose, bison, elk, caribou, deer, sheep, goats, and musk-oxen. Most of the prey animals present formidable defenses. (Photo by L. David Mech)*

*The red wolf of the southeastern United States has long been an enigma to wolf biologists. Intermediate in size and appearance between a wolf and a coyote, the animal has been considered a separate species (Canis rufus). Just as its appearance suggests, recent genetic studies also suggest that the creature may actually be a wolf-coyote hybrid. Whatever the case, the animal is almost extinct in the wild except for a small population recently reintroduced by the U.S. Fish and Wildlife Service into northeastern North Carolina. (Photo by Tom Brakefield)*

## ARE WOLVES DANGEROUS TO PEOPLE?

What do you think? Was Little Red Riding Hood really in danger? What about campers in national parks and national forests that contain wolves? The short answer is, NO! For example, the Superior National Forest of Minnesota has always harbored two hundred to four hundred wolves. Some nineteen million visitor-days have been logged in there, and not a single soul has turned up missing due to wolf predation.

There are several documented cases of wolves in other areas of North America possibly attacking people. One involved a scientist trying to break up a fight between a wolf and his sled dogs; the man ended up with a torn arm when he tried to grab the wolf by the back of the neck. In Minnesota, a wolf apparently mistook a deer-scent-soaked hunter for a deer and knocked him over. When the wolf realized its mistake, it fled. And a few other similar instances exist.

What about Eurasia? Tales of wolves attacking people still emanate from the Middle East, China, India, and the Soviet Union. Whether or not these reports prove true is not clear because often when traced, such stories fall apart. So far, no carefully checked, well-documented, recent records have been published that shed light on the question. With such uncertainty, we must keep an open mind about the issue in that region.

I have no doubt that, if a single wolf—let alone a pack—wanted to kill someone, it could do so without trouble. When I have watched wolves close-up killing prey, they were swift and silent. A few good bites, and a human would be dead. The fact remains, however, that there is no record of an unprovoked, non-rabid wolf in North America seriously injuring a person.

*Most wolves are gray, hence the name "gray wolf" for the species. However, especially in Canada and Alaska, black wolves are common, and in the highest latitude, generally on the high arctic islands of Canada and in Greenland wolves are white. Some of the white arctic wolves have grayish hues on their back. Blacks and grays can occur in the same litter, and the author once observed a Minnesota pack containing grays, blacks, and a very light, whitish wolf. In other cases, some gray wolves tend to turn light as they get older. The genetic aspects of coat color in wolves are completely unknown, but the appearance of occasional "chocolate," silver-black, and other intermediate-colored individuals suggests that matings of different colored wolves sometimes result in blends. (Photo by Tom Brakefield)*

Wolves cannot grow further after about one year. They may gain weight after that time, but their basic size stays the same. A ten- to twelve-month-old captive pup whose food my colleagues and I rationed remained forever smaller and lighter weight than its littermate that we let eat all it wanted.

Presumably a wolf pup's fast growth is related to the need for pups to travel with the adults by fall. Since the wolf is a northern species, it must contend with snow for much of the year. If the pups were not adult size by snowfall, they would struggle hard to keep up with their parents during the pack's travels. In some areas of northern Canada and Alaska, where the wolf's main prey is caribou, the pups must follow their migrating food supply as far as three hundred miles to its winter range.

Each wolf has a distinct personality, just as dogs do. People who have raised wolves in captivity, including me, have noticed this. Some are shy, some outgoing, others aloof, others puzzling. One male I raised in a pen for observation would wag its tail, assume a relaxed face, and act very friendly to its keepers and various visitors until they walked up to the cage and greeted it. At that point, if anyone got too close to the chainlink fence, the wolf would suddenly grab the person right through the wire. It's hard to explain this behavior.

In the High Arctic where I spent five summers living with the pack of arctic wolves near their den, I got to know each wolf personally. "Mom" was shy, timid, and jumpy, frequently looking up above her. The only airborne intrusion came from long-tailed jaegers, pigeon-sized birds with long wings and pointed tail. Jaegers regularly dive-bombed the wolves to keep them from harassing their nests. This shy wolf seemed to react more extremely to these assaults than did any other of the pack members.

On the other hand, "Mid-Back," a female colleague of this wolf, was confident and bold and not easily upset. Presumably a variety of personalities is useful within a group, for it would tend to reduce competition among individuals. In addition, each personality might just help each member secure food in a different way. For example, a more timid wolf might spend its time catching hares, lemmings, and young birds, rather than musk-oxen.

One very important factor that shapes wolf personality is the individual's position in the pack's social ladder, which will be discussed in detail later. Suffice it to say now that when top-ranking or alpha, a wolf is confident, self-assured, outgoing, and initiating. When bottom-ranking, it is just the opposite. When a top-ranking animal is deposed, it loses the personality that accompanies being dominant. When a subor-

*The coyote is often referred to as the "little brother of the wolf." Only one-third to one-half the size of the wolf, the coyote generally feeds on much smaller prey such as rabbits, hares, mice, squirrels, and birds, and also eats a variety of fruits and vegetable matter. Generally coyotes tend to live in pairs, and their offspring usually disperse their first autumn rather than remaining with the pack for one to four years as wolf young do. Nevertheless, coyotes look like small wolves, are referred to in some areas as "brush wolves," and can interbreed with wolves, although this rarely happens in the wild. (Photo by Tom Brakefield)*

*Male and female wolves differ primarily in size, with males generally weighing 20 percent more than females. Actual weights of wolves vary considerably over the animal's entire geographic range. Wolves in the Middle East, for example, may weigh as little as 30 pounds, whereas those from Canada and Alaska often weigh from 100 to 135 pounds. In midlatitudes, adult females tend to weigh about 55 to 65 pounds and adult males, 75 to 95 pounds. (Photo by L. David Mech)*

*Overleaf: Whether making its way on bare ground, through vegetation, or over ice and snow, the wolf is well adapted to pursue its prey. (Photo by Tom Brakefield)*

23

dinate animal becomes dominant, it gains that personality.

Wolves possess keen senses and excellent learning ability—both to be expected from a hunter. Under some conditions, wolves can hear as far as six miles away in the forest and ten miles away on the open tundra. I've watched them seem to smell a moose a mile and a quarter away, and they appear to see at least as well as humans. Dogs, too, possess keen senses, but in their domesticated lives, they rarely depend on their senses the way wolves must.

Wolves show a great breadth of learning ability, even greater than that of dogs. We teach our companions to do tricks for food or to come when called. They are more easily trained than wolves, showing a type of behavior based on associative learning. But wolves reveal themselves capable of more types of learning, such as problem solving, and are particularly adept at learning by observing. Dr. Harry Frank of Michigan State University kept both wolves and dogs as house pets and tested them on various learning skills. He found that the wolves caught on quite quickly about how to open a door by turning the knob merely by watching a human do so, whereas his dogs never learned.

Certainly, wolves also seem to be very good at insightful behavior, that is, behavior implying that the wolf might actually understand certain relationships. Once a wolf has learned how to escape from a pen, for example, it is almost impossible to keep the animal in. One such escape artist I knew learned to raise a drop door in its pen by jumping to the top of the eight-foot-high pen, and grabbing with its teeth the door cable on the outside of the pen, which was exposed to the inside through a three-inch gap. By jumping up and grabbing the cable, the wolf could lift the door at the bottom of the cage. After the wolf raised the door many times, it stuck in the "up" position, and the wolf ran out!

*The leaders of a wolf pack are the alpha male and alpha female, often distinguishable by their raised tails. Being parents of most of the other pack members, the alpha pair holds the allegiance of the rest of the pack. They maintain this allegiance by continually asserting themselves over their offspring from birth through maturation. For example, on small kills, yearlings and other subordinate pack members can only feed by deferring to the alpha pair and often by begging from them. Alpha animals are usually mature adults, and they sometimes can hold their alpha position for as long as eight years. Wolves can live up to sixteen years in captivity and up to at least thirteen years in the wild. Probably most wild wolves die before they reach five years of age, however. (Photo by Rolf Peterson)*

26

# • THE PACK •

*When a pack makes a kill, the alpha members, being the most experienced, lead the attack and are the most aggressive. Subordinate members, usually being younger and less experienced, follow the lead of the alphas and imitate, learning the attack process for themselves. For example, here the alphas have gripped the musk-ox calf by the nose and ear, and the subordinates have grabbed the head as close to the alphas as they could. From the standpoint of good hunting strategy, it would seem to make more sense for some members to bite the rump and flanks, bringing down the animal quickly. In some cases that actually happens, presumably when subordinates gain more experience. (Photo by L. David Mech)*

The wolf pack is basically a family, composed of a mated pair and their offspring. Although there are some exceptions, such as a mated pair plus a close relative, such assemblages are rare and usually temporary. The pack lives, hunts, and raises its young in a territory, an area it will defend against other packs or individual wolves.

The typical pack begins when two lone wolves of opposite sex meet, court, and pair-bond. I have seen two variations on this theme. In most areas, single wolves disperse from a pack, find the same vacant territory to settle in, and meet. However, in northwestern Minnesota, some singles would locate mates first and travel together until they found a vacant spot. After the wolves mate, their litters of pups each year add to the pack. Although some young may die or disperse in their first two years, others may stay with the pair for up to four years.

Since litters average five to six pups, a wolf pack can reach a size of six to nine within a year. Larger packs, such as those in northern Canada and Alaska, may number into the twenties. Large packs result when older offspring fail to disperse. Indications are that this takes place when food is abundant.

At such times of abundance, and contrary to the usual birth of a single litter by the top-ranking female, a second female in the pack may produce pups and raise them along with the alpha pair's pups. Presumably, this extra female is a daughter of the alpha female. Whether she is bred by her father, by a brother, or by an unrelated male that the pack takes in is still unknown, but in any case, her young add to the burgeoning of a large pack.

Wolf packs generally are largest in late fall. By this time, the pups have become almost adult size and can travel widely. As the adults go hunting, the pups follow along. These novices begin to learn their territory, where to find

*Ears erect, eyes ahead, the running wolf focuses its attention on its quarry. (Photo by Tom Brakefield)*

*In large packs of wolves, there is often a lowest-ranking member who becomes the focus of the pack's social aggression. Referred to by behaviorists as the "omega" wolf, this animal seems to be a scapegoat and may actually become an outright outcast. In this scene from Isle Royale, the alpha male punishes a subordinate while the rest of the pack watches. This may be part of the process by which pack members disperse and become independent, rather than remain to live at the bottom of the pecking order or on the fringes of the pack. (Photo by Rolf Peterson)*

*Overleaf: A dominance order is a very important part of the wolf's social system. The adults dominate the pups, and as young wolves begin to mature, the alpha male dominates the males, and the alpha female the females. In this way, the pack leaders control breeding rights and food distribution amongst the pack members. Here, a high-ranking wolf dominates a subordinate. Such dominance displays become a regular part of wolf interactions, and their incidence peaks as breeding season approaches. However, even when pups are only a few weeks old, the adults dominate them regularly. Although most dominance interactions are among individuals of the same sex, the alpha male dominates the alpha female, which is necessary for the pair to copulate. (Photo by Layne Kennedy)*

prey, and how to hunt. Over winter, some wolves may die and others leave, causing the pack size to diminish. By mid-spring, the pack is at its lowest annual size. When the new pups are born, the cycle repeats itself, and the social group enlarges.

Two reasons perhaps account for large packs: Many members help make it easier to catch and kill prey, or many members help make more efficient use of large and/or abundant prey. Possibly, big packs form for both reasons. Although a single wolf can actually kill even an adult moose, the wolf's largest prey, no doubt it is easier for several wolves to do so. Nevertheless, beyond five or six, extra wolves apparently add little advantage to the hunt. On the other hand, a large pack would consume the prey quickly, and make the best of each kill by leaving little for scavengers to usurp.

Basically, wolf packs are smaller where their prey is smaller and largest where their prey is largest. Minnesota wolves, which prey primarily on deer, generally live in packs of about five to ten (although sometimes up to seventeen). Denali National Park wolves in Alaska, which prey considerably on moose, number from ten to twenty and sometimes up to twenty-nine. However, the largest of these Alaskan packs tend to concentrate on Dall sheep, which are as small as deer, and this exception suggests that the last word on factors determining pack size is still not in.

The wolf pack functions as a unit. The glue that holds the pack together is social bonds, bonds similar to the ties of affection that hold human families together. The alpha male and the alpha female bond as mates, and their young remain with the group through parent-offspring bonding. Furthermore, bonds between siblings probably also play a role in creating a strong, cohesive family group. These bonds form and strengthen as the littermates constantly interact with each other from their earliest days: the pups sleep and feed together, follow each other around, and regularly wrestle with each other. As they mature, they help care for the next litter of pups just as though they were parents.

Order is maintained in the pack through a dominance hierarchy or social ladder. This is the wolf's version of the well-known "pecking order," in which top-ranking animals or alphas dominate all the others. Middle-ranking animals are dominated by the alphas, but they in turn dominate the lowest-ranking ones. In larger packs, there are even "scapegoat" wolves. These "omegas" (meaning "last," from the Greek) are picked on by all the other members and eventually may become so harassed that they leave the pack.

A wolf's position on the pack social ladder is strongly related to its age. The oldest animals are usually the alphas,

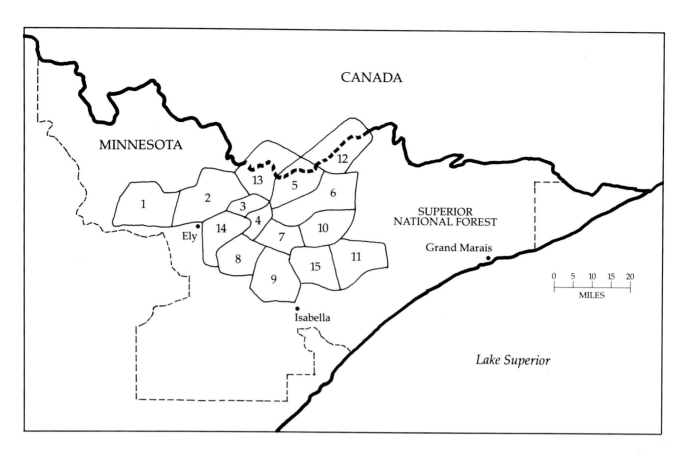

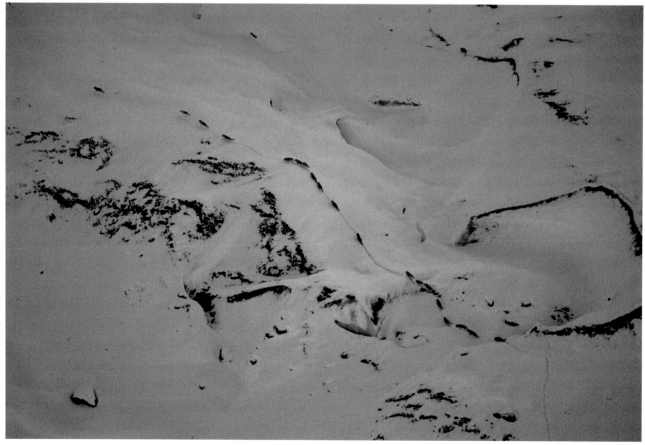

Wolf packs live in territories of from thirty to over one thousand square miles each, which are defended against neighboring packs and most strange wolves wandering through the area. Territories interconnect much like cells in a beehive. However, the thin strip around the edge of each overlaps with that of the neighboring territory in a buffer zone, in which either pack is dominant. Most wolf killings of other wolves occur close to the edges of the adjacent territories. Here, wolf pack territories are delineated by aerial radio-tracking of members of fifteen contiguous packs in the Superior National Forest. Packs live outside the delineated area as well, but were not studied intensively enough for the territories to be described.

Wolf packs vary in size up to about thirty members. However most packs are much smaller, consisting primarily of the alpha pair, their last litter of pups, and offspring of a few previous litters, for a total of six to ten members. The largest packs usually contain offspring from more than one female. (Photo by Thomas Meier)

their oldest offspring fall next in line, and the yearlings and pups fall below them. An exception would be an old former breeder who stays with the pack as a subordinate member.

Younger pack members are continually subjected to the dominance of the adults. This feature of wolf pack life helps keep order in the group and insures that the alpha pair retains its privileges. At kills, for example, they get to eat the best parts and the largest quantities. If food is short, the alphas get it, although they still share it with the pups. Both a male and a female dominance hierarchy operate in a wolf pack, and during mating season, each alpha tries to prevent its same-sex offspring from breeding. This system insures the breeding rights of the higher-ranking wolves.

To maintain dominance over other pack members, the alphas begin asserting themselves over pups when the pups are very young. I have watched adults pounce on tiny pups continually and bowl them over when the pups took too much initiative. Even the older brothers and sisters dominate the pups.

This dominance hierarchy explains much of the social behavior seen when watching wolves. When a dominant wolf approaches a subordinate, the dominant raises its tail, ears, and mane, and may bare its teeth and growl. In a physical and psychological sense, it enlarges itself. Meanwhile the subordinate diminishes itself, lowering its tail, body, and ears, and whining. It may lie down or roll over in submission, or may paw at the dominant animal solicitously.

Watch your pet dog. It dominates or submits to other dogs in the same way wolves do. Because you are an alpha member of your dog's pack, your dog submits to you. If it doesn't, you are in trouble!

Who is the actual leader of the pack? That is still an unanswered question, probably because the concept of leadership is a human one. We tend to think in terms of the leader of an organization or a government. However, in a wolf pack, both alpha animals hunt, both care for the pups, and both dominate the offspring. The alphas get to feed on the kill together, even when they exclude subordinates. Both fight intruding strange wolves, presumably those of their own sex.

So what other test of leadership can be used? Perhaps we can say that the alpha male is the leader because he dominates the alpha female. He also provides food for her when she is caring for the pups. On the other hand, the alpha female might be called the leader because she often seems to be able to grab food away from the alpha male and tends to dominate activities around the pups, especially when they are very young. For example, she is the one that moves the pups in case of danger.

Preliminary information reveals that the alpha male

usually heads the pack and chooses the route when traveling, but the female is close to him in line. Before and during breeding season, the female often travels out ahead, with the male just behind her. Perhaps with more close-up wolf watching under various circumstances, we eventually will be able to say for sure whether the pack leader is the male or the female, or whether leadership is by both.

For much of each year—most of fall, winter, and early spring—the members of the wolf pack travel together nomadically over their territory to hunt and to hold these lands. In midspring, the birth of pups suddenly changes the basic social mode of the pack: The pups become the center of social activities. For a wolf to get in on the pack activities in winter, it must travel with the other members. In summer, however, a wolf's social life revolves around the den. By merely remaining at the den, a wolf is guaranteed of interacting with the pups and with its packmates. Generally, all the adults return to the den at least every day or two. If a pack fails to produce pups some year, then the pack members tend to travel together year-round.

Furthermore, during summer wolves often hunt alone rather than as a pack. This is probably for two reasons. First, they can always find packmates and socialize merely by returning to the den. Second, there is a new crop of small, easier-to-catch prey throughout summer, and it is more efficient for each wolf to hunt a separate area. That way the pack covers much more ground than when traveling together. In the High Arctic, the four adult members of the pack I watched in the summer of 1988 left the den to forage individually about 80 percent of the time.

A wolf pack is basically a family that stays together while the offspring learn to function well enough to live on their own. In that respect, it can be viewed as a finishing school for young wolves. Remaining in the pack furthers the survival of the young and helps insure that their own genes have the greatest chance of persisting in the population.

The mother and father wolves, the alpha pair who dominate the pack, guide almost all of the family's activities: where to go, when to hunt, which prey to attack, and when to call off the chase. The rest of the pack are usually all younger offspring of the alpha pair. As such, they are less experienced and less self-assured. They are apprentices, learning hunting by imitating the alpha pair and older offspring. I once saw an alpha male and an older female grab a musk-ox calf by the ear and nose. The younger wolves immediately followed and grabbed the stricken calf as close to these points as they could, stacking right up against their parents.

Even when doing something as simple and essential to

*A wolf pup begs food from a subordinate pack member. Subordinate wolves are usually young animals, but occasionally are former alphas who have lost their positions. If they remain with the pack, subordinates play a strong and important role in helping care for and feed the pups. An unknowing observer watching subordinates around a den would be unable to distinguish their behavior from that of the actual parents. At times, the nurturing by these subordinate "helpers" may even allow more of the pups to survive. (Photo by L. David Mech)*

*Long and muscular, the wolf's legs carry the animal mile after mile, whether it's pursuing prey or merely accompanying its packmates. Wolves often travel ten to twenty miles in a day, loping from one area to the next, chasing prey, and then heading on once again. (Photo by Tom Brakefield)*

*When in pursuit of a playful packmate, the wolf may exercise its legs almost as much as when after prey. With mighty bursts, the animals chase one another as if in deadly earnest. (Photo by Tom Brakefield)*

being wolves as traveling, these animals show the organization and cohesiveness that make them a pack. Members generally trot along single file, with the parents or alpha wolves ahead and the offspring strung out behind. During winter this is an obviously effective way to travel, for the stronger adults break trail through the snow, and the younger and weaker members merely follow in their footsteps. However, even when wolves travel together in summer, they usually stay in single file, alphas in the lead.

Of course, younger pack members do not always follow the pack. Especially in summer when the new pups are the pack's focal point, the yearlings and two-year-olds may wander off by themselves. Like teenagers, they practice independence. They even start to earn part of their own living, hunting smaller prey such as hares. Nevertheless, they return regularly to the den area and often bring their catch home to the new pups.

The apprenticeship of young wolves even carries over into their care of the new pups around the den. An observer not knowing the identity of pack members would be unable to tell which were the parents. The yearlings and two-year-olds (and any older offspring left) feed, play with, and tend the pups as much as do the parents. In fact, most of the adult members seem to compete to care for the pups.

Because younger pack members deliver food to the den area, they, as well as the alpha male, feed the alpha female. She remains with the newborn pups for most of their first three weeks to keep them warm and nurse them. When a wolf arrives with food, the alpha female either grabs part of it or begs it away. The help that other pack members provide can be crucial to the alpha female and pups during this sensitive period.

Wolf packs can show variations in the organization and the composition that human observers have come to expect as typical. For example, occasionally a pack may accept an outside member. Usually, the only time this happens is when one of the alphas is killed, and the remaining alpha accepts a new mate. But there are exceptions to this pattern. In the few such cases recorded, the ultimate origins of the newcomers were unknown: They could have been pack dispersers that returned, or they could have been totally unknown individuals.

In Denali National Park, however, my assistants observed a pack of wolves accepting a lone male that had been born to a pack two territories away. Neither alpha animal that accepted him could have been a relative with whom this wolf was acquainted, for we knew their histories. This lone male was not renewing a social and familial bond, and I still do not

understand why the pack accepted him.

In another instance, a radio-collared female my colleagues and I studied in Minnesota left her pack and joined a neighboring pack, remaining with it for at least two years. Perhaps such individuals end up becoming mates of subordinate pack members. If so, this could also explain how pack splitting takes place.

In Minnesota's Superior National Forest, the Malberg Lake pack that I studied from 1978 to 1985 split one spring. Four members including a radioed male moved adjacent to the pack's former territory in spring 1984 and lived there through at least 1986. The remaining six members apparently remained in the old territory.

One of the strangest deviations from the usual pack organization I have ever seen involved the high arctic pack in 1989. The alpha male, a two-year-old male, and four yearlings traveled together, rarely visiting the den or associating with the nursing female for at least several weeks. What is more, another adult female, very probably a two-year-old animal seen in previous years, socially dominated the nursing female and raised her leg while urinating, a definite sign of top status. In two weeks of observing the den, my assistants and I never saw the alpha male there. During four other years of observations, the alpha male usually frequented the den daily and was never recorded away for more than fifty-eight hours.

Clearly, there is much more to learn about the details of wolf pack life and social structure.

*Just as quickly as they start a chase, wolves can suddenly stop and use their legs as brakes to change direction, feint, or prepare for another long dash. (Photo by Tom Brakefield)*

41

## WOLF MALADIES

As might be expected, wolves are subject to the same diseases, parasites, and other pathologies that affect dogs. The life of the wolf in the wild, however, makes these maladies more hazardous for the animal. Coupled with starvation or wounds from prey animals, for example, worms, lice, or disease may be enough to overwhelm a wolf and cause its death.

Of special consequence are new diseases affecting the wolf. In the United States these include canine parvovirus, Lyme disease, and heartworm (*Dirofilaria immitis*).

Parvovirus was first discovered in dogs about 1977 and quickly spread to wild canid populations. "Parvo" is fatal to both dog pups and wolf pups. It is common in wolves that live anywhere near dogs from whom it spreads, but its effect on wolf populations remains unknown. Preliminary information indicates that large wolf populations may build up resistance to the disease. Nevertheless, small, disjunct populations may be more seriously affected.

Lyme disease, a human disease carried by certain ticks, also infects dogs and wolves and potentially could be devastating. However, work on its effects in dogs and wolves is still in its infancy.

Heartworm is a disease of the South that has recently found its way northward. It was probably spread through southern dogs participating in field trials held in the North. Dogs and wolves serve as the reservoir for the worm, which sheds tiny microfilariae into the blood stream. Mosquitoes carry the microfilariae from infected animals to healthy ones, and these microscopic worms then lodge in the heart or larger blood vessels and become adults. Several adults can reduce blood flow to the lungs and impair the wolf's ability to run long distances at top speed. The older a wolf gets, the greater the parasite load and the lower the wolf's endurance. Such a condition could make traveling and successful hunting increasingly difficult for the wolf. The wolf's life span most likely is shortened by this parasite.

*Many of the wolf's prey animals frequent areas around beaver ponds, marshes, swamps, lakes, and rivers. The wolf, therefore, visits such areas often and is almost as comfortable in water as on land. Its long legs allow the wolf to function well in the shallows as it tries to stop escaping prey from reaching deeper water. (Photo by Tom Brakefield)*

# ◆ COMMUNICATION ◆

As we might expect of any social animal, the wolf uses a rich vocabulary to communicate. At least three separate systems are involved: visual signaling, vocalizations, and scent marking. Each system is useful in different ways, so they tend to complement each other. The best way to familiarize yourself with wolf communication is to observe your dog.

The wolf's visual signals consist mostly of body language. Just as humans and dogs show their emotions through various facial expressions, so too does the wolf. We smile when we're happy, and our dogs assume a "happy face" when they do something we think they enjoy. The wolf and dog happy expression includes an open mouth, tongue hanging loosely, and ears forward.

Or, consider threat behavior. Most of us and our dogs have met it in the shape of another dog protecting its yard or possessions. The threatening animal—dog or wolf—wrinkles its nose, opens its mouth, bares its teeth, pulls its lips forward, and erects its ears. Usually this expression is accompanied by a growl or a snarl. The anxious dog or wolf on the receiving end of the threat puts on a very different face: It keeps its mouth closed and its lips drawn way back, slicks back its ears, and whines.

One of the most useful expressions of an alpha wolf is the "fixed stare," or glare. Often, all an alpha has to do is stare at a subordinate wolf, and that animal will immediately cringe, turn, and slink away. The glare is an alpha's way of controlling subordinate pack members.

A wolf or dog also uses certain tail and body positions to communicate. For example, a threatening wolf not only snarls and bares its teeth, but also raises its hackles and tail and essentially inflates its size. Conversely, the wolf being threatened pulls its lips back in a defensive "grin," lowers itself, holds its tail between its legs, and may even roll over on

*Howling serves several functions in a wolf's life. Maintaining contact when the pack is split up, advertising the pack's presence to other packs so as to maintain the territory, and helping solidify social bonds within the pack are all important functions of howling. (Photo by L. David Mech)*

45

its side or back; it seems to make itself look smaller.

Such dominant and subordinate posturing are important to maintaining the social structure in a wolf pack. Usually, many times each day the alpha wolves dominate the subordinates. They do so through fixed stares and aggressive threats, or by actually pinning the subordinates to the ground with their jaws. When the pups are small, the alphas commonly bowl them over with their muzzle or feet and hold them down for a second. This no doubt teaches the pups just who is boss.

Another aspect of the submissive behavior of lower-ranking wolves is their food begging. Eventually the subordinate wolves learn that when an alpha possesses food, the best way they can grab some is to wheedle it away. Like a pup, the subordinate paws at the muzzle of the alpha, lays its ears back, and points its muzzle upward with mouth closed and lips drawn way back, probably whining. The subordinate may then "fawn" in front of the alpha. The alpha's response is to quickly pin the subordinate to the ground. Every now and then, however, the subordinate manages to snatch some food from the alpha and go off and devour it.

In legend and in life, howling is the best-known of the various types of vocal communication that wolves use. Although wolves also whimper, growl, bark, and squeak, everyone has heard about the wolf baying at the moon. Wolves don't really do that, but they do howl regularly for a variety of reasons. One function of wolf howling is to assemble the various pack members when they're split up after having chased prey over a large area, or when they become separated in a forest and can't see each other but want to reassemble.

Second, wolves seem to howl as a group when they hear the howl of a strange pack. Studies by Fred Harrington and me in the Superior National Forest have indicated that packs tend to reply more often when they have something to defend like a fresh kill or the den of pups. This led us to believe that such "chorus howling" functions like bird song: It threatens potential intruders—Stay out of my lands or be challenged!

Some people, knowing this, howl to wolves during summer when they are at their dens or rendezvous sites with their pups. Often these human choristers are greeted with a group

*Facial expressions form an important part of the wolf's constant communication with its packmates. Taut, forward ears, staring eyes, and bared teeth signal a strong dominance threat, whereas lowered ears, drawn-back lips, and a protruding or licking tongue indicate submission. Wolves also show a "happy" face when playing with each other or with their young, just as dogs and people do. (Photo by Rick McIntyre)*

howl in response. Various parks in Canada, as well as the International Wolf Center in Ely, Minnesota, offer special wolf-howling trips for the public.

A third function of wolf howling seems to be social in nature, rather than a call to reassemble or a means of defense. Frequently when the wolves awaken, they stretch, urinate and defecate, nose each other, get all excited, and break into a group howl. But in contrast with other occasions for howling, the howl under these circumstances is often accompanied by a great deal of ritualistic display and domination, including pinning. This all involves much growling and whining. Then the wolves may break into a run and chase each other around for a few minutes in friendly, rambunctious play.

At other times, the intense socializing begins first and leads to a chorus howl. Similar observations I have made have led me to think that such howling may be merely manifestation of the wolves' excitement. Or, it may be a way for each wolf to remind the others that it too is present at the social get-together. Lois Crisler, in her book *Arctic Wild*, described such socializing as: "Like a community sing, a howl is . . . a happy social occasion. Wolves love a howl. When it is started, they instantly seek contact with one another, troop together, fur to fur. Some wolves . . . will run from any distance, panting and bright-eyed, to join in, uttering, as they near, fervent little wows, jaws wide, hardly able to wait to sing."

Group howling also can be a sign of the wolves' being alarmed or upset at an intruder. Sometimes when I have been away from "my" high arctic pack for a long period and camp back in their territory, they come to within one hundred feet of the tent, stand, and howl. Later, when they are accustomed to my presence, they still visit but usually do not howl.

The other major system of wolf communication is scent marking. Wolves urinate and defecate throughout their territory apparently to maintain their territory and to make their claims clear to neighboring packs and lone wolves. All the wolves urinate and defecate of course, and thus they automatically mark. Typically most pack members squat (females) or stand on all fours (males) when urinating. However, an alpha animal, especially the alpha male (but also the alpha female on occasion), lifts its leg when urinating and elevates the urine off the ground onto conspicuous scent posts including logs, sticks, rocks, ice chunks, and snowbanks. Presumably this is to maximize its advertising power.

Wolves raise-leg urinate most frequently in key travel spots around the territory, creating a preponderance of

*When food is scarce, which is usually the case, subordinate wolves go hungry more often than the alphas do. They constantly try to beg and wheedle food from the alphas. To do so requires a great deal of submissiveness: they fawn, whine, lower their head—sometimes even sliding it along the ground beneath an alpha's head—to get as close as possible to the animal with the food. Then, they may quickly snatch one end of a food item or a loose piece and dash off with it. (Photo by Rick McIntyre)*

*Overleaf: Chorus howling, in which the entire pack, including pups, howl together usually signals a heightened state of arousal. Wolves often howl in chorus upon awakening, after breaking into a run-and-play session, or when disturbed. (Photo by Karen Hollett)*

As an assertive gesture and an advertisement of rank and sexual status, alpha wolves mark their territories with urine. Usually this is done with a raised-leg urination (RLU), which allows urine to be squirted on objects above the ground where it may be more prominent and easy to detect. Both alpha males and females raise-leg urinate and increase their frequency around the breeding season. Males tend to raise-leg urinate more often than females. (Photo by L. David Mech)

A pack of wolves on Isle Royale reacts to a scent post of a neighboring pack. Note that after having sniffed the scent mark under the evergreens to the right, several of the trespassing wolves have turned and run from it. Depending on weather, scent marks may assert their effectiveness for weeks. (Photo by Rolf Peterson)

raised-leg urinations, or scent marks, around trail junctions. There are twice as many marks around the edges of wolf pack territories as in the centers. On the average, wolves raise-leg urinate along trails about every three hundred yards during winter. We have some preliminary evidence that during winter marks can be detected for up to two weeks.

Wolves increase their rate of scent marking as breeding season approaches, and alpha females seem to scent mark much more then than at other times. This suggests a second function for scent marking: courtship and preparation for breeding. However, I often saw a dominant female in the High Arctic raise-leg urinate during summer. This animal attended a den at which the only other regular den attendant was her mother, a subordinate, nursing female. It seemed like the dominant female had taken the place of the alpha male which did not visit the den for many days, if not weeks, on end.

Wolves use urinations in another way: to mark empty food caches. After the wolf removes food from the cache, it urinates there. Presumably this tells any other wolf not to bother looking for the food, for it is gone. In a related use that I still do not understand, an alpha wolf will urinate on food it has not killed. I have seen captive wolves urinate on carcasses or chunks of food provided them, and wild wolves urinate on food they have found but did not want to eat, such as the intestines of a hare.

Besides raised-leg urinations, wolf feces no doubt also act as scent marks. Wolves possess complex scent glands just inside the anus. When the anus everts to release a scat, the secretions can pass out and coat each side of the scat. Very likely, each scat could contain the peculiar chemical mix of any given wolf's glands.

Between the urinations and these defecations, a wolf pack's territory is dotted with olfactory hot spots. Any pack wolf probably is reassured that it is in its territory or knows when it is about to leave it. Any stranger should know when it is trespassing.

Scent marking nicely complements howling in territory advertisement because it tells where the pack has been and lasts for long periods. In contrast, howling tells where the pack is at a given instant, but it would have no lasting function. With these two methods, backed up by outright attack, territorial wolves insure that they continue to own an area where they can gain a living.

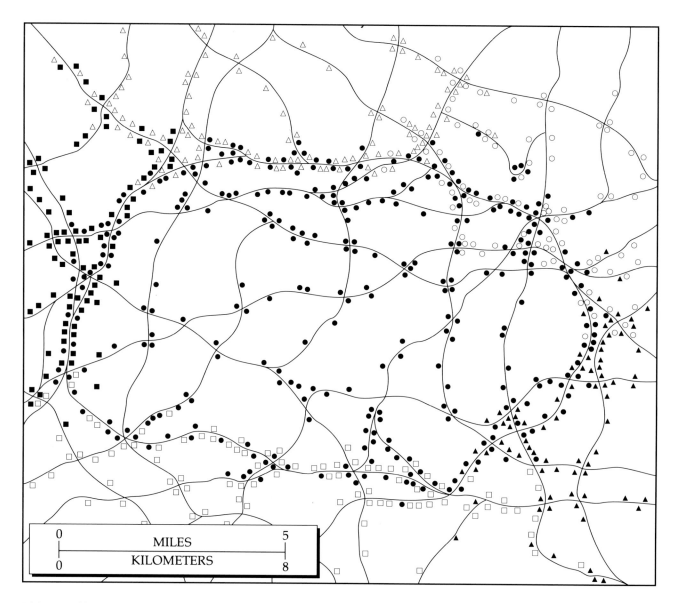

*This map of hypothetical scent-mark distribution around a wolf pack territory indicates the relative frequency and distribution of the marks. Any given wolf pack territory (center) is usually surrounded by several other territories in a network of trails. Wolves tend to mark more along established trails than when just traveling for the first time off a trail. They also tend to mark about twice as often around the edge of the territory as in the center, and they mark the most around the junctions of trails. There, presumably, they maximize the chances of their marks being detected. Here each dot represents a scent mark, with each symbol indicating a different pack.*

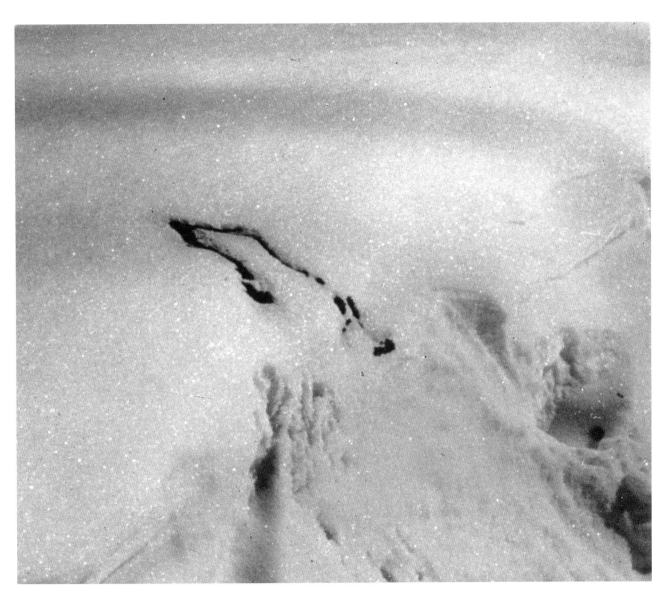

*A double urine mark on a snowbank is part of the pair-bonding ceremony of the alpha pair. As breeding season approaches, double marking increases, and newly formed pairs double mark at a higher rate than old, established pairs of wolves. Probably, chemicals in the urine of each sex help tell the other how ready each is to copulate. The presence of double marks probably also informs other pack members and any strange wolves passing through the area that a pair is already bonded. (Photo by L. David Mech)*

# HUNTING AND
# ◆ FEEDING ◆

*Teeth are the tools of the wolf. Instead of knives, cleavers, grinding machines, and saws, the wolf has only its forty teeth to catch, kill, and cut up such large animals as moose and musk-oxen. Four long, sharp fangs do most of the damage, while the front incisors help rip and tear, and the carnassials do the cutting. The wolf's teeth last for many years, but by the time an animal reaches twelve to fourteen years of age, they have grown blunt and worn. (Photo by Tom Brakefield)*

Like a dog or cat, the wolf is a meat eater or carnivore. Unlike deer, cows, mice, rabbits, and most other mammals, the wolf cannot live on leaves, stems, roots, or branches. It has what is known as a simple stomach which cannot digest the thick cellulose of most plants. Instead, the wolf can best digest meat and fat.

In addition, the wolf's teeth are shaped entirely differently from the teeth of plant eaters. The latter are usually flattened, rough, or blocky. The wolf's teeth, on the other hand, are sharp and pointed—ideal for grabbing, holding, tearing, and shearing. It is just as ludicrous to imagine a wolf munching branches or gnawing tree bark as it is to think of a deer trying to catch and tear apart another animal. A wolf is destined, by its whole anatomy, to be a meat eater.

For a mammal to feed as consistently on meat as a wolf must, it cannot rely on merely finding dead animals. Though that sometimes happens, it would be easy to starve to death waiting for such a find. Instead of waiting, the wolf takes a more active role and hunts its food.

Of course, not only do the wolf's specialized teeth and digestive system cause the animal, and adapt it, to be a hunter, so does most everything else about the wolf. The animal's temperament, behavior, sensory abilities, and even social tendencies all adapt the wolf to a hunting nature. Probably every cell of its body compels a wolf to be a hunter.

Because the wolf is a large animal and lives in packs, it cannot meet its needs in the long run by hunting small animals. Although it will eat any kind of creature including mice, birds, and rabbits, it must invest most of its time trying to capture large animals. While they may be harder to catch and kill than smaller ones, they yield enough food for a long period or for several members of the pack all at once. Depending on where the wolf lives, the main animals it preys on are deer, elk, caribou, moose, bison, mountain sheep, mountain goats, or musk-oxen. In some areas, beavers or arctic hares form secondary parts of the wolf's diet.

Nowhere has any scientist found a population of wolves that relies consistently on smaller prey animals. (Farley Mowat's book *Never Cry Wolf* claimed that the wolves in his story relied mostly on mice during summer. However, Mowat is not a scientist, and his book, although presented as truth, is fiction.)

To find, catch, and kill large prey animals is a very hard job. The hunted all have numerous ways to thwart hunters, and the wolf must spend much time trying to overcome these defenses. To do so, the carnivore relies on all its adaptations: fine senses to help it find prey animals, an ability to travel long distances tirelessly and to sustain speed, and a certain deftness that allows it to dash in and out quickly at a prey animal while trying to dodge horns or hooves.

Let's look at the defensive traits of the wolf's prey one by one. Locating prey is the wolf's first problem. Usually prey animals are scattered few and far between over a large area. Or they are grouped in large herds in a small part of a vast area, and they move often.

Some large prey animals change their defense strategies seasonally. The white-tailed deer, for example, lives scattered during snow-free periods, making any individual hard to find. However, come snowfall, and deer may migrate up to twenty-six miles to congregate in winter "yards." This strategy provides more eyes, ears, and noses to detect approaching wolves. It produces trails through snow for deer to run on. It probably also introduces a "confusion factor" to a wolf who must decide on which deer to focus. Furthermore, grouping tends to spread the risk for any given individual.

When chased, deer are fleet. If cornered, they can strike with sharp hooves and cave in a wolf's skull. Males in autumn and early winter can kill a wolf with their pointed antlers.

Caribou are larger than deer, and both sexes have larger racks of antlers. Although their hooves are not sharp, they are large and blocky, and could probably easily break a wolf's back. Caribou travel constantly in large herds except when about to calve. Then they disperse individually to isolated knife-ridges or to islands or to other remote, protected, or less accessible areas to bear their calves. Because caribou calves are weak and helpless for their first day or two of life, a wolf only needs to find them to kill them.

I once watched a wolf locating a newborn calf on the tundra of Denali National Park in Alaska. The birthing spot was unlike most of the less accessible ones I had seen, and the

*The hare's ability to zigzag in shorter, sharper turns than the longer-legged wolf helps the hare to hold its lead. Healthy adult hares thus can often escape wolves. (Photo by Tom Brakefield)*

*Deer are not much larger than wolves, but their acute senses and alertness, their speed and endurance, and their sharp hooves and horns are all part of a successful defense system that causes most chases by wolves to end in failure. (Photo by Todd Fuller)*

folly of such a choice was dramatically demonstrated. The wolf merely ran to the caribou cow, which then left her hunkered-down calf. The wolf bit the calf once or twice, and dinner was served.

When a few days old, caribou calves can run quickly. Their mothers then assemble with other cows and calves and form nursery herds. The defensive benefit of such groupings are probably similar to those described for deer.

Moose, the wolf's largest prey, rely mostly on their size and strength. Many merely stand their ground when wolves approach, and they are safe. Wolves must get them running to attack safely, and even then most moose outrun or outlast wolves. One well-placed blow by a moose hoof, and a wolf is a goner.

The rest of the wolf's prey present equally jawbreaking defenses. Elk herd up and possess formidable hooves and antlers. Musk-oxen and bison group and greet wolves head-on with sharp recurved horns; their young tuck themselves in the circle of safety or between the flanks of the adult warriors. Mountain goats and sheep inhabit rugged, rocky terrain where they cling to pinnacles and ledges that wolves are hard-pressed to reach. Beavers surround themselves with watery moats.

The wolf, of course, has senses, abilities, and strengths almost comparable to each of those of its prey. But not quite. If their hunting skills surpassed their prey's defenses, wolves would be able to kill any animal they wanted most any time. They would have wiped out their prey, and eaten themselves out of house and home and into extinction. Instead, a system has evolved that maintains itself: In general, wolves are barely able to catch enough prey to survive and reproduce, and their prey usually can escape only when in the best condition and circumstances.

Because the wolf cannot quite match the defenses of most prey, it must hunt far and wide to find an animal it can catch and kill. It helps that for each wolf there usually exists a multitude of prey. On Isle Royale in Lake Superior, for example, there have been up to seventy moose per wolf; in Minnesota, fifty to one hundred deer per wolf; and in Denali Park, some thirty-five large prey animals (caribou, Dall sheep, and moose) per wolf.

*Although wolves are primarily killers of large mammals, they will take smaller creatures such as mice and hares, which they must chase and run down. These form a very low proportion of the wolf's diet but may be important when raising pups. This is because younger and less experienced wolves in the pack can hunt smaller prey and help feed themselves and the pups when food demand is especially high. (Photo by Tom Brakefield)*

60

*Throughout most of Canada and Alaska, one of the wolf's most important prey species is the caribou. Although caribou generally live in large herds, in summer they are sometimes alone and less protected. Still, it is difficult for a wolf to catch an alert healthy animal. Unless the wolf can sneak to within a few yards of an animal, its quarry can usually make a fast break and, if in good condition, can pull away from a wolf in a hurry. (Photo by Rick McIntyre)*

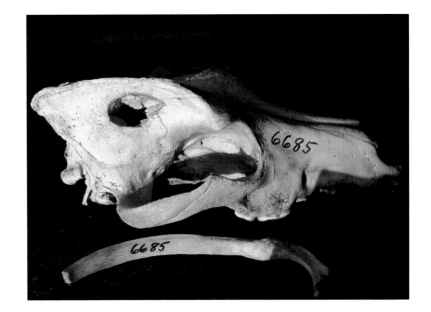

*A deer-hoof-shaped hole in the skull of this alpha male wolf attests to the danger wolves face when trying to catch their prey. This wolf also had two healed broken ribs, which indicate that at least once before he probably was injured by a blow from a prey animal. Wolves have also been impaled by the sharp horns of bucks. (Photo by L. David Mech)*

*Dall sheep are small and not especially formidable to the wolf. However, they inhabit rocky crags and precipices, so their main defense is to remain near such escape terrain where they can quickly get out of reach of wolves. The wolf's strategy is to try to catch sheep away from such terrain, for example, by approaching them from above or by catching them out on open flats crossing from one mountain range to another. (Photo by Thomas Meier)*

Of all the prey a wolf has to choose from, some individuals are bound to be old, injured, weak, sick, or otherwise debilitated. Each year, prey animals produce fragile, untested, vulnerable young. Adult prey all have intense rutting seasons in which males wear themselves out and lose their healthy condition. Wolves find such animals, and they eat. (This is not said to cast the wolf in a better light. It merely describes the way the wolf lives and explains how the creature is able to make its living against the formidable defenses of its prey.)

Once a wolf or pack finds its quarry, it usually tries to sneak up, regardless of whether the area is tree-covered or open. Eyeing the animal intently, the stalker strides slowly and carefully towards it. Ever ready to rush headlong towards the prey, the hunter holds itself in check trying to gain every last inch unnoticed.

If the prey detects the wolf but hesitates, the wolf hesitates too. However, the instant the intended dinner bolts, the wolf springs after it. To rush an animal, the wolf seems to need the stimulus of a fleeing quarry. Aware of similar behavior in our domesticated "wolves," we warn a child not to run from a strange dog approaching, lest the child become the dog's victim. Truly, the wolf catches most of its meals on the run. Often the outcome of the chase is determined in the first few seconds. It's almost as though a quick gain spurs the wolf on. In fact, often if the wolf does not gain on its target in a few minutes, it quickly gives up.

There are exceptions, however. One wolf I know of chased a deer for thirteen miles; unfortunately, the outcome of this contest took place out of sight. Or sometimes, wolves will harass musk-oxen for hours—waiting for the flank-to-flank defenses to break, for a calf to fall away from the herd, or for a fleeing adult to falter. Nevertheless, these examples remain exceptions. Most meals are caught on the run, and a short one at that.

Wolves generally attack large prey in the rump area simply because it offers the closest hold to the pursuers and is well out of the way of death-dealing hooves. However, as soon as the quarry is stopped, the hunters try to grab it by the head, usually by the nose. A good hold here focuses the prey's attention on the wolf with the nose hold. Meanwhile, other pack members grab at the animal's rump, flanks, neck, and throat. Within a few minutes, the prey is usually dead.

The alpha animals then begin boring into the abdomen and tugging at the entrails. Other pack members work on the wounded areas where they can most easily reach the meat. All kinds of snarling, growling, and threatening pervade the scene as each wolf tries to guard its own share of the take. No

*Usually it is some defect in the prey's defense system that enables wolves to succeed. In this case, a large, old buck has probably weakened from fighting with other bucks and from paying more attention to defending his females during the rutting season than to gaining enough sustenance. During the autumn rut, old males of many species form one of the main prey items of wolves. (Photo by Diane Boyd)*

*Arthritis in the spine of a moose killed by wolves may have been a contributing factor to the animal's demise. Because wolves tend to kill disproportionate numbers of old animals of all prey and because old animals are particularly prone to arthritis, the stiffness and soreness during movement may make them easier for wolves to kill without danger to themselves. Other debilitations that may make animals easier prey are lung cysts, massive infestations of ticks, and various diseases. Many animals killed by wolves are so afflicted. (Photo by Thomas Meier)*

Moose, one of the wolf's largest prey, can best defend themselves by standing their ground and defying the pack. The wolves often maneuver around their standing prey, perhaps sizing up the animal or trying to detect any weaknesses. Meanwhile, the prey acts belligerent and tries to intimidate the wolves by charging and striking at them with its hooves. These wolves tried for five minutes to attack this moose, but failing to get it running, they left and continued their hunt for other moose they could catch. (Photo by L. David Mech)

Sometimes moose run instead of standing their ground, and in all such cases, if the wolves are close enough, they give chase and try to catch and kill the animal. However, most often, even in these cases, the moose are able to lash out at the wolves with their hooves and keep them from attacking. The chase may continue for a mile or more until finally the wolves either attack or abandon the chase. (Photo by Rolf Peterson)

When wolves do attack moose, they tend to grab their quarry by the rump or flanks and slow it down. Eventually, an alpha wolf dashes around and tries to grab the moose by the nose. If it succeeds, the moose stops and tries to dislodge this wolf; meanwhile, the other pack members continue to rip at its rump and flanks and bring down the prey. (Photo by Rolf Peterson)

Wolves preying on musk-oxen harass the herd and try to get it to run, leaving the calves less protected. If the herd stands its ground, the adults form a defensive front against the wolves, keeping the calves behind them or within their circle. Sometimes the contest lasts for hours. (Photo by L. David Mech)

wonder then that when a wolf does detach a large chunk of the carcass, the animal heads away and eats it alone and in peace!

With food suddenly in abundance, wolves often set some aside for leaner times. After taking their fill, they may carry off a chunk of prey and bury it, bunting the soil back over it with forward sweeps of their down-turned nose. Or, they may disgorge chunks of the prey from their stomach into a hole and bury them. Sometime later, when hunting is harder, they will dig up their cache and gain a free meal.

After gorging on some ten to twenty pounds of the booty from their kill, each pack member, with bulging belly, finds a comfortable spot, lies down, and snoozes. All the long, hard hours of hunting, all the chasing and failures, all the close calls and near-misses fade behind them. For a while, they are content.

*As with other prey, most often the Dall sheep killed by wolves are old adults or young of the year. In the scene above, an eleven-year-old ram that appeared to be healthy was taken. Witnesses to the feeding were heard to actually proclaim what a healthy sheep it was. A closer look, however, revealed that the ram had severe arthritis of its jaw joint, probably greatly affecting its ability to eat properly and maintain its strength and energy. (Photo by L. David Mech)*

*Once wolves have finally killed a prey animal, they immediately tear open its undersides and eat its entrails. The heart, lungs, liver, and other soft organs are especially rich in fat and nutrients, so they are progressively sought after. The alphas take the choicest parts first. (Photo by L. David Mech)*

*Besides transporting food in their bellies, adult wolves also carry chunks of prey home to the pups. Kills are sometimes more than twenty miles from the den, so the adults must spend much time shuttling food from the kill to the pups. (Photo by Rick McIntyre)*

*Wolves often bury chunks of food and dig them up later when hunting is hard and they or their pups are hungry. Food is cached around kills and also around dens and rendezvous sites. Caching thus becomes a method of buffering against the vagaries of an intermittent food supply. (Photo by L. David Mech)*

Because wolves are hunters, they travel widely. To locate vulnerable prey, wolves must spend a great deal of time and effort. They hunt continually whenever they are not feeding or resting, and they try as often as possible to catch prey. To do so, they must hunt far and wide, traveling many miles in a day.

In Isle Royale National Park, I followed wolf tracks in the snow from an airplane and found that a pack of fifteen wolves covered an average of thirty-one miles a day to hunt moose. A pack of six wolves, which I followed with my all-terrain vehicle in the High Arctic one July, traveled thirty miles away from the den before they were able to kill a musk-ox.

But wolves are well adapted for travel. Their long legs allow them to travel rapidly and tirelessly, even through deep snow. Their feet, while not as specialized as the hooves of their prey, are nevertheless large and blocky and thus well adapted for running. The blockiness is especially noticeable when compared to the feet of their relatives and fellow hunters, the cats and weasels.

Despite the blockiness of the wolf's foot, the arrangement of its toes and heel pad gives the foot much flexibility when wolves really need it. For example, when wolves are trying to reach mountain sheep on a rocky pinnacle, their toes sprawl out widely, and their leathery toe pads cling tenaciously to steeply sloping rock, allowing them to come as close as possible to the sheep. Or, when running on uneven terrain, over rocks and logs, the wolf's foot automatically conforms to the irregularities. This helps the wolf minimize any impediments and maximize its speed.

The wolf is also a tireless traveler. It can run thirty-five to forty miles per hour. It can lope for many miles at a time without rest if necessary. Although most of the wolf's chases are relatively short, the wolf can continue a pursuit for a long dis-

*Running is one of the wolf's most important abilities, since it allows the carnivore to chase down its quarry. Accordingly, an old Russian proverb states that "the wolf is kept fed by its feet." The animal can attain speeds of thirty-five to forty miles per hour and has enough endurance to run for miles. (Photo by Tom Brakefield)*

tance. One of my wildlife technicians, Mark Korb, once followed a radio-tagged wolf from an aircraft while the wolf chased and followed a deer one autumn for thirteen miles. Mark was unable to determine the outcome of the hunt, but his observation did illustrate the predator's great persistence. The wolf's ability to travel extensively also means that the creature can roam far from its den, and that dispersers from a pack can travel great distances to find new places to live.

From an airplane, I have tracked wolves crossing large lakes and other expanses of known distance. I have also timed their pace of travel in the High Arctic following with my all-terrain vehicle. During their regular excursions, wolves trot at five to nine miles per hour. The faster rate applies to a yearling male that I trailed over the tundra as he headed back to a den. At times he would break into a lope. I was uncertain as to whether it was because I was following, or because he was getting excited as he approached the den. Wolves returning to the den often speed up as they approach. One alpha female that I paced for over two hundred meters as she approached the den traveled at six miles per hour.

It should not be surprising that an animal like the wolf, which is such a widespread traveler, should have a large home area. In other words, a wolf travels far and wide, covering a large expanse, not only in a given day, but also over the period of several weeks or months.

To appreciate just how extensive an area a wolf pack uses, we must compare it to the home ranges of some other animals. Deer, for example, usually use an area of about one-quarter to one-half square mile. They may travel many miles between their summer range and their winter range, but for most of the year each deer lives in a small area. A female bear with cubs will occupy a territory of five or six square miles.

Wolf packs, however, cover territories of from about thirty square miles where they prey on deer up to eight hundred square miles where they live on moose and caribou. The high arctic pack I studied ranged over at least one thousand square miles. One pack in Alaska covered five thousand square miles in six weeks. Such large areas allow each wolf pack to obtain enough food to supply itself, reproduce, feed the pups, and continue living there over a long period. For this system to work, however, each pack must assure itself

*The wolf's foot is a marvelous adaptation for the animal's way of life. Although thick, rugged, and blocky when the toes are together, the foot can also sprawl, allowing the toes to grasp sloping rocks, logs, and other uneven or steep surfaces. When walking, the wolf holds its foot in the blocky fashion, reducing area and friction. However, during tricky maneuvering, the toes can spread far apart, much increasing the surface and friction. (Photo by Tom Brakefield)*

74

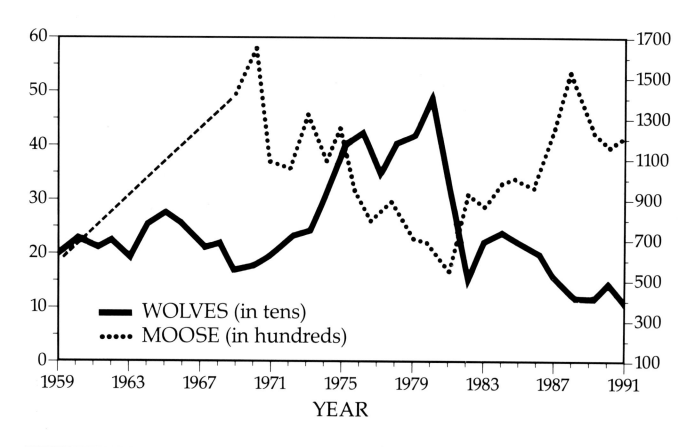

WOLVES (in tens)
MOOSE (in hundreds)

YEAR

*The Isle Royale wolf–moose population relationship. (Graph courtesy of Rolf Peterson)*

*The wolf's long legs are a great help in wading through snow, in bounding through the brush and blown-down trees, and during a straight-out run. Standing thirty inches at the chest, the wolf is often mistaken for a deer at first glance because it looks so tall. (Photo by Tom Brakefield)*

## ISLE ROYALE WOLF STUDIES

One of the best-known studies of wolves or any other predator has been conducted in Isle Royale National Park. Isle Royale is a 210-square-mile island in Lake Superior within twenty miles of the Minnesota-Ontario border. Wolves colonized the island about 1949 after having crossed the ice from the mainland. Probably no more than two individuals were involved. The only year-round prey available is the moose, although beavers supplement the wolves' diet in the warm months.

In 1958, Dr. Durward L. Allen of Purdue University initiated the Isle Royale study, assigning a series of scientists to the project. It has since become the longest running predator-prey study anywhere. I was fortunate enough to conduct the first three years of the study, which has now run more than three decades. Dr. Rolf Peterson of Michigan Technological University has directed the project since 1970. The Isle Royale wolf population remained at about twenty-five animals through the late 1960s. However, by 1980 it had reached fifty and become the densest wolf population recorded. Wolf numbers then crashed, and bottomed out about 1989 when there were only twelve. Since then they have increased to fifteen and dropped to fourteen and then twelve, as shown in the accompanying graph.

Because of the recent low in the number of wolves, biologists and park administrators have expressed concern about the causes. Various diseases and/or "inbreeding depression" have been suspected. Inbreeding depression is a reduction in a population resulting from lower production or survival caused by closely related individuals breeding. Because favorable conditions rarely exist for wolves to travel to Isle Royale, the wolf population there must be thoroughly inbred.

Inbreeding has been confirmed by laboratory studies of Isle Royale wolf genetics, and sooner or later, inbreeding depression may affect the population. However, sorting out its effects from those of nutritional, pathological, or other causes will be most difficult. Meanwhile, the Isle Royale wolf population continues to survive as one of the world's best-known.

It is not unusual for wolves to die by attack from other wolves, and in some areas such "intraspecific strife" comprises the majority of natural wolf mortality. Most such killings result from territorial disputes, involve adult wolves, and occur a few months before and after breeding season, suggesting some involvement of breeding rights as well as territorial competition. (Photo by L. David Mech)

that it is the only pack cropping its resources on its lands. To insure this exclusive use, wolves defend their territories.

Wolves maintain their territories in several ways. If they find a neighboring pack or a strange wolf on home ground, the resident pack will chase the intruders and attack them, often killing them. However, packs cannot afford to be fighting their neighbors constantly. Because such bellicose behavior endangers them and takes valuable time away from their hunting opportunities, wolves depend on at least the two elaborate warning systems, howling and scent marking, discussed in detail earlier.

Howling warns neighbors where a resident pack is and announces that the howlers are willing to defend their area. However, howling is very temporary. It says little about where the pack's boundaries are or where the pack may suddenly show up some day. That is where the second system, scent marking, comes in, as a pack assiduously posts its territory with signs of urine and feces.

The result of scent marking, howling, and direct attacks by resident packs on intruding wolves is a mosaic of territories covering the wolf's range, as shown on the accompanying map. The exact edges of each territory in the mosaic are not necessarily precise. There appears to be a buffer zone between territories in which neither pack is supreme, a zone of continuing contest. Either pack may try to assert itself there against the other, and true ownership might shift continually.

Every year as the wolf pack produces new pups, the previous year's pups become yearlings, and the pack starts to overflow. At least some of the yearlings usually leave the pack and the territory and disperse. Some dispersers merely move next door if there is a vacant area. Others travel around the population as transients, or "floaters." These lone wolves may cover over one thousand square miles, drifting around the population and trying to avoid the territorial packs.

If intruding lone wolves are detected, they will be chased and attacked, and often they are killed. To survive, they tend to hang around the edges of the territories or in the corners among several territories. Sometimes, they frequent favorite areas many miles apart. If a member of the opposite sex doing the same thing is found, the two animals may court, pair-bond, mate, and produce pups.

Where prey abounds, the newly formed pair may be able to establish itself among the other territories, which then compress. A new pack with a new territory is formed. However, where prey is scarce, the new pair may be killed by neighboring wolves, which then retake the territory.

Another type of disperser takes off in a set direction and leaves its natal area. Some of these animals, both males and

79

females, travel several hundred miles straight-line distance. A few that have been studied have ended up over five hundred miles from where they were originally captured. These directional dispersers are also looking for a mate and a vacant area with enough prey. Then they can settle down, establish their own territory, and start a new pack.

Other young wolves, rather than disperse, may leave the pack but stay within the territory. A few young actually remain with the pack. These animals seem to be biding their time as though waiting to breed in their own pack's territory. They probably eventually mate with their own parents or siblings. That certainly takes place in captive packs. And on Isle Royale, where all the wolves are closely related, it has to be the situation.

The question often arises about the possible ill effects of inbreeding in wolves. The answer is not clear. The best example to draw from is the Isle Royale wolf population. No doubt, that population started from at most two unrelated wolves in the late 1940s. Genetic studies in 1988 and 1989 confirmed that the island wolves are as closely related as brothers and sisters. Nevertheless, the wolves increased to fifty as recently as 1980. Although they have declined since, they still numbered fifteen in 1990 and twelve in 1991, according to Dr. Rolf Peterson, director of the study. If inbreeding caused noticeable problems at all, it took forty years!

Most wolf populations that have been intensively studied are organized into territories. However, a few must resort to other types of spacing in order to exploit their prey populations enough to survive. Where wolves depend on migrating herds of caribou, the wolves themselves must migrate to follow the herds. This approach requires wolves to den and produce pups within reach of the caribou's calving grounds. Then, by late summer the whole pack, including still-growing pups, must pick up and leave. They spend the next several weeks trailing the bands of caribou heading south some 125 miles or more to their wintering range.

The wolves then remain over winter with the caribou, usually in the high taiga or conifer areas of central Canada or Alaska. Because of the size of such caribou herds and the expanses they cover during summer, they generally support several wolf packs. All these packs then follow the herd to their wintering ground. They keep company with the caribou as well as with their neighboring wolf packs throughout winter and spring. How these wolf packs get along with each other and keep from battling in competition for the caribou, biologists don't know yet. However, we surmise that in this situation howling may be most useful in keeping wolf packs apart, by alerting each about the others' movements.

*The lone wolf is an animal that has left its pack and lives alone. Most lone wolves are one to three years old, maturing, and looking for a mate and a large enough area vacant of other wolves but containing enough prey to support a pack. In saturated wolf populations, lone wolves are doomed to wander for many months or longer before finding a place to settle. Occasionally, they can infiltrate a strange pack, but little is known about this behavior. Some lone wolves disperse in a set direction for hundreds of miles. These movements take the animals into new areas that may not be occupied by other wolves. In such cases, the loners become colonizers helping to found a new population. (Photo by Rick McIntyre)*

*Hares can give a wolf a good chase. With long, powerful hind legs, hares spring forth mightily. They can stay ahead of a wolf running at full speed for long periods. This allows them to take advantage of changes in terrain and vegetation, which may eventually help them elude their pursuer. (Photo by Tom Brakefield)*

*A wolf breaks through the ice while attempting to cross a newly frozen river. Although this individual eventually made it to shore, wolves do suffer mortality from numerous natural hazards such as drowning. In Denali National Park, Alaska, two radio-tagged alpha wolves were killed in an avalanche. Probably they were traveling along a mountain ridge on an overhanging snow cornice, causing it to give way and precipitating the snowslide. (Photo by Mike Nelson)*

*When traveling, the alpha male usually heads the wolf pack and chooses the route, but the alpha female is close to him in line. (Photo by Tom Brakefield)*

# COURTSHIP AND
# ⬥REPRODUCTION⬥

*Wolf pups play with each other for hours on end, rolling, wrestling, pouncing, and chasing. One of the important functions of such play is to help the animals exercise and maintain good muscle tone. (Photo by Tom Brakefield)*

*Overleaf: As part of their play, pups practice behavior that eventually will serve them well when they need to defend themselves as adults or when they begin to prey on other animals. Such playfighting goes on daily throughout most of the pups' first few months. (Photo by Tom Brakefield)*

Courtship and reproduction are among the most interesting aspects of the wolf's life. Several puzzles about wolf courtship and reproduction when solved will probably clarify many unknowns in other aspects of the wolf's natural history.

Your own wolf, the dog, seems to exhibit a simplified version of the wolf's reproductive life. Dogs generally mature fast enough to produce pups at less than a year of age. And dogs come into estrus (sexual heat) twice a year, while wolves breed only once annually.

Captive wolves can sometimes produce pups when one year of age, and they can achieve heat at the age of ten months. In the best-documented case of this, a brother of a ten-month-old female in a zoo bred the female, and the pups survived. Such early reproduction has been found a few times in other captive wolf colonies. However, it has never been demonstrated in the wild and probably rarely, if ever, happens there. Just why is unknown. It may have to do with the pack's parents, the alphas, so thoroughly dominating the mating rites among members.

Although wild wolves often reach adult size within their first year, and certainly by the end of their second, their reproductive abilities do not necessarily mature until much later. In terms of its hormones, a wolf is not fully mature— comparable to a human of about twenty-five years of age— until about five years of age. Nevertheless, female wolves in the wild sometimes breed at two or three years of age. Probably many wild wolves do not breed until four or five. Of course, this disparity in age of first breeding does not necessarily mean that such differences exist in their physiological ability to breed. It may only reflect a wolf's ability to find, attract, or hold a mate or territory.

Mating season for any given wolf population takes place over a period of a month in late winter or spring, depending

on the geographic latitude of the animals' range. Southern wolves mate earlier in the season; northern wolves later. During that period, individual females come into estrus for one to two weeks; younger wolves reach estrus about two weeks later. For periods of one to seven weeks before estrus, females undergo proestrus and bleed from the vagina, no doubt advertising their condition to males. The blood is expelled with urine and shows up well on scent posts in snowbanks. There, any wolf spotting it can come up and sniff.

Furthermore, both male and female adults increase their rate of scent marking as breeding season approaches. Especially prominent is double marking, where the alpha female urinates and then the alpha male responds by urinating over or near the female's mark. On snowbanks, two marks, including one with proestral blood, are often seen. In newly formed pairs, the marking rate is higher than in old established pairs. This is evidence that double marking is part of pair-bonding, the process by which the male and the female form affectionate ties to one another.

Wolves can bond to each other at any time of the year, but little is known about the process outside of winter. Once the bond is formed, the pair tends to travel together and to scent mark its territory. Usually a male only bonds and mates with one female. However, in the Superior National Forest, a male I studied once bred two females who were probably sisters. When it was time to den, the male stuck with one female and helped her raise the pups. The other female denned thirteen miles away and raised her pups alone. There was some evidence that the male visited the extra female at least once while she was raising the pups, but he certainly did not visit her often.

In established packs, primarily the top-ranking, or alpha, male and female breed with each other. However, 20 to 40 percent of the packs containing at least two adult females produce two litters. In many cases the subordinate pair's pups do not survive, but sometimes the two litters are moved together and raised together. In Denali Park, Alaska, an extra female in the East Fork pack in 1988 denned a mile from the main den. When the pups were four weeks old, the mother picked up each in her mouth. Then she trotted along the park road in full view of hundreds of tourists until, one by one, she delivered her whole litter to the main den.

As breeding season approaches, members of the alpha pair become increasingly friendly to each other. They sleep closer and closer together, and the male tends to hang close to the female as they travel. Both alphas threaten competitors from within the pack with stares, growls, and grimaces. Meanwhile, male and female groom each other, place fore-

*Although pups do not develop a stable social order, they do practice dominating each other through their play. Here, one pup, with tail erect, stands over the other, imitating a dominant wolf trying to suppress a subordinate individual. Tables will soon turn, however, and the underdog will get a chance to assert itself as well. (Photo by Tom Brakefield)*

paws over the other's shoulders, and touch each other more and more.

Often when about to copulate, individual mated pairs move out of the main pack for a few days. This is probably to avoid interference from other pack members. Sometimes pack associates try to get in on the mating, or they harass the mated pair during copulation.

Wolves copulate like dogs, the male mounting the female from behind. The male inserts his penis, and during the mating process the base of the penis swells and the female's vaginal sphincter muscle locks, forming a copulatory tie between the pair. After the tie is made, the male dismounts and swivels his body around while still coupled with the female. The two animals are then "hung up" tail to tail the same way as dogs are during mating, for up to thirty minutes. During this time the male ejaculates frequently. No one knows exactly why the copulatory tie occurs. However, it may help to insure passage of sperm to the eggs and make certain no competitor sneaks in on the act.

Previously, people thought that wolves mate for life, and one male and female I studied mated for nine consecutive years and produced pups. However, if one wolf of a pair dies, the other may mate with a different wolf. I knew one male wolf that over several years bonded consecutively to at least three females and produced pups from at least two of them. This male in turn had been the last mate of a female that had had two other mates; her first partner was killed, and her second mate had left her territory for unknown reasons.

Although biologists do not know for certain what factors promote pair-bonding in wolves, females do not have to be sexually mature to pair-bond. One female who dispersed from a pack at seventeen months of age paired at nineteen months. The two set up a territory and localized in an area of about a square mile during the first month of denning season. The pair then split, and the female returned to her natal pack. There she remained for the next six months. When she died at the age of thirty-four months, an autopsy revealed she had never ovulated and thus had not yet sexually matured. In another case, a thirty-two-month-old female pair-bonded and maintained the same mate through two breeding seasons before she produced any pups that survived.

It is clear that female wolves have complex courtship, pair-bonding, and reproductive behavior as well as complex hormonal characteristics, for female wolves are capable of a reproductive state called "pseudopregnancy." Apparently, once a female matures sexually, she either becomes pregnant or pseudopregnant each year. During pseudopregnancy the wolf's hormonal state is precisely the same as if the animal

*Mature female wolves come into estrus or heat only once a year, whereas dogs achieve heat twice a year. This is one of the main differences between wolves and dogs. The alpha male follows his mate around faithfully before and during the heat period, waiting for a chance to copulate. After mounting the female and inserting his penis, the male dismounts while still attached, swivels 180 degrees, and faces away from his mate. The two animals then either stand or lie locked together for a period up to a half hour while the sperm rush in to fertilize the eggs. (Photo by Jane Packard)*

were pregnant even though she is not. This includes the ability to produce milk and possibly even to nurse the offspring of another female. Dogs also become pseudopregnant.

Conceivably, pseudopregnancy would allow pupless females to become "wetnurses" in the pack. This phenomenon, while not yet documented in the wild, has been seen in captive wolves. It may explain the situation I saw in the High Arctic where for three years I observed a low-ranking female nursing the pups. The alpha female, who should have been the one that produced the pups (and perhaps was), spent her time hunting and bringing food back to them.

Pseudopregnancy would certainly prepare females to take at least as much care of the pups as the actual mother. That readiness to nurture is one of the most predominant traits of a wolf pack. The strongest impression I had of the high arctic wolves with whom I lived centers on the great care that every pack member paid to the pups. Each wolf, including yearlings and males, brought food to the pups, played with them, kept them around the den, and in all other ways treated them as their own. In spring, the hormone prolactin, which causes nurturing behavior, surges up even in male and immature wolves. Evidently, this explains why all pack members tend the pups so well.

The pups' chances for healthy development are also maximized in another way and while they are still *in utero*. The timing of wolf mating seems nicely synchronized with the season when wolves find it easiest to kill prey. Most wolf prey lose weight over winter, so any inferior animals reach their poorest condition by late winter or early spring. As a result, wolves appear to be best fed around the mating season and for the next few months while the fetuses are developing, a period of about sixty-three days.

As birth approaches, the pregnant female searches for a shelter in which she can bear the pups and care for them during their first several weeks of age. Dens can take many forms, but are most often a rock cave or a crevice or a hole in the ground. Either the wolf usurps the den from a smaller animal like a fox and enlarges it, or she digs it herself. However, other shelters, such as old beaver houses and hollow logs, are sometimes used. I have known of four instances when wolves bore their pups on top of the ground in no shelter. In one case, the pups all died; in two cases, the female later moved the pups to better locations; and in the last instance, their fate remains unknown.

Dens are often reused from year to year, especially where scarce. Sometimes the same den may be used over long periods. For example, a den which Adolph Murie studied in the early 1940s in Denali National Park is still being used regu-

*Occasionally wolves bear their pups in shallow pits in the ground, and at least in some such cases, they move the pups to a den several days later. Biologists know little about why wolves use pits in which to bear their young, but some think that the wolves resort to them when they are suddenly caught in labor away from a den. While it is tempting to suggest that perhaps first-breeders are the ones who use pits, there is at least one record of an experienced female using a pit for her second litter. (Photo by L. David Mech)*

*Most wolf dens are holes dug into the ground leading to tunnels extending several feet to a nesting chamber. The pups spend their first three weeks in the den being kept warm by their mother's body wrapped around them. After the third week, the pups begin to venture to the mouth of the den, and within another two or three weeks spend much time outside the den. When eight weeks old, the wolves generally abandon the den and may even move long distances with the pack to a nest above ground called a rendezvous site. There all pack members meet each other as they care for and feed the pups. (Photo by L. David Mech)*

*Overleaf: In some regions, rock caves are used for dens. This cave in the High Arctic, where permafrost prevents digging in most places, showed sign of having been used by wolves as long ago as seven hundred to eight hundred years. (Photo by L. David Mech)*

larly, nearly fifty years later.

In the High Arctic, I discovered a den that was a spacious cave which the wolves used for at least three consecutive years and probably much longer. The area around the den was littered with bones of prey that the adults had brought back, fresh, moderately old, and very old. Two old bones dated by the radiocarbon technique were 232 and 783 years old. This may indicate that the den had been used over a period of almost eight hundred years.

The den is known not just by the female who produces the pups, but also by other pack members. When the alpha female of one of my study packs in the Superior National Forest trespassed into foreign territory and was killed by other wolves, a new alpha female from outside the pack moved in. She produced pups the next year and used the same den where the errant female had borne her pups a year earlier. Perhaps the new female found the old den independently. More probably, she learned its location from the alpha male or yearlings that remained in the pack.

Wolves produce an average of five or six pups per litter, although they sometimes bear up to nine pups, and perhaps eleven. They only produce one litter a year, but once mature, they usually whelp annually.

During the first three weeks, the pups remain inside the den with their mother. They cannot yet regulate their own heat, so their mother's presence is very important. The mother is then pretty well restricted to the den to keep the pups warm, and she is dependent on the alpha male or other pack members to regurgitate food to her. At about two weeks of age, the pups' eyes open, and when three weeks old, the pups can hear. Their milk teeth break through then, and the pups begin to eat small pieces of meat.

During their fourth week, the pups first show up outside the den. Their mother can then go off for hours on end to hunt. I recorded one mother wolf that once stayed away from her lone, four- to five-week-old pup for twenty hours at a time. The other pack members were gone as well. Every few hours, the lonely little fuzzball would wander to the front of the den and let out plaintive, pleading pup-howls advertising its empty belly.

As pups develop, they eat more and more solid food regurgitated to them by adults, or carried back to them. By five to six weeks of age, they are very robust and can follow the adults as far away as a mile from the den.

Pups grow rapidly, and they are weaned at about nine weeks of age. About that time, the pups generally forsake the den. They are then moved to a "rendezvous site," which is essentially a den above the ground. In forested areas, rendez-

*Newborn pups are blind and deaf, and weigh about a pound each. Unable to maintain their body heat until about three weeks of age, pups must rely on warmth from their mother. Their eyes open when they are about two weeks old, and they can hear when about three weeks old. Even when newborn, the pups are very muscular and strong. They can crawl and compete with each other to get at their mother's teats. (Photo by L. David Mech)*

*By four weeks of age, the wolf pups' ears stand erect, and the animals somewhat resemble kittens. They spend more time outside the den and may venture as far away as fifty feet from the entrance. Any sudden sound or frightening noise, however, sends them scurrying back to the safety of the den. (Photo by L. David Mech)*

vous sites are often situated in low, shaded areas. The pups spend much time huddled together in a pile in one part of the site, and then travel back and forth a few hundred yards around it. They headquarter there, while the adults hunt and bring food back to them. In open areas, pups are just kept in willow thickets, around rock piles, or near holes in the ground.

Sometimes, if the adults kill a large animal, they take the pups to it rather than carrying food from the carcass back to the pups. As the pups hang around the carcass, they essentially develop a rendezvous site right there. Some wolf families use the same rendezvous site throughout summer, but other adults may move their pups to a series of rendezvous sites, some often many miles from the others.

Pups remain in rendezvous sites until about mid-September, when they begin traveling with the pack more and more. On the other hand, runty pups may remain at the rendezvous site for several more weeks. Adults do continue to return with food, but probably not as often since they are frequently traveling far away with the healthier pups. The laggards then either die or gain enough weight to eventually join the traveling pack.

This is a no-nonsense system of reproduction that forges strong, competent animals. Life is generally rough for wolves, so there is little room for individuals that cannot make it. The survivors then are the best prepared for contending with the formidable challenges they must face.

*At about three weeks of age, the wolf pup first emerges from the den. Sharp, prickly teeth begin to emerge, and the pup can begin eating solid food regurgitated by the adults. It already growls at its competing littermates, and it readily fights and wrestles with them. (Photo by Fred Harrington)*

When about two months old, wolf pups start growing adult hair around their noses and eyes, and their bodies begin taking on the conformation of adults'. They may weigh fifteen to twenty pounds during this stage. (Photo by Tom Brakefield)

Wolf pups nurse four to five times a day for periods ranging from three to five minutes each. One pup, however, was known to go some eighteen hours without nursing because its mother remained away hunting all that time. A full litter of pups is weaned at about nine weeks of age, and a single pup may be weaned as early as six weeks. (Photo by L. David Mech)

Left: Five weeks old, wolf pups are larger but still show the same basic conformation as four-week-old pups. They have learned to wander farther from the den and have become much bolder. (Photo by L. David Mech)

# WOLF RENDEZVOUS SITES

Wolves move pups from dens to rendezvous sites after about eight weeks of age. The rendezvous site is an area where the whole pack headquarters, a sort of den above ground. The pups spend much of the time at the site huddled together in a pile to keep warm, but they also venture for several hundred yards in various directions, giving the site a well-used look.

In the Superior National Forest of Minnesota, wolf rendezvous sites are often heavily shaded lowlands thick with dense vegetation. One such site I checked included the edge of a birch-aspen forest and an almost impenetrable (to me!) alder swamp, interwoven with tall grass. Well-worn trails led towards the center of the site. There, freshly chewed bones and numerous scats, complete with flies, littered the padded-down beds and paths that in many places were only tunnels through the northern jungle. One especially large bed evidenced the favorite spot where the pups had piled up to sleep.

Although thick vegetation is non-exitent in the High Arctic, wolf rendezvous sites there still afford the pups protection by being located near rock crevices. Usually such crevices are too small for the adults. However, so long as the pups can squeeze into them should danger arise, the adults apparently feel comfortable leaving the pups nearby while they go off to hunt.

Rendezvous sites are sometimes traditional, being used in several consecutive years. Other times, they are used once and abandoned. Sometimes rendezvous sites seem to be chosen purely for convenience, especially when the pups are older and less fragile. In such cases, the adults may lead the pups for miles to an adult moose or other large prey animal they have killed. Rather than transport the prey, piece by piece, back to the pups, they merely transport the pups to the prey. The whole pack then headquarters there until the wolves literally eat themselves out of house and home!

The differences in habitats that support wolves and their young, that afford them places to make dens and rendezvous sites, astonish humans. Wolves continue to live in a great variety of northern habitats: barren grounds, tundra, taiga, plains or steppes, savannahs, deserts, mountains, and forests—wherever wilderness remains. The function of rendezvous sites is, of course, the same: to provide the growing pups with a safe headquarters at which all the adult pack members can rendezvous when they are not out hunting.

*When the pups are hungry, which is most of the time except right after they have eaten, they often get more food by persistently licking an adult's muzzle, sometimes trying to get their tongue into the adult's mouth. Fervent enough displays trigger food disgorgement. As wolves get older, this food-begging behavior eventually transforms into a greeting ritual by adult wolves towards the pack leaders. (Photo by L. David Mech)*

*Yearling and adult wolves bring home food in their bellies to the pups, and regurgitate it to the young. The pups madly rush any arriving adult, swarm around it, and excitedly jump at its mouth, until the adult brings up its partly digested booty. The pups gobble up the food instantly. From any one stomach load, the adult can regurgitate at least three times, and probably still have some left for itself. (Photo by L. David Mech)*

# · WOLF ·
# CONSERVATION

*Wolves are completely at home in and around water, and in much of their range probably swim across waterways daily. They often prey on beavers, which requires their regular patrol of lakes and streams. (Photo by Tom Brakefield)*

Wolves were once the most widely distributed mammal in the world. As mentioned earlier, they lived everywhere outside of Africa above about 20 degrees north latitude, which runs through Mexico City and southern India. In much of their former range, however, they have been wiped out. This resulted from habitat destruction and deliberate persecution, primarily by official government programs well supported by the public. Because wolves kill livestock and pets, they competed directly with humans. Thus, in extensive agricultural areas, it was inevitable that wolves had to go.

However, in many cases wolves were exterminated from areas even without livestock. One of the best examples is Yellowstone National Park, located at the juncture of northwestern Wyoming, eastern Idaho, and southern Montana. National parks are supposed to help preserve their natural plant, animal, and geologic systems. Although all other prominent components of the Yellowstone ecosystem have been preserved, its major predator was deliberately destroyed. The official mentality of that era is manifest in the May 1922 monthly report of the Yellowstone Park superintendent: "It is evident that the work of controlling these animals must be vigorously prosecuted by the most effective means available whether or not this meets with the approval of certain game conservationists."

An official program of extermination in Yellowstone cleaned out the wolf population there by the early 1930s. The same was true for several other areas of the western United States and the upper Midwest. In other areas of the world, such as Norway, Sweden, Finland, and parts of the Soviet Union, much the same approach was used.

Today, most wolves in the world are found primarily in wilderness—unarable, steep, remote, or otherwise inaccessible areas. It really can never be otherwise. Conservation

*Whether it be to nab a swimming beaver or to chase a deer or moose trying to escape into water, wolves must be ever ready to jump in. (Photo by Tom Brakefield)*

efforts, then, must be devoted primarily to restoring wolves to suitable areas where they have been eliminated, and to preserving extensive wilderness where the wolf still lives.

But conservationists must also recognize that when and where wolves are established in wilderness, young dispersers will try to colonize adjacent areas used or settled by people. Eventually these wolves or their offspring will prey on livestock and pets. And where human and wolf interests collide, control programs will be necessary: Some wolves will have to be killed.

In most cases, such wolves cannot be translocated elsewhere. First, once these intelligent hunters have learned to kill pets and livestock in one area, they would tend to do so in the new areas. Second, by the time such a translocation might be needed, most suitable wolf range would already have been saturated with wolves.

Neither could livestock-depredating wolves be held in captivity, for they remain shy and fearful and only languish when penned or controlled by people. They do not make good display animals. It is unfortunate that some wolves will have to be killed. However, this should be regarded as the necessary price for allowing wolves to live elsewhere.

A program that dispatches errant wolves has been in effect in northern Minnesota and has worked well for years. There, both state and federal government programs have kept the livestock-depredation problem under control. Some 230,000 to 360,000 cattle, 16,000 to 58,000 sheep, and 680,000 turkeys are raised in certain parts of Minnesota's 25,000-square-mile wolf range on about 7,200 farms. On average, the annual wolf-caused losses claimed by farmers have been about 70 cattle, 90 sheep, and 320 turkeys, and damage has been confirmed at 21 farms.

When a farmer or rancher believes livestock have suffered wolf damage, the individual calls government officials, and they respond within twenty-four hours. If physical sign of a kill is found, as well as evidence of wolf involvement, the Minnesota Department of Agriculture pays the owner compensation for the loss. The U.S. Department of Agriculture sends a wolf trapper to try to kill the offending animal. From 1975 through 1987, an average of thirty-six wolves a year were taken.

In 1988 and 1989, wolf-caused losses increased, and sixty-four and ninety-five wolves were trapped. At this writing, it is unclear whether these figures represent a permanent increase in wolf numbers and/or wolf damage, or whether some other factor was involved. Whatever the case, a combination of wolf control in agricultural areas and compensation for wolf damages to livestock seems a reasonable price to pay for allowing wolves to live in our wildernesses.

## WOLF POPULATION REGULATION

One of the main questions facing wolf researchers is: What regulates wolf population trends? Three decades of wolf population studies on Isle Royale in Lake Superior and two decades of such studies in the Superior National Forest of Minnesota have been devoted to the question. Much information has been obtained and many aspects of the question answered; shorter studies from other areas have also helped. Basically, it is known that the higher the wolf food supply, the higher the wolf population. Thus, areas having more "biomass" of total prey tend to have higher wolf numbers.

Nevertheless, higher amounts of existing prey do not necessarily mean that more food is available to wolves. What seems to count is the amount of *vulnerable* prey, and that can vary by season and by year. Just what factors make prey vulnerable and how these translate into changes in wolf numbers are some of the main questions still occupying wolf biologists. For example, on Isle Royale there has been little relationship between the number of moose in a given year and the number of wolves.

*Always with an eye on their prey, wolves enter water effortlessly in pursuit. (Photo by Tom Brakefield)*

Wolf control can take the form of government programs or of well-regulated public harvest. Killing individual "nuisance" wolves is more precise but more expensive. Public hunting or trapping is best suited to extensive areas where wolves must be reduced or eliminated because of too much conflict with humans.

Control of wolves to increase big game herds is highly controversial. When the numbers of such prey animals as elk, moose, or deer are low as a result of overhunting or adverse weather, wolf control may speed recovery of these herds. However, when prey numbers are not low, or when prey are limited by other factors, wolf control has little effect. Wildlife managers generally have been learning these facts, so there now are few widespread wolf-control efforts to benefit big game animals and the people who want to hunt them.

Nevertheless, even local wolf-control programs, set up in response to severely dwindling herds, are often condemned by the public. While these are noble sentiments, they may fail to consider that when prey numbers fall, wolf pups die slowly from starvation, disease, and parasitism, while adults often end up killing each other.

Wildlife managers favoring control under these conditions argue that faster recovery of prey herds allows faster wolf population recovery as well. Certainly with prescription

*A pursuing wolf plunges ahead—in water shallow or deep. A wolf in northeastern Minnesota was seen swimming behind a deer until it caught up, killing the deer while both swam. (Photo by Tom Brakefield)*

110

*Where wolves inhabit agricultural areas, they may prey on livestock. This habit has led to official destruction of wolves the world over. Current, more enlightened wolf-depredation control includes killing only the wolves actually involved in the depredations, compensating ranchers for the losses wolves have caused, and educating livestock owners in good husbandry practices that minimize wolf depredations. (Photo by Bill Paul)*

*Populations of caribou herds across northern Canada and Alaska have risen and fallen over the decades, and wolves have often been blamed for the declines. As a result, wolves have been controlled in some local areas in an attempt to promote increases in herd size. In some instances, wolf control seems to have resulted in caribou population increases. In other cases, caribou have increased in the face of uncontrolled wolf populations. Wildlife biologists currently disagree among themselves about the effect of wolf predation on caribou numbers. (Photo by L. David Mech)*

wolf control in local areas, wolves usually repopulate within a few years. For example, when wolves in south-central Alaska were reduced by 58 percent, the survivors increased to within 80 percent of their previous number within a year. Within three years, their numbers exceeded pre-control levels. Fortunately, regardless of a person's view on wolf control, the wolf populations in these areas as a whole continue to survive despite temporary control.

The public has shown that in general it has a strong positive interest in the wolf. A Yale University survey of Minnesota residents, for example, indicated that most citizens, including those in wolf range, looked favorably upon the wolf. They felt that the creature should be an integral part of Minnesota's wilderness. Although farmers were less favorably inclined towards the wolf, still most farmers held positive attitudes towards wolves.

The U.S. public's interest in the wolf is also reflected in the federal Endangered Species Acts. These laws declare the wolf endangered in all the lower forty-eight states, except Minnesota where it is on the endangered species list although classified as threatened. "Endangered" means that a group of animals is in danger of extinction in all, or a significant portion, of its range, while "threatened" means that in the foreseeable future, they may become endangered. In keeping with the laws, the federal government has appointed special wolf recovery teams, one for the eastern timber wolf, one for the northern Rocky Mountain wolf, one for the Mexican wolf, and one for the red wolf. The wolf recovery teams have produced plans that are idealized proposals for the recovery of each subspecies in danger. While the plans may never be fulfilled, they are useful guidelines for government agencies involved with wildlife or land management in wolf range.

The northern Rocky Mountain wolf recovery plan calls for reintroduction of the wolf into Yellowstone National Park. As mentioned earlier, the wolves there were killed off by people about sixty years ago. Congressman Wayne Owens (Democrat, Utah) in 1989 and Senator James McClure (Republican, Idaho) in 1990 introduced bills into the U.S. Congress to facilitate wolf reintroduction into the park, and Congress even appropriated monies to study the situation. Healthy populations of prey animals wander the parklands, and few natural predators hunt these elk, moose, bison, bighorn sheep, and pronghorn antelope. Human hunters periodically must thin some of the herds just outside the park.

The major opposition to the plan comes from local ranchers who must bear at least some livestock losses when wolves disperse from the park. However, the recovery plan calls for control of wolves where necessary outside the park.

Furthermore, the Defenders of Wildlife, a nationwide organization, has instituted a compensation fund to pay farmers for their losses. Surveys of Yellowstone Park visitors indicate overwhelming support for wolf reintroduction. It appears to be only a matter of time before wolves will once again roam the hills and valleys of Yellowstone.

Another significant development favoring wolf conservation is the International Wolf Center in Ely, Minnesota. This center combines a variety of vibrant, wolf-related educational activities in a single setting. It does not propagandize for or against the wolf; it provides factual education about the wolf.

A unique and important part of the wolf center is a program for the public to experience the wolf in its own environment. Field trips include hikes to find wolf tracks, abandoned dens, and other signs of wolves; evening trips to hear wolves howl; ski, snowshoe, and dogsled excursions to snowtrack wolves and see remains of their kills; winter flights to actually observe wolves; and guided wolf research in which the public participates. These activities enliven the education offered by exhibits, lectures, demonstrations, and audiovisual presentations.

Because the wolf originally was the most widely distributed mammal in the world, there is strong international interest in the creature. The international component of the wolf center is provided by appropriate displays and by periodic visits from foreign wolf specialists who present programs about wolves in their countries.

The International Wolf Center's new building, to open during the next few years, will house the Science Museum of Minnesota's six-thousand-square-foot exhibit "Wolves and Humans." The exhibit includes a mounted wolf pack around a kill, video displays of wolf behavior, a booth where one can listen to howling, videotaped interviews with people of diverse views about wolves, a computerized wolf predation game, and numerous other artifacts and audiovisuals about wolves and their interactions with humans. This exhibit has been traveling around the United States and Canada, and more than two million people have already seen it.

Elsewhere in the world, wolf conservation efforts are proceeding well in many areas. The Council of Europe has adopted the "Manifesto and Guidelines for Wolf Conservation" established by the International Union for the Conservation of Nature and Natural Resources' Species Survival Commission (IUCN/SSC) Wolf Specialist Group, which is the world's foremost wolf conservation organization. Wolves are increasing in Italy, Spain, and Portugal. Canada's population of fifty thousand wolves remains relatively intact, and al-

*(Photo by Thomas Meier)*

*At the International Wolf Center in Ely, Minnesota, the public can participate in guided field activities to observe wolves, listen to them howl, and to see their tracks, scats, and kills. Here a weekend group skis across a wilderness lake after examining a wolf-killed deer. The International Wolf Center combines such field activities with formal courses about wolf biology, audiovisual presentations, viewing of a captive wolf pack, and will eventually feature a tour through the six-thousand-square-foot, award-winning "Wolves and Humans" exhibit. (Photo by the International Wolf Center)*

though wolf hunting is permitted throughout the country, some provinces only permit taking during part of the year. Alaska has banned aerial wolf hunting but does allow hunting and trapping of its wolves, guaranteeing survival of its populations through closed seasons during part of the year.

In other parts of the world, wolves fare quite differently. Mexico's wolves are almost gone. The few wolves in Norway and Sweden cause great controversy when they prey on livestock, thus jeopardizing their future. The Soviet Union has greatly reduced its wolf population, even in its nature preserves. The wolves in Israel are barely hanging on, while those of India have yet even to be counted. Worldwide the picture is mixed.

Nevertheless, several countries that still harbor wolves have set an example. Wolves can be allowed to live in wild areas or can be reestablished there so long as appropriate management is planned. We can only hope that elsewhere these lessons will be learned. Then, perhaps someday the wolf will again inhabit every suitable wilderness throughout the world.

# SUGGESTED
# ·READINGS·

For readers interested in digging deeper into the way of the wolf, the following books will provide a wealth of solid facts:

Allen, D. L. 1979. *The Wolves of Minong: Their Vital Role in a Wild Community*. Houghton Mifflin Co., Boston.

Boitani, L. 1987. *Dalla Parte del Lupo*. L'Airone di Giorgio Mondadori e Associati Spa, Milano.

Harrington, F. H. and P. C. Paquet (Eds.). 1982. *Wolves of the World*. Noyes Publications, Park Ridge, NJ.

Klinghammer, E. (Ed.). 1979. *The Behavior and Ecology of Wolves*. Garland STPM Press, New York, London.

Mech, L. D. 1988. *The Arctic Wolf: Living with the Pack*. Voyageur Press, MN.

Mech, L. D. 1970, reprint 1981. *The Wolf: Ecology and Behavior of an Endangered Species*. University of Minnesota Press, Minneapolis, MN.

Murie, A. 1944. *The Wolves of Mount McKinley*. Fauna of the National Parks of the United States. Fauna Series No. 5. U.S. Government Printing Office.

National Geographic Video. 1988. *White Wolf*. National Geographic Society, Washington, D.C.

Peterson, R. O. 1977. *Wolf Ecology and Prey Relationships on Isle Royale*. National Park Service Scientific Monograph Series No. 11.

Savage, Candace. 1988. *Wolves*. Sierra Club Books, San Francisco, CA.

Walberg, K. I. 1987. *Ulven*. Grondahl & Sons, Forlag A. S., Oslo.

Zimen, E. 1981. *The Wolf: A Species in Danger*. Delacorte, NY.

*The first ice of winter intrigues a wolf and needs to be explored. Wolves cross waterways daily in many areas, so knowing when the ice is safe presents a constant problem during fall and winter. (Photo by Tom Brakefield)*

# ABOUT THE AUTHOR
# AND THE PHOTOGRAPHERS

*(Photo by L. David Mech)*

A noted wildlife research biologist, "wolfman" Dr. L. David Mech has studied wolves and their prey full-time since 1958, except for a four-year period when he studied radio-tracking. During this record-long career as a wolf biologist, he has published four previous books, including the international best-seller *The Arctic Wolf: Living with the Pack,* published by Voyageur Press in 1988. His classic book, *The Wolf,* was originally published in 1970 and has sold over 60,000 copies. He has written hundreds of scientific and popular articles on wildlife topics for such publications as *National Geographic, Audubon, Defenders, Natural History,* and *Science.*

Known internationally, Mech has studied wolves in the United States, Italy, Canada, and elsewhere; leopards and lions in Kenya; tigers in India; and has done wildlife censusing in the Soviet Union. Mech's studies have included major investigations of the wolves and moose of Isle Royale National Park in Lake Superior, wolves and white-tailed deer in Minnesota, wolves and musk-oxen in the High Arctic, as well as wolves and moose, caribou, and Dall sheep in Denali National Park, Alaska. He is probably the only person who has watched wolves kill moose, deer, caribou, musk-oxen, and arctic hares. He is also most likely the only person who has had his boot laces untied by a wild wolf pup. Working for the future of the wolf, Mech chairs the Wolf Specialist Group of the International Union for the Conservation of Nature and Natural Resources (IUCN), is a member of several wolf recovery teams, and is founder and vice chair of the Committee for an International Wolf Center. Mech has a bachelor of science degree in conservation from Cornell University and a doctorate in wildlife ecology from Purdue. He is a wildlife research biologist for the U.S. Fish and Wildlife Service and an adjunct professor of the University of Minnesota.

Photographing wolves, like studying them, poses a major challenge. Almost all the world's wolf photographs result from four approaches: (1) opportunistic shots of wild wolves taken during wolf studies, primarily from aircraft, (2) close-ups of captive wolves in natural-looking surroundings, (3) photos of wild wolves in far-off areas, such as the High Arctic, and in national parks, where they are relatively unafraid of people, and (4) images of tame wolves temporarily released into the natural environment for the sake of photography. The last technique was pioneered by wolf biologist Douglas Pimlott when he released several wolves he had raised into Algonquin Provincial Park, Ontario, Canada, and then took spectacular black-and-white photos that appeared in his book *The World of the Wolf.*

To illustrate this undertaking, *The Way of the Wolf,* it was necessary to select photos obtained by all these means. Here, we have the advantage of viewing most major aspects of wolf biology through remarkable work by such photographers as Dr. Rolf Peterson from his Isle Royale study; Mr. Layne Kennedy and Miss Karen Hollett of captive wolves; Mr. Rick McIntyre of the wolves in Denali National Park; and Mr. Tom Brakefield who has been able to magnificently simulate numerous scenes that occur in the wild, but which would be impossible to capture there. We are indeed fortunate to be able to present this fine collection, to which I have added some of my own photos taken in the High Arctic.

# ◆ INDEX ◆

# So-Sweet Baby Wardrobe
## to mix & match

Carol Holding knows what a busy new mom is looking for—options!

Each of these stylish crochet pattern sets for Baby includes a cardigan, hat or bonnet, and booties, and gives you the choice of creating pants and a top or a one-piece romper.

Crochet your favorite outfit and see how happy your wee one will be in these playful, lively designs!

# Darlin' Duds

**INTERMEDIATE**

"I'm all dressed up just ready to go visiting so I can show off my new duds."

## SPECIAL STITCHES

**To change color:**

Work st until 2 lps rem on hook, drop old color, pick up new color and draw through both lps on hook, cut dropped color.

**Sc decrease (sc dec):**

Insert hook in first specified st and draw up a lp, insert hook in second specified st and draw up a lp; YO and draw through all 3 lps on hook: sc dec made.

**Front Post dc (FPdc):**

YO, insert hook from front to back to front around post of st one row below specified st and draw up a lp, (YO and draw through 2 lps on hook) 2 times: FPdc made.

# Blanket

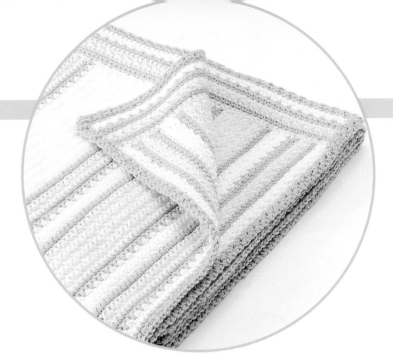

**Size:** 37" x 44"

**Materials**
Light worsted weight yarn
   13 oz white
   8 oz lt blue
   4 oz med blue
   3 oz lime
Size F (3.75 mm) crochet hook (or size required for gauge)

**Gauge**
19 sc = 4"; 20 rows in pattern = 4"

## Instructions

### CENTER

With white, ch 182.

**Row 1 (wrong side):** Sc in 2nd ch from hook and in each rem ch across: 181 sc; ch 1, turn.

**Row 2 (right side):** Work (sc, dc) in first sc; *skip next sc, (sc dc) in next sc; rep from * across to last 2 sc; skip next sc, sc in last sc, changing to lime: 181 sts. With lime, ch 1, turn. Finish off white.

**Row 3:** With lime, sc in first st and in each st across, changing to med blue in last sc. With med blue, ch 1, turn. Finish off lime.

**Row 4:** With med blue, sc in first sc and in each sc across, changing to lt blue in last sc. With lt blue, ch 1, turn. Finish off med blue.

**Row 5:** With lt blue, rep Row 4. Do not change color.

**Row 6:** With lt blue, rep Row 2. Do not change color.

**Row 7:** With lt blue, rep Row 3, changing to med blue in last sc. With med blue, ch 1, turn. Finish off lt blue.

**Row 8:** With med blue, rep Row 4, changing to lime in last sc. With lime, ch 1, turn. Finish off med blue.

**Row 9:** With lime, rep Row 4, changing to white in last sc. With white, ch 1, turn. Finish off lime.

**Rows 10 and 11:** With white, rep Rows 2 and 3. Do not change color.

**Rows 12 through 17:** Rep Rows 2 through 7. At end of Row 17, do not change color.

**Rows 18 and 23:** With lt blue, rep Rows 2 and 3 three times more. Do not change color. At end of Row 23, change to med blue in last sc. With med blue, ch 1, turn. Finish off lt blue.

**Rows 24 through 27:** Rep Rows 8 through 11.

**Rows 28 through 37:** Rep Rows 2 through 11.

**Rows 38 through 49:** With white, rep Rows 2 and 3 six times more. Do not change color.

**Rows 50 through 145:** Rep Rows 2 through 49 two times more.

**Rows 146 through 181:** Rep Rows 2 through 37. At end of Row 181, do not ch 1. Finish off; weave in ends.

### Right Edging

**Row 1:** With right side facing, join lt blue with sl st in edge of last sc on Row 1 of Center, ch 1, sc in edge of same row, work 161 more sc evenly spaced across right edge of rows, changing to lime in last sc: 162 sc. With lime, ch 1, turn. Finish off lt blue.

**Row 2:** With lime, sc in first sc and in each sc across, changing to med blue in last sc. With med blue, ch 1, turn. Finish off lime.

**Row 3:** With med blue, rep Row 2, changing to lt blue in last sc. With lt blue, ch 1, turn. Finish off med blue.

**Row 4:** With lt blue, rep Row 2. Do not change color.

**Row 5:** With lt blue, (sc, dc) in first sc; *skip next sc, (sc, dc) in next sc; rep from * across to last 3 sc; skip next sc, sc in last 2 sc: 162 sc; ch 1, turn.

**Row 6:** Sc in first st and in each st across, changing to med blue in last sc. With med blue, ch 1, turn. Finish off lt blue.

**Row 7:** With med blue, rep Row 2, changing to lime in last sc. With lime, ch 1, turn. Finish off med blue.

**Row 8:** With lime, rep Row 2, changing to white in last sc. With white, ch 1, turn. Finish off lime.

**Rows 9 and 10:** With white, rep Rows 5 and 6. Do not change color. At end of Row 6, do not ch 1. Finish off; weave in ends.

### Left Edging

**Row 1:** With right side facing, join lt blue with sl st in edge of first sc on Row 181 of Center, ch 1, sc in edge of same row, work 161 more sc evenly spaced across left edge of rows, changing to lime in last sc: 162 sc. With lime, ch 1, turn. Finish off lt blue.

**Rows 2 through 10:** Rep Rows 2 through 10 on Right Edging. At end of Row 10, change to med blue in last sc. With med blue, ch 1, turn. Finish off white.

### Border

**Rnd 1 (right side):** Work 2 sc in first sc on Row 10 of Left Edging (corner started); work 159 more sc evenly spaced across Row 10 to last sc, 3 sc in last sc (corner made); work 7 sc evenly spaced across edge of rows on Left Edging, sc in free lp of each foundation ch across bottom of Center; work 7 sc evenly spaced across edge of rows on Right Edging, 3 sc in last sc on Row 10 of Right Edging (corner made); work 159 more sc evenly spaced across Row 10 to last sc, 3 sc in last sc (corner made); work 7 sc evenly spaced across edge of rows on Right Edging, sc in each sc on Row 181 of Center; work 7 sc evenly spaced across edge of rows on Left Edging, sc in same sc as first 2 sc (corner completed): 720 sc; join with sl st in first sc.

**Rnd 2:** Ch 1, (sc, dc) in same sc as joining (center sc of corner), (sc, dc) in next sc; *skip next sc, (sc, dc) in next sc; rep from * across each side, working (sc, dc) in each of 3 sc in each corner and ending with (sc, dc) in first sc of first corner; join as before. Finish off; weave in ends

# Little Boy's Cardigan

**Size:** 3 to 6 months

**Materials**

Light worsted weight yarn
   2 oz  lt blue
   2 oz white
   1 oz med blue
   small amount lime
Size F (3.75 mm) crochet hook
   (or size required for gauge)
Five 5/8" diameter buttons
Matching sewing thread
Sewing needle

**Gauge**

In pattern, 18 sts = 4"; 20 rows = 4"

## Instructions

### BACK

Starting at bottom with lt blue, ch 49.

**Row 1 (wrong side):** Sc in 2nd ch from hook and in each rem ch across: 48 sc; ch 1, turn.

**Row 2 (right side):** Work (sc, dc) in first sc; *skip next sc, (sc, dc) in next sc; rep from * across to last 3 sc; skip next sc, sc in last 2 sc: 48 sts; ch 1, turn.

**Row 3:** Sc in first st and in each st across; ch 1, turn.

**Rows 4 through 16:** Rep Rows 2 and 3 six times more, the rep Row 2 once more, changing to med blue in last sc. With med blue, ch 1, turn. Finish off lt blue.

**Row 17:** With med blue, rep Row 3. At end of row, do not ch 1. Finish off; weave in ends.

### Armhole Shaping

**Row 1:** With right side facing, skip first 2 sc, join white with sl st in next sc, ch 1, (sc, dc) in same sc as joining; *skip next sc, (sc, dc) in next sc; rep from * across to last 5 sc; skip next sc, sc in next 2 sc: 44 sts; ch 1, turn, leaving rem sts unworked.

**Row 2:** Sc in first st and in each st across: 44 sc; ch 1, turn.

**Row 3:** Work (sc, dc) in first sc; *skip next sc, (sc, dc) in next sc; rep from * across to last 3 sc; skip next sc, sc in last 2 sc; ch 1, turn.

**Rows 4 through 20:** Rep Rows 2 and 3 eight times more, then rep Row 2 once more.

**Row 21:** Sc in first sc and in each sc across; ch 1, turn.

### Left Neck Shaping

**Row 1 (wrong side):** Sc in first 12 sc: 12 sc; ch 1, turn, leaving rem sts unworked.

**Row 2 (right side):** Sc in first sc and in each sc across. Finish off; weave in ends.

### Right Neck Shaping

**Row 1:** With wrong side facing, skip next 20 sc on Row 21 of Armhole Shaping, join white with sl st in next sc, ch 1, sc in same sc as joining and in each sc across: 12 sc; ch 1, turn.

**Row 2:** Sc in first sc and in each sc across. Finish off; weave in ends.

### LEFT FRONT

Starting at bottom with lt blue, ch 23.

**Row 1 (wrong side):** Sc in 2nd ch from hook and in each rem ch across: 22 sc; ch 1, turn.

**Row 2 (right side):** Work (sc, dc) in first sc; *skip next sc, (sc, dc) in next sc; rep from * across to last 3 sc; skip next sc, sc in last 2 sc: 22 sts; ch 1, turn.

**Row 3:** Sc in first st and in each st across; ch 1, turn.

**Rows 4 through 16:** Rep Rows 2 and 3 six times more, then rep Row 2 once more, changing to med blue in last sc. With med blue, ch 1, turn. Finish off lt blue.

**Row 17:** With med blue, rep Row 3. At end of row, do not ch 1. Finish off; weave in ends.

### Armhole Shaping

**Row 1:** With right side facing, skip first 2 sc on Row 17 of Left Front, join white with sl st in next sc, ch 1, (sc, dc) in same sc as joining; *skip next sc, (sc, dc) in next sc; rep from * across to last 3 sc; skip next sc, sc in last 2 sc: 20 sts; ch 1, turn.

**Row 2:** Sc in first st and in each st across: 20 sc; ch 1, turn.

**Row 3:** Work (sc, dc) in first sc; *skip next sc, (sc, dc) in next sc; rep from * across to last 3 sc; skip next sc, sc in last

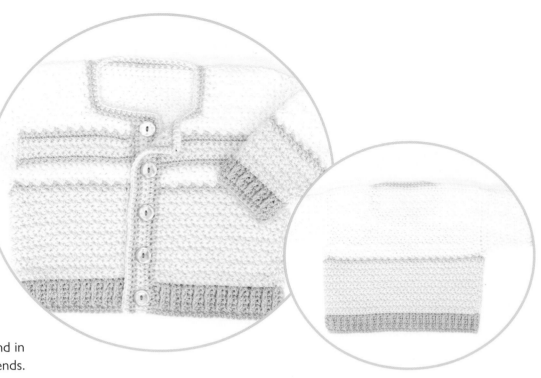

2 sc, changing to lime in last sc. With lime, ch 1, turn. Finish off white.

**Row 4:** With lime, rep Row 2, changing to med blue in last sc. With med blue, ch 1, turn. Finish off lime.

**Row 5:** With med blue, sc in first sc and in each sc across, changing to lt blue in last sc. With lt blue, ch 1, turn. Finish off med blue.

**Row 6:** With lt blue, rep Row 5. Do not change color.

**Row 7:** With lt blue, rep Row 3. Do not change color.

**Row 8:** With lt blue, rep Row 2, changing to med blue in last sc. With med blue, ch 1, turn. Finish off lt blue.

**Row 9:** With med blue, rep Row 5, changing to lime in last sc. With lime, ch 1, turn. Finish off med blue.

**Row 10:** With lime, rep Row 5, changing to white in last sc. With white, ch 1, turn. Finish off lime.

**Rows 11 and 12:** With white, rep Rows 3 and 2. Do not change color.

### Neck Shaping

**Row 1 (right side):** Work (sc, dc) in first sc; *skip next sc, (sc, dc) in next sc; rep from * 3 times more; skip next sc, sc in next 2 sc: 12 sts; ch 1, turn, leaving rem sts unworked.

**Row 2:** Sc in first st and in each st across: 12 sc; ch 1, turn.

**Row 3:** Work (sc, dc) in first sc; *skip next sc, (sc, dc) in next sc; rep from * across to last 3 sc; skip next sc, sc in next 2 sc; ch 1, turn.

**Rows 4 through 9:** Rep Rows 2 and 3 three times more. At end of Row 9, do not ch 1. Finish off; weave in ends.

## RIGHT FRONT

Starting at bottom with lt blue, ch 23.

**Row 1 (wrong side):** Sc in 2nd ch from hook and in each rem ch across: 22 sc; ch 1, turn.

**Row 2 (right side):** Sc in first sc, (sc, dc) in next sc; *skip next sc, (sc, dc) in next sc; rep from * across to last 2 sc; skip next sc, sc in last sc: 22 sts; ch 1, turn.

**Row 3:** Sc in first st and in each st across; ch 1, turn.

**Rows 4 through 16:** Rep Rows 2 and 3 six times more, then rep Row 2 once more, changing to med blue in last sc. With med blue, ch 1, turn. Finish off lt blue.

**Row 17:** With med blue, rep Row 3, changing to white in last sc. With white, ch 1, turn. Finish off med blue.

### Armhole Shaping

**Row 1 (right side):** With white, sc in first sc, (sc, dc) in next sc; *skip next sc, (sc, dc) in next sc; rep from * across to last 4 sc; skip next sc, sc in next sc: 20 sts; ch 1, turn, leaving rem sts unworked.

**Row 2:** Sc in first st and in each st across: 20 sc; ch 1, turn.

**Row 3:** Sc in first sc, (sc, dc) in next sc; *skip next sc, (sc, dc) in next sc; rep from * across to last 2 sc; skip next sc, sc in last sc, changing to lime. With lime, ch 1, turn. Finish off white.

**Row 4:** With lime, rep Row 2, changing to med blue in last sc. With med blue, ch 1, turn. Finish off lime.

**Row 5:** With med blue, sc in first sc and in each sc across, changing to lt blue in last sc. With lt blue, ch 1, turn. Finish off med blue.

**Row 6:** With lt blue, rep Row 5. Do not change color.

**Row 7:** With lt blue, rep Row 3. Do not change color.

**Row 8:** With lt blue, rep Row 2, changing to med blue in last sc. With med blue, ch 1, turn. Finish off lt blue.

**Row 9:** With med blue, rep Row 5, changing to lime in last sc. With lime, ch 1, turn. Finish off med blue.

**Row 10:** With lime, rep Row 5, changing to white in last sc. With white, ch 1, turn. Finish off lime.

**Rows 11 and 12:** With white, rep Rows 3 and 2. Do not change color. At end of Row 12, do not ch 1. Finish off; weave in ends.

### Neck Shaping

**Row 1:** With right side facing, skip first 8 sc on Row 12 of Armhole Shaping, join white with sl st in next sc, ch 1, sc in same sc as joining, (sc, dc) in next sc; *skip next sc, (sc, dc) in next sc; rep from * across to last 2 sc; skip next sc, sc in last sc: 12 sts; ch 1, turn.

**Row 2:** Sc in first st and in each st across: 12 sc; ch 1, turn.

**Row 3:** Sc in first st, (sc, dc) in next sc; *skip next sc, (sc, dc) in next sc; rep from * across to last 2 sc; skip next sc, sc in last sc; ch 1, turn.

**Rows 4 through 9:** Rep Rows 2 and 3 three times more. At end of Row 9, do not ch 1. Finish off; weave in ends.

Sew shoulder and side seams.

## RIBBING

**Row 1:** With right side facing and foundation ch at top, join med blue with sl st in free lp of first foundation ch on Left Front, ch 1, sc in same ch as joining, sc in free lp of next 21 chs, sc in free lp of next 48 chs on Back, sc in free lp of next 22 chs on Right Front: 92 sc; ch 1, turn.

**Row 2:** Sc in first sc and in each sc across; ch 1, turn.

**Row 3:** Sc in first sc, FPdc around next sc; *sc in next sc, FPdc around next sc; rep from * across to last 2 sc; sc in last 2 sc: 47 sc and 45 FPdc; ch 1, turn.

**Row 4:** Sc in first st and in each st across; ch 1, turn.

**Row 5:** Sc in first sc, FPdc around next FPdc; *sc in next sc, FPdc around next FPdc; rep from * across to last 2 sc; sc in last 2 sc; ch 1, turn.

**Rows 6 through 8:** Rep Rows 4 and 5 once, then rep Row 4 once more. At end of Row 8, do not ch 1 and do not turn.

### Left Placket

**Row 1 (wrong side):** Sc in edge of last sc made, work 35 more sc evenly spaced in edge of Ribbing, Left Front and Left Front Armhole Shaping, ending with sc in edge of Row 12 of Left Armhole Shaping, changing to lt blue in last sc: 36 sc. With lt blue, ch 1, turn. Finish off med blue.

**Row 2:** With lt blue, sc in first sc and in each sc across: 36 sc; ch 1, turn.

**Row 3:** Sc in first sc; *ch 2, skip next 2 sc, sc in next 6 sc; rep from * 3 times more; ch 2, skip next 2 sc, sc in last sc: 26 sc and 5 ch-2 sps; ch 1, turn.

**Row 4:** Sc in first sc; *2 sc in next ch-2 sp, sc in next 6 sc; rep from * 3 times more; 2 sc in next ch-2 sp, sc in next sc: 36 sc. Finish off; weave in ends.

## Right Placket

**Row 1:** With wrong side facing, join med blue with sl st in last sc on Row 12 of Right Front Armhole Shaping, ch 1, sc in same sc as joining, work 35 more sc evenly spaced in edge of Right Front Armhole Shaping, Right Front and Ribbing, ending with sc in edge of Row 8 of Ribbing, changing to lt blue in last sc: 36 sc. With lt blue, ch 1, turn. Finish off med blue.

**Row 2:** With lt blue, sc in first sc and in each sc across: 36 sc; ch 1, turn. At end of Row 4, do not ch 1. Finish off; weave in ends.

## Neck Edging

With right side facing, join lt blue with sl st in top edge of Row 4 on Right Placket, ch 1, sc in edge of same row, sc in edge of next 3 rows, sc in next 7 sc on Row 12 of Right Front Armhole Shaping, sc dec in next sc of Right Front Armhole Shaping and in edge of Row 1 on Right Front Neck Shaping, work 9 sc evenly spaced in edge of rows on Right Neck Shaping (Front and Back), sc dec in edge of Row 1 on Right Back Neck Shaping and in next sc on Row 21 of Back Armhole Shaping, sc in next 18 sc on Row 21, sc dec in next sc on Back Armhole Shaping and in edge of Row 1 on Left Back Neck Shaping, work 9 sc evenly spaced in edge of rows on Left Neck Shaping (Back and Front), sc dec in edge of Row 1 on Left Front Neck Shaping and in next sc on Row 12 of Left Front Armhole Shaping, sc in next 7 sc on Row 12, sc in edge of next 4 rows of Left Placket: 62 sc. Finish off; weave in ends.

## Placket and Neck Edging

**Row 1:** With wrong side facing, join med blue with sl st in last sc on Row 4 of Left Placket, ch 1, sc in same sc and in each sc on Row 4, sc in edge of Neck Edging, sc in edge of last sc made, sc in each sc on Neck Edging, working sc dec in sc before and after sc dec in each of 4 corners (skipping each sc dec), sc in edge of last sc made, sc in edge of Neck Edging, sc in each sc on Row 4 of Right Placket, changing to lt blue in last sc: 130 sc. With lt blue, ch 1, turn. Finish off med blue.

**Row 2 (right side):** With lt blue, sc in first 38 sc across Right Placket, sc in edge of last sc made, sc in next 56 sc around neck, sc in edge of last sc made, sc in last 38 sc across Left Placket: 134 sc. Finish off; weave in ends.

Sew buttons onto Right Placket.

## SLEEVES (MAKE 2)

With lt blue, ch 27.

**Row 1 (wrong side):** Sc in 2nd ch from hook and in each rem ch across: 26 sc; ch 1, turn.

**Row 2 (right side):** Work (sc, dc) in first sc; *skip next sc, (sc, dc) in next sc; rep from * across to last 3 sc; skip next sc, sc in last 2 sc: 26 sts; ch 1, turn.

**Row 3:** Work 2 sc in first sc, sc in each st across to last sc, 2 sc in last sc: 28 sc; ch 1, turn.

**Row 4:** Sc in first sc, (sc, dc) in next sc; *skip next sc, (sc, dc) in next sc; rep from * across to last 2 sc; skip next sc, sc in last sc: 28 sts; ch 1, turn.

**Row 5:** Sc in first st and in each st across; ch 1, turn.

**Row 6:** Rep Row 4.

**Row 7:** Rep Row 3: 30 sc.

**Row 8:** Rep Row 2, changing to med blue in last sc. With med blue, ch 1, turn. Finish off lt blue.

**Row 9:** With med blue, rep Row 5, changing to white in last sc. With white, ch 1, turn. Finish off med blue.

**Rows 10 through 13:** With white, rep Rows 2 through 5. At end of Row 11: 32 sc.

**Rows 14 through 24:** With white, rep Rows 6 through 13 once, then rep Rows 6 through 8 once more. Do not change color. At end of Row 15: 34 sc. At end of Row 19: 36 sc. At end of Row 23: 38 sc.

**Row 25:** Rep Row 3: 40 sc. At end of row, do not ch 1. Finish off; weave in ends.

## Sleeve Ribbing

**Row 1:** With right side facing and foundation ch at top, join med blue with sl st in free lp of first foundation ch on Sleeve, ch 1, sc in free lp of same ch as joining and in free lp of each ch across: 26 sc; ch 1, turn.

**Row 2:** Sc in first sc and in each sc across; ch 1, turn.

**Row 3:** Sc in first sc, FPdc around next sc; *sc in next sc, FPdc around next sc; rep from * across to last 2 sc; sc in last 2 sc; 14 sc and 12 FPdc; ch 1, turn.

**Row 4:** Sc in first st and in each st across; ch 1, turn.

**Row 5:** Sc in first sc, FPdc around next FPdc; *sc in next sc, FPdc around next FPdc; rep from * across to last 2 sc; sc in last 2 sc; ch 1, turn.

**Row 6:** Rep Row 4. At end of row, do not ch 1. Finish off; weave in ends.

Rep Ribbing on other sleeve. Set in sleeves. Sew sleeve seams.

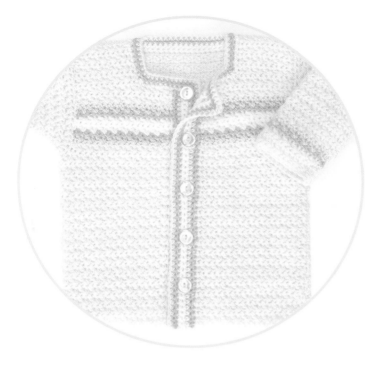

# Little Girl's Cardigan

**Size:** 3 to 6 months

**Materials**

Light worsted weight yarn
- 6 oz lt pink
- 1 oz med pink
- small amount white
- smalll amount lime
- small amount mint

Size F (3.75 mm) crochet hook (or size required for gauge)
Five ⅝" diameter buttons
Matching sewing thread
Sewing needle

**Gauge**

In pattern, 19 sts = 4"; 20 rows = 4"

## Instructions

### BACK

Starting at bottom with lt pink, ch 49.

**Row 1 (wrong side):** Sc in 2nd ch from hook and in each rem ch across: 48 sc; ch 1, turn.

**Row 2 (right side):** Work (sc, dc) in first sc; *skip next sc, (sc, dc) in next sc; rep from * across to last 3 sc; skip next sc, sc in last 2 sc: 48 sts; ch 1, turn.

**Row 3:** Sc in first st and in each st across; ch 1, turn.

**Rows 4 through 35:** Rep Rows 2 and 3 sixteen times more. At end of Row 35, do not ch 1. Turn.

#### Armhole Shaping

**Row 1 (right side):** Sl st in first 3 sc, ch 1, (sc, dc) in same sc; *skip next sc, (sc, dc) in next sc; rep from * across to last 5 sc; skip next sc, sc in next 2 sc: 44 sts; ch 1, turn, leaving rem sts unworked.

**Row 2:** Sc in first st and in each st across: 44 sc; ch 1, turn.

Row 3: Work (sc, dc) in first sc; *skip next sc, (sc, dc) in next sc; rep from * across to last 3 sc; skip next sc, sc in last 2 sc; ch 1, turn.

**Rows 4 through 20:** Rep Rows 2 and 3 eight times more, then rep Row 2 once more.

**Row 21:** Sc in first sc and in each sc across; ch 1, turn.

#### Left Neck Shaping

**Row 1 (wrong side):** Sc in first 12 sc: 12 sc; ch 1, turn, leaving rem sts unworked.

**Row 2 (right side):** Sc in first sc and in each sc across. Finish off; weave in ends.

#### Right Neck Shaping

**Row 1:** With wrong side facing, skip next 20 sc on Row 21 of Armhole Shaping, join lt pink with sl st in next sc, ch 1, sc in same sc as joining and in each sc across: 12 sc; ch 1, turn.

**Row 2:** Sc in first sc and in each sc across. Finish off; weave in ends.

### LEFT FRONT

Starting at bottom with lt pink, ch 23.

**Row 1 (wrong side):** Sc in 2nd ch from hook and in each rem ch across: 22 sc; ch 1, turn.

**Row 2 (right side):** Work (sc, dc) in first sc; *skip next, (sc, dc) in next sc; rep from * across to last 3 sc; skip next sc, sc in last 2 sc: 22 sts; ch 1, turn.

**Row 3:** Sc in first st and in each st across; ch 1, turn.

**Rows 4 through 35:** Rep Rows 2 and 3 sixteen times more. At end of Row 35, do not ch 1. Turn.

#### Armhole Shaping

**Row 1 (right side):** Sl st in first 3 sc, ch 1, (sc, dc) in same sc; *skip next sc, (sc, dc) in next sc; rep from * across to last 3 sc; skip next sc, sc in last 2 sc, changing to mint in last sc: 20 sts. With mint, ch 1, turn. Finish off lt pink.

**Row 2:** With mint, sc in first st and in each st across,

8

changing to lime in last sc: 20 sc. With lime, ch 1, turn. Finish off mint.

**Row 3:** With lime, work (sc, dc) in first sc; *skip next sc, (sc, dc) in next sc; rep from * across to last 3 sc; skip next sc, sc in last 2 sc, changing to med pink in last sc. With med pink, ch 1, turn. Finish off lime.

**Row 4:** With med pink, rep Row 2, changing to white in last sc. With white, ch 1, turn. Finish off med pink.

**Rows 5 and 6:** With white, rep Rows 3 and 2. Do not change color.

**Row 7:** With white, rep Row 3, changing to med pink in last sc. With med pink, ch 1, turn. Finish off white.

**Row 8:** With med pink, rep Row 2, changing to lime in last sc. With lime, ch 1, turn. Finish off med pink.

**Row 9:** With lime, rep Row 3, changing to mint in last sc. With mint, ch 1, turn. Finish off lime.

**Row 10:** With mint, rep Row 2, changing to lt pink in last sc. With lt pink, ch 1, turn. Finish off mint.

**Rows 11 through 13:** With lt pink, rep Row 3 once, then rep Rows 2 and 3 once more. At end of Row 13, do not ch 1. Finish off; weave in ends.

### Neck Shaping

**Row 1:** With wrong side facing, skip first 8 sts on Row 13 of Armhole Shaping, join lt pink with sl st in next st, ch 1, sc in same st as joining and in each st across: 12 sc; ch 1, turn.

**Row 2:** Work (sc, dc) in first sc; *skip next sc, (sc, dc) in next sc; rep from * across to last 3 sc; skip next sc, sc in last 2 sc: 12 sts; ch 1, turn.

**Row 3:** Sc in first st and in each st across; ch 1, turn.

**Rows 4 through 8:** Rep Rows 2 and 3 two times more, then rep Row 2 once more. At end of Row 8, do not ch 1. Finish off; weave in ends.

### RIGHT FRONT

Starting at bottom with lt pink, ch 23.

**Row 1 (wrong side):** Sc in 2nd ch from hook and in each rem ch across: 22 sc; ch 1, turn.

**Row 2 (right side):** Sc in first sc, (sc, dc) in next sc; *skip next sc, (sc, dc) in next sc; rep from * across to last 2 sc; skip next sc, sc in last sc: 22 sts; ch 1, turn.

**Row 3:** Sc in first st and in each st across; ch 1, turn.

**Rows 4 through 35:** Rep Rows 2 and 3 sixteen times more.

### Armhole Shaping

**Row 1 (right side):** Sc in first sc, (sc, dc) in next sc; *skip next sc, (sc, dc) in next sc; rep from * across to last 4 sc; skip next sc, sc in next sc, changing to mint: 20 sts. With mint, ch 1, turn, leaving rem sts unworked. Finish off lt pink.

**Row 2:** With mint, sc in first st and in each st across, changing to lime in last sc: 20 sc. With lime, ch 1, turn. Finish off mint.

**Row 3:** With lime, sc in first sc, (sc, dc) in next sc; *skip next sc, (sc, dc) in next sc; rep from * across to last 2 sc; skip next sc, sc in last sc, changing to med pink. With med pink, ch 1, turn. Finish off lime.

**Row 4:** With med pink, rep Row 2, changing to white in last sc. With white, ch 1, turn. Finish off med pink.

**Rows 5 and 6:** With white, rep Rows 3 and 2. Do not change color.

**Row 7:** With white, rep Row 3, changing to med pink in last sc. With med pink, ch 1, turn. Finish off white.

**Row 8:** With med pink, rep Row 2, changing to lime in last sc. With lime, ch 1, turn. Finish off med pink.

**Row 9:** With lime, rep Row 3, changing to mint in last sc. With mint, ch 1, turn. Finish off lime.

**Row 10:** With mint, rep Row 2, changing to lt pink in last sc. With lt pink, ch 1, turn. Finish off mint.

**Rows 11 through 13:** With lt pink, rep Row 3 once, then rep Rows 2 and 3 once more. Do not change color.

### Neck Shaping

**Row 1 (wrong side):** Sc in first 12 sts: 12 sc; ch 1, turn, leaving rem sts unworked.

**Row 2:** Sc in first sc, (sc, dc) in next sc; *skip next sc, (sc, dc) in next sc; rep from * across to last 2 sc; skip next sc, sc in last sc: 12 sts; ch 1, turn.

**Row 3:** Sc in first st and in each st across; ch 1, turn.

**Rows 4 through 8:** Rep Rows 2 and 3 two times more, then rep Row 2 once more. At end of Row 8, do not ch 1. Finish off; weave in ends.

### Left Placket

**Row 1:** With wrong side facing, join med pink with sl st in edge of last sc on Row 1 of Left Front, ch 1, sc in edge of same row, work 44 more sc evenly spaced in edge of rows on Left Front and Left Front Armhole Shaping, ending with sc in edge of Row 13 of Left Front Armhole Shaping, changing to white in last sc: 45 sc. With white, ch 1, turn.

Finish off med pink.

**Row 2:** With white, sc in first sc and in each sc across; ch 1, turn.

**Row 3:** Sc in first 6 sc; *ch 2, skip next 2 sc, sc in next 7 sc; rep from * 3 times more; ch 2, skip next 2 sc, sc in last sc: 35 sc and 5 ch-2 sps; ch 1, turn.

**Row 4:** Sc in first sc; *2 sc in next ch-2 sp, sc in next 7 sc; rep from * 3 times more; 2 sc in next ch-2 sp, sc in next 6 sc: 45 sc. Finish off.

### Right Placket

**Row 1:** With wrong side facing, join med pink with sl st in edge of first sc on Row 13 of Right Front Armhole Shaping, ch 1, sc in edge of same row, work 44 more sc evenly spaced in edge of rows on Right Front Armhole Shaping and Right Front, ending with sc in edge of Row 1 of Right Front, changing to white in last sc: 45 sc. With white, ch 1, turn. Finish off med pink.

**Rows 2 through 4:** With white, sc in first sc and in each sc across; ch 1, turn. At end of Row 4, do not ch 1. Finish off; weave in ends.

Sew shoulder seams.

### Neck Edging

**Row 1:** With right side facing, join white with sl st in top edge of Row 4 on Right Placket, ch 1, sc in edge of same row, sc in edge of next 3 rows, sc in next 7 sc on Row 13 of Right Front Armhole Shaping, sc dec in next sc of Right Front Armhole Shaping and in edge of Row 1 of Right Front Neck Shaping, work 9 sc evenly spaced in edge of rows on Right Neck Shaping (Front and Back), sc dec in edge of Row 1 on Right Back Neck Shaping and in next sc on Row 21 of Back Armhole Shaping, sc in next 18 sc on Row 21, sc dec in next sc on Back Armhole Shaping and in edge of Row 1 on Left Back Neck Shaping, work 9 sc evenly spaced in edge of rows on Left Neck Shaping (Back and Front), sc dec in edge of Row 1 on Left Front Neck Shaping and in next sc on Row 13 of Left Front Armhole Shaping, sc in next 7 sc on Row 13, sc in edge of next 4 rows of Left Placket: 62 sc. Finish off; weave in ends.

### Placket and Neck Edging

**Row 1:** With wrong side facing, join med pink with sl st in last sc on Row 4 of Left Placket, ch 1, sc in same sc and in each sc on Row 4, sc in edge of Row 1 of Neck Edging, sc in edge of last sc made, sc in each sc on Row 1 of Neck Edging, working sc dec in sc before and after sc dec in each of 4 corners (skipping each sc dec), sc in edge of last sc made, sc in edge of Row 1 of Neck Edging, sc in each sc on Row 4 of Right Placket, changing to lt pink in last sc: 148 sc. With lt pink, ch 1, turn. Finish off med pink.

**Row 2 (right side):** With lt pink, sc in first 47 sc across Right Placket, sc in edge of last sc made, sc in next 56 sc around neck, sc in edge of last sc made, sc in last 47 sc across Left Placket: 152 sc. Finish off; weave in ends.

Sew buttons onto Right Placket.

### SLEEVES (MAKE 2)

With lt pink, ch 27.

**Row 1 (wrong side):** Sc in 2nd ch from hook and in each rem ch across: 26 sc; ch 1, turn.

**Row 2 (right side):** Work (sc, dc) in first sc; *skip next sc, (sc, dc) in next sc; rep from * across to last 3 sc; skip next sc, sc in last 2 sc: 26 sts; ch 1, turn.

**Row 3:** Sc in first st and in each st across; ch 1, turn.

**Row 4:** Rep Row 2, changing to med pink in last sc. With med pink, ch 1, turn. Finish off lt pink.

**Row 5:** With med pink, rep Row 3, changing to lime in last sc. With lime, ch 1, turn. Finish off med pink.

**Row 6:** With lime, rep Row 2, changing to mint in last sc. With mint, ch 1, turn. Finish off lime.

**Row 7:** With mint, work 2 sc in first st, sc in each st across to last st, 2 sc in last st, changing to lt pink in last sc: 28 sc. With lt pink, ch 1, turn. Finish off mint.

**Row 8:** With lt pink, sc in first sc; *(sc, dc) in next sc, skip next sc; rep from * across to last sc, sc in last sc: 28 sts; ch 1, turn.

**Row 9:** Rep Row 3.

**Rows 10 through 14:** Rep Rows 8 and 9 two times more, then rep Row 8 once more.

**Row 15:** With lt pink, rep Row 7: 30 sc. Do not change color.

**Rows 16 through 18:** Rep Rows 2 and 3 once, then rep Row 2 once more.

**Rows 19 and 20:** With lt pink, rep Rows 7 and 8. Do not change color. At end of Row 19: 32 sc.

**Row 21:** Rep Row 3.

**Row 22:** Rep Row 8.

**Rows 23 through 28:** Rep Rows 15 through 20. At end of Row 23: 34 sc. At end of Row 27: 36 sc.

**Row 29:** With lt pink, rep Row 7: 38 sc. Do not change color.

**Row 30:** Rep Row 2.

**Row 31:** With lt pink, rep Row 7: 40 sc. Do not change color. At end of row, do not ch 1. Finish off; weave in ends.

Set in sleeves. Sew sleeve and side seams.

# Shirt

**Size:** 3 to 6 months

## Materials
Light worsted weight yarn
    4 oz white
    ¹/₂ oz lt Pink
    small amount med pink
    small amount mint
    small amount lime
Size F (3.75 mm) crochet hook (or size required for gauge)
Two ⁵/₈" diameter buttons
Matching sewing thread
Sewing needle

## Gauge
In sc, 18 sts = 4"; 21 rows = 4"

## Instructions

### FRONT

Starting at bottom with white, ch 43.

**Row 1 (wrong side):** Sc in 2nd ch from hook and in each rem ch across: 42 sc; ch 1, turn.

**Row 2 (right side):** Sc in first sc and in each sc across; ch 1, turn.

**Rows 3 through 27:** Rep Row 2 twenty five times more. At end of Row 27, change to mint in last sc. With mint, ch 1, turn. Finish off white.

**Row 28:** With mint, rep Row 2, changing to lime in last sc. With lime, ch 1, turn. Finish off mint.

**Row 29:** With lime, rep Row 2, changing to med pink in last sc. With med pink, ch 1, turn. Finish off lime.

**Row 30:** With med pink, rep Row 2. At end of row, do not ch 1. Finish off. Turn.

### Armhole Shaping

**Row 1:** With wrong side facing, skip first 2 sc on Row 30, join lt pink with sl st in next sc, ch 1, sc in same sc as joining and in each sc across to last 2 sc: 38 sc; ch 1, turn, leaving rem sts unworked.

**Row 2:** Work (sc, dc) in first sc; *skip next sc, (sc, dc) in next sc; rep from * across to last 3 sc; skip next sc, sc in last 2 sc: 38 sts; ch 1, turn.

**Row 3:** Sc in first st and in each st across, changing to med pink in last sc. With med pink, ch 1, turn. Finish off lt pink.

**Row 4:** With med pink, sc in first sc and in each sc across, changing to lime in last sc. With lime, ch 1, turn. Finish off med pink.

**Row 5:** With lime, rep Row 4, changing to mint in last sc. With mint, ch 1, turn. Finish off lime.

**Row 6:** With mint, rep Row 4, changing to white in last sc. With white, ch 1, turn. Finish off mint.

**Rows 7 through 11:** With white, rep Row 4 five times more.

### Left Neck Shaping

**Row 1 (right side):** Sc in first 10 sc: 10 sc; ch 1, turn, leaving rem sts unworked.

**Rows 2 through 9:** Sc in first sc and in each sc across; ch 1, turn. At end of Row 9, do not ch 1. Finish off; weave in ends.

### Right Neck Shaping

**Row 1:** With right side facing, skip next 18 sc on Row 11 of

Armhole Shaping, join white with sl st in next sc, ch 1, sc in same sc as joining and in each sc across: 10 sc; ch 1, turn.

**Rows 2 through 9:** Sc in first sc and in each sc across; ch 1, turn. At end of Row 9, do not ch 1. Finish off; weave in ends.

### BACK

Starting at bottom with white, ch 43.

**Rows 1 through 30:** Rep Rows 1 through 30 on Front.

### Armhole Shaping

**Row 1:** With wrong side facing, skip first 2 sc on Row 30, join white with sl st in next sc, ch 1, sc in same sc as joining and in each sc across to last 2 sc: 38 sc; ch 1, turn, leaving rem sts unworked.

**Rows 2 through 4:** Sc in first sc and in each sc across; ch 1, turn.

### Left Back

**Row 1 (wrong side):** Sc in first 17 sc: 17 sc; ch 1, turn, leaving rem sts unworked.

**Rows 2 through 14:** Sc in first sc and in each sc across; ch 1, turn.

### Neck Shaping

**Row 1 (wrong side):** Sc in first 10 sc: 10 sc; ch 1, turn, leaving rem sts unworked.

**Row 2:** Sc in first sc and in each sc across. Finish off; weave in ends.

### Right Back

**Row 1:** With wrong side facing, skip next 4 sc on Row 4 of Armhole Shaping, join white with sl st in next sc, ch 1, sc in same sc as joining and in each sc across: 17 sc; ch 1, turn.

**Rows 2 through 14:** Sc in first sc and in each sc across; ch 1, turn. At end of Row 14, do not ch 1. Finish off; weave in ends.

### Neck Shaping

**Row 1:** With wrong side facing, skip first 7 sc on Row 14 of Right Back, join white with sl st in next sc, ch 1, sc in same sc as joining and in each sc across: 10 sc; ch 1, turn.

**Row 2:** Sc in first sc and in each sc across. Finish off; weave in ends.

### Right Placket

**Row 1:** With wrong side facing, join lt pink with sl st in edge of first sc on Row 1 of Right Back, ch 1, sc in edge of same row, work 12 more sc evenly spaced in edge of rows on Right Back, ending with sc in edge of Row 14 of Right Back: 13 sc; ch 1, turn.

**Rows 2 and 3:** Sc in first sc and in each sc across; ch 1, turn.

**Row 4:** Sc in first sc; *ch 2, skip next 2 sc, sc in next 4 sc; rep from * once more: 9 sc and 2 ch-2 sps. Finish off.

### Left Placket

**Row 1:** With wrong side facing, join lt pink with sl st in edge of first sc on Row 14 of Left Back, ch 1, sc in edge of same row, work 12 more sc evenly spaced in edge of rows on Left Back, ending with sc in edge of Row 1 of Left Back: 13 sc; ch 1, turn.

**Rows 2 through 4:** Sc in first sc and in each sc across; ch 1, turn. At end of Row 4, do not ch 1. Finish off.

Sew shoulder seams.

### Neck Edging

With right side facing, join lt pink with sl st in top edge of Row 4 on Left Placket, ch 1, sc in edge of same row, sc in edge of next 3 rows, sc in next 6 sc on Row 14 of Left Back, sc dec in next sc of Left Back and in edge of Row 1 of Neck Shaping, sc in edge of next 9 rows on Left Neck Shaping (Back and Front), sc dec in edge of Row 1 of Front Left Neck Shaping and in next sc on Row 11 of Front Armhole Shaping, sc in next 16 sc on Row 11, sc dec in next sc on Row 11 of Front Armhole Shaping and in edge of Row 1 of Front Right Neck Shaping, sc in edge of next 9 rows on Right Neck Shaping (Front and Back), sc dec in edge of Row 1 of Back Right Neck Shaping and in next sc on Row 14 of Right Back, sc in next 6 sc on Row 14, sc in edge of next 4 rows on Right Placket: 58 sc. Finish off.

### Placket and Neck Edging

**Row 1:** With wrong side facing, join lt pink with sl st in last sc on Row 4 of Right Placket, ch 1, sc in same sc as joining and in next 3 sc, 2 sc in next ch-2 sp, sc in next 4 sc, 2 sc in next ch-2 sp, sc in next sc, sc in edge of Neck Edging, sc in edge of last sc made, sc in each sc of Neck Edging, working sc dec in sc before and after sc dec in each of 4 corners (skipping each sc dec), sc in edge of last sc made, sc in edge of Neck Edging, sc in each sc on Row 4 of Left Placket, changing to med pink in last sc: 80 sc. With med pink, ch 1, turn. Finish off lt pink.

**Row 2:** With med pink, sc in first 15 sc, sc in edge of last sc, sc in next 52 sc, sc in edge of last sc, sc in next 15 sc: 84 sc. Finish off; weave in ends.

Sew bottom edges of Plackets to skipped sc on Row 4 of Back Armhole Shaping between Left Back and Right Back. Sew buttons onto left Placket.

## SLEEVES (MAKE 2)

With white, ch 23.

**Row 1 (wrong side):** Sc in 2nd ch from hook and in each rem ch across: 22 sc; ch 1, turn.

**Row 2 (right side):** Sc in first sc and in each sc across; ch 1, turn.

**Row 3:** Rep Row 2, changing to mint in last sc. With mint, ch 1, turn. Finish off white.

**Row 4:** With mint, work 2 sc in first sc, sc in each sc across to last sc, 2 sc in last sc, changing to lime in last sc: 24 sc. With lime, ch 1, turn. Finish off mint.

**Row 5:** With lime, rep Row 2, changing to med pink in last sc. With med pink, ch 1, turn. Finish off lime.

**Row 6:** With med pink, rep Row 2, changing to lt pink in last sc. With lt pink, ch 1, turn. Finish off med pink.

**Row 7:** With lt pink, rep Row 4: 26 sc. Do not change color.

**Row 8:** Work (sc, dc) in first sc; *skip next sc, (sc, dc) in next sc; rep from * across to last 3 sc; skip next sc, sc in last 2 sc: 26 sts; ch 1, turn.

**Row 9:** Sc in first st and in each st across, changing to med pink in last sc. With med pink, ch 1, turn. Finish off lt pink.

**Row 10:** With med pink, rep Row 2, changing to lime in last sc. With lime, ch 1, turn. Finish off med pink.

**Row 11:** With lime, rep Row 4, changing to mint in last sc: 28 sc. With mint, ch 1, turn. Finish off lime.

**Row 12:** With mint, rep Row 2, changing to white in last sc. With white, ch 1, turn. Finish off mint.

**Rows 13 and 14:** With white, rep Row 2 two times more.

**Row 15:** With white, rep Row 4: 30 sc. Do not change color.

**Rows 16 through 18:** With white, rep Row 2 three times more.

**Row 19:** With white, rep Row 4: 32 sc. Do not change color.

**Rows 20 through 25:** With white, rep Rows 13 through 15 two times more. At end of Row 22: 34 sc. At end of Row 25: 36 sc. Finish off; weave in ends.

Set in sleeves. Sew sleeve and side seams.

## Pants with Booties

**Size:** 3 to 6 months

**Materials**
Light worsted weight yarn
   3 1/2 oz lt pink
   small amount mint (for pompons and ties)
Size F (3.75 mm) crochet hook (or size required for gauge)
1/2" wide elastic, 17" long

**Gauge**
In pattern, 19 sts = 4"; 20 rows = 4"

## Instructions

### PANTS FRONT

#### Left Leg

Starting at bottom of leg with lt pink, ch 13.

**Row 1 (wrong side):** Sc in 2nd ch from hook and in each rem ch across: 12 sc; ch 1, turn.

**Row 2 (right side):** Work (sc, dc) in first sc; *skip next sc, (sc, dc) in next sc; rep from * across to last 3 sc; skip next sc, sc in last 2 sc: 12 sts; ch 1, turn.

**Row 3:** Work 2 sc in first st, sc in each st across: 13 sc; ch 1, turn.

**Row 4:** Work (sc, dc) in first sc; *skip next sc, (sc, dc) in next sc; rep from * across to last 2 sc; skip next sc, sc in last sc: 13 sts; ch 1, turn.

**Row 5:** Sc in first st and in each st across; ch 1, turn.

**Row 6:** Rep Row 4.

**Row 7:** Rep Row 3: 14 sc.

**Row 8:** Rep Row 2.

**Row 9:** Rep Row 5.

**Rows 10 through 13:** Rep Rows 2 through 5. At end of **Row 11:** 15 sc.

**Rows 14 through 21:** Rep Rows 6 through 13. At end of **Row 15:** 16 sc. At end of Row 19: 17 sc.

**Rows 22 through 24:** Rep Rows 6 through 8. At end of **Row 23:** 18 sc.

**Rows 25 and 26:** Rep Rows 3 and 4. At end of Row 25: 19 sc. At end of Row 26, do not ch 1. Finish off; weave in ends.

### Right Leg

Starting at bottom of leg with pink, ch 13.

**Row 1 (wrong side):** Sc in 2nd ch from hook and in each rem ch across: 12 sc; ch 1, turn.

**Row 2 (right side):** Sc in first sc, (sc, dc) in next sc; *skip next sc, (sc, dc) in next sc; rep from * across to last 2 sc; skip next sc, sc in last sc: 12 sts; ch 1, turn.

**Row 3:** Sc in first st and in each st across to last st, 2 sc in last st: 13 sc; ch 1, turn.

**Row 4:** Work (sc, dc) in first sc; *skip next sc, (sc, dc) in next sc; rep from * across to last 2 sc; skip next sc, sc in last sc; 13 sts; ch 1, turn.

**Row 5:** Sc in first st and in each st across; ch 1, turn.

**Row 6:** Rep Row 4.

**Row 7:** Rep Row 3: 14 sc.

**Row 8:** Rep Row 2.

**Row 9:** Rep Row 5.

**Rows 10 through 13:** Rep Rows 2 through 5. At end of Row 11: 15 sc.

**Rows 14 through 21:** Rep Rows 6 through 13. At end of **Row 15:** 16 sc. At end of Row 19: 17 sc.

**Rows 22 through 24:** Rep Rows 6 through 8. At end of Row 23: 18 sc.

**Rows 25 and 26:** Rep Rows 3 and 4. At end of Row 25: 19 sc.

### Body

**Row 1 (wrong side):** Sc in first st and in each st across Right Leg, pick up Left Leg, with wrong side facing, sc dec in same st as last sc on Right Leg and in first st on Left Leg, sc in same st as last st on Left Leg and in each st across Left Leg: 39 sc; ch 1, turn.

**Row 2:** Work (sc, dc) in first sc; *skip next sc, (sc, dc) in next sc; rep from * across to last 2 sc; skip next sc, sc in last sc: 39 sts; ch 1, turn.

**Row 3:** Work 2 sc in first st, sc in each st across to last st, 2 sc in last st: 41 sc; ch 1, turn.

**Row 4:** Sc in first sc, (sc, dc) in next sc; *skip next sc, (sc, dc) in next sc; rep from * across to last 3 sc; skip next sc, sc in last 2 sc; 41 sts; ch 1, turn.

**Row 5:** Sc in first st and in each st across; ch 1, turn.

**Rows 6 through 22:** Rep Rows 4 and 5 eight times more, then rep Row 4 once more.

**Row 23:** Sc dec in first 2 sts, sc in each st across to last 2 sts, sc dec in last 2 sts: 39 sc; ch 1, turn.

**Row 24:** Rep Row 2.

**Row 25:** Rep Row 5.

### Waistband

**Row 1:** Sl st in front lp of each sc across: 39 sl sts; ch 1, turn.

**Row 2:** Sc in back lp of each sc on Row 25 of Body: 39 sc; ch 1, turn.

**Rows 3 and 4:** Sc in first sc and in each sc across; ch 1, turn.

**Rows 5 through 8:** Rep Rows 1 through 4, working sc in Row 6 in back lp of each sc on Row 4 of Waistband. At end of Row 8, do not ch 1. Finish off; weave in ends.

## PANTS BACK

### Right Leg
Work same as Front Left Leg.

### Left Leg
Work same as Front Right Leg.

## Body

**Row 1 (wrong side):** Sc in first st and in each st across Left Leg, pick up Right Leg, with wrong side facing, sc dec in same st as last sc on Left Leg and in first st on Right Leg, sc in same st as last st on Right Leg and in each st across Right Leg: 39 sc; ch 1, turn.

**Rows 2 through 25:** Work same as Rows 2 through 25 on Front Body.

## Waistband

Work same as Front Waistband.

## Assembly

With wrong sides facing, joining front and back together, sew side and crotch seams. Sew ends of elastic together. Fold Row 8 of Waistband back over elastic to wrong side and sew Waistband seam.

## BOOTIES (MAKE 2)

### Instep

With pink, ch 7. Place marker in first ch.

**Row 1 (right side):** Sc in 2nd ch from hook and in each rem ch across: 6 sc; ch 1, turn.

**Rows 2 through 7:** Sc in first sc and in each sc across; ch 1, turn. At end of Row 7, do not ch 1 and do not turn.

### Sides

**Rnd 1 (right side):** Ch 18, being careful not to twist ch, join with sl st in free lp of marked ch (move marker to 9th ch of ch-18), ch 1, sc in same ch, sc in free lp of next 5 chs, work 6 sc evenly spaced across edge of rows, sc in each sc in Row 7 of Instep, sc in each ch around: 36 sc; join with sl st in first sc; ch 1, turn.

**Rnds 2 through 5:** Sc in first sc and in each sc around; join as before; ch 1, turn. At end of Rnd 5, do not turn.

### Sole

**Rnd 1 (right side):** Sc in same sc as joining and in next 5 sc, sc dec in next 2 sc, sc in next 4 sc, sc dec in next 2 sc, sc in next 11 sc, sc dec in next 2 sc, sc in next 2 sc, sc dec in next 2 sc, sc in next 5 sc: 32 sc; join with sl st in first sc.

**Rnd 2:** Ch 1, sc in same sc as joining and in next 5 sc, sc dec in next 2 sc, sc in next 2 sc, sc dec in next 2 sc, sc in next 11 sc, (sc dec in next 2 sc) 2 times, sc in last 5 sc: 28 sc; join as before.

**Rnd 3:** Ch 1, sc in same sc as joining and in next 4 sc, (sc dec in next 2 sc) 2 times, sc in next 10 sc, (sc dec in next 2 sc) 2 times, sc in last 5 sc: 24 sc; join. Finish off.

Sew bottom seam on Sole.

## Cuff

**Row 1:** With right side facing, join pink with sl st in free lp of marked ch on Rnd 1 of Sides, ch 1, sc in same ch, sc in free lp of next 8 chs, work 6 sc evenly spaced across edge of Instep rows, sc in free lp of next 9 chs: 24 sc; ch 1, turn.

**Row 2:** Sc in first sc and in each sc across; ch 1, turn.

**Row 3:** Sc in first sc; *ch 1, skip next sc, sc in next sc; rep from * across to last sc; sc in last sc: 13 sc and 11 ch-1 sps; ch 1, turn.

**Row 4:** Sc in each sc and in each ch-1 sp across: 24 sc. Finish off; weave in ends.

Sew back seam on Cuff. Sew bootie to pants leg. Weave in all ends.

## TIES (MAKE 2)

Cut two 8 foot long pieces of mint. With both pieces held together, ch 75. Finish off.

Weave ties through ch-1 sps on Row 3 of each Cuff.

## POMPONS

Make 4 pompons with mint according to pompon instructions on page 80. Attach pompons to each end of ties.

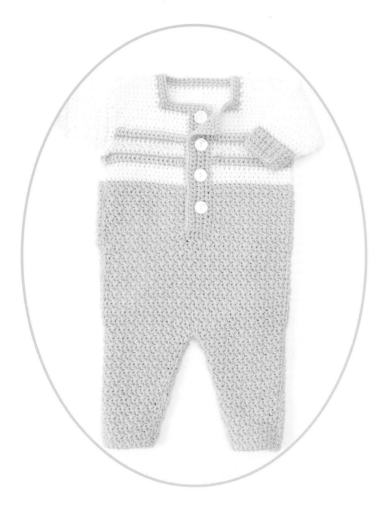

# Romper

**Size:** 3 to 6 months

**Materials**

Light worsted weight yarn

   $3^1/_2$ oz lime

   $2^1/_2$ oz white

   $^1/_8$ oz lt pink

   small amount med pink

   small amount mint

Size F (3.75 mm) crochet hook (or size required for gauge)

Four $^5/_8$" diameter buttons

Matching sewing thread

Sewing needle

**Gauge**

In pattern, 18 sts = 4"; 19 rows = 4"

## Instructions

### FRONT

**Left Leg**

Starting at bottom of leg with lime, ch 13.

**Row 1 (wrong side):** Sc in 2nd ch from hook and in each rem ch across: 12 sc; ch 1, turn.

**Row 2 (right side):** Work (sc, dc) in first sc; *skip next sc, (sc, dc) in next sc; rep from * across to last 3 sc; skip next sc, sc in last 2 sc: 12 sts; ch 1, turn.

**Row 3:** Work 2 sc in first st, sc in each st across: 13 sc; ch 1, turn.

**Row 4:** Work (sc, dc) in first sc; *skip next sc, (sc, dc) in next sc; rep from * across to last 2 sc; skip next sc, sc in last sc: 13 sts; ch 1, turn.

**Row 5:** Sc in first st and in each st across; ch 1, turn.

**Row 6:** Rep Row 4.

**Row 7:** Rep Row 3: 14 sc.

**Row 8:** Rep Row 2.

**Row 9:** Rep Row 5.

**Rows 10 through 13:** Rep Rows 2 through 5. At end of Row 11: 15 sc.

**Rows 14 through 21:** Rep Rows 6 through 13. At end of Row 15: 16 sc. At end of Row 19: 17 sc.

**Rows 22 through 24:** Rep Rows 6 through 8. At end of Row 23: 18 sc.

**Rows 25 and 26:** Rep Rows 3 and 4. At end of Row 25: 19 sc. At end of Row 26, do not ch 1. Finish off; weave in ends.

### Right Leg

Starting at bottom of leg with lime, ch 13.

**Row 1 (wrong side):** Sc in 2nd ch from hook and in each rem ch across: 12 sc; ch 1, turn.

**Row 2 (right side):** Sc in first sc, (sc, dc) in next sc; *skip next sc, (sc, dc) in next sc; rep from * across to last 2 sc; skip next sc, sc in last sc: 12 sts; ch 1, turn.

**Row 3:** Sc in first st and in each st across to last st, 2 sc in last st: 13 sc; ch 1, turn.

**Row 4:** Work (sc, dc) in first sc; *skip next sc, (sc, dc) in next sc; rep from * across to last 2 sc; skip next sc, sc in last sc: 13 sts; ch 1, turn.

**Row 5:** Sc in first st and in each st across; ch 1, turn.

**Row 6:** Rep Row 4.

**Row 7:** Rep Row 3: 14 sc.

**Row 8:** Rep Row 2.

**Row 9:** Rep Row 5.

**Rows 10 through 13:** Rep Rows 2 through 5. At end of Row 11: 15 sc.

**Rows 14 through 21:** Rep Rows 6 through 13. At end of Row 15: 16 sc. At end of Row 19: 17 sc.

**Rows 22 through 24:** Rep Rows 6 through 8. At end of Row 23: 18 sc.

**Rows 25 and 26:** Rep Rows 3 and 4. At end of Row 25: 19 sc.

## Body

**Row 1 (wrong side):** Sc in first st and in each st across Right Leg, pick up Left Leg, with wrong side facing, sc dec in same st as last sc on Right Leg and in first st on Left Leg, sc in same st as last st on Left Leg and in each st across Left Leg: 39 sc; ch 1, turn.

**Row 2:** Work (sc, dc) in first sc; *skip next sc, (sc, dc) in next sc; rep from * across to last 2 sc; skip next sc, sc in last sc: 39 sts; ch 1, turn.

**Row 3:** Work 2 sc in first st, sc in each st across to last st, 2 sc in last st: 41 sc; ch 1, turn.

**Row 4:** Sc in first sc, (sc, dc) in next sc; *skip next sc, (sc, dc) in next sc; rep from * across to last 3 sc; skip next sc, sc in last 2 sc; 41 sts; ch 1, turn.

**Row 5:** Sc in first st and in each st across; ch 1, turn.

**Rows 6 through 18:** Rep Rows 4 and 5 six times more, then rep Row 4 once more.

**Row 19:** Rep Row 3: 43 sc; ch 1, turn.

**Row 20:** Rep Row 2.

**Row 21:** Rep Row 5.

## Left Front

**Row 1 (right side):** Work (sc, dc) in first sc; *skip next sc, (sc, dc) in next sc; rep from * 7 times more; skip next sc, sc in next sc: 19 sts; ch 1, turn, leaving rem sts unworked.

**Row 2:** Sc in first st and in each st across: 19 sc; ch 1, turn.

**Row 3:** Work (sc, dc) in first sc; *skip next sc, (sc, dc) in next sc; rep from * across to last 2 sc; skip next sc, sc in last sc; ch 1, turn.

**Rows 4 through 12:** Rep Rows 2 and 3 four times more, then rep Row 2 once more, changing to white in last sc. With white, ch 1, turn. Finish off lime.

**Row 13:** With white, sc in first sc and in each sc across; ch 1, turn.

**Rows 14 through 16:** Rep Row 13 three times more. At end of Row 16, change to mint in last sc. With mint, ch 1, turn. Finish off white.

**Row 17:** With mint, rep Row 13, changing to lime in last sc. With lime, ch 1, turn. Finish off mint.

**Row 18:** With lime, rep Row 13, changing to med pink in last sc. With med pink, ch 1, turn. Finish off lime.

**Row 19:** With med pink, rep Row 13, changing to lt pink in last sc. With lt pink, ch 1, turn. Finish off med pink.

## Armhole Shaping

**Row 1 (wrong side):** With lt pink, sc in first 17 sc: 17 sc; ch 1, turn, leaving rem sts unworked.

**Row 2 (right side):** Work (sc, dc) in first sc; *skip next sc, (sc, dc) in next sc; rep from * across to last 2 sc; skip next sc, sc in last sc: 17 sts; ch 1, turn.

**Row 3:** Sc in first st and in each st across, changing to med pink in last sc. With med pink, ch 1, turn. Finish off lt pink.

**Row 4:** With med pink, sc in first sc and in each sc across, changing to lime in last sc. With lime, ch 1, turn. Finish off med pink.

**Row 5:** With lime, rep Row 4, changing to mint in last sc. With mint, ch 1, turn. Finish off lime.

**Row 6:** With mint, rep Row 4, changing to white in last sc. With white, ch 1, turn. Finish off mint.

**Rows 7 through 11:** With white, rep Row 4 five times more. Do not change color.

## Neck Shaping

**Row 1 (right side):** Sc in first 10 sc: 10 sc; ch 1, turn, leaving rem sts unworked.

**Rows 2 through 9:** Sc in first sc and in each sc across; ch 1, turn. At end of Row 9, do not ch 1. Finish off; weave in ends.

## Right Front

**Row 1:** With right side facing, skip next 5 sc on Row 21 of Body, join lime with sl st in next sc, ch 1, (sc, dc) in same sc as joining; *skip next sc, (sc, dc) in next sc; rep from * across to last 2 sc; skip next sc, sc in last sc: 19 sts; ch 1, turn.

**Row 2:** Sc in first st and in each st across: 19 sc; ch 1, turn.

**Row 3:** Work (sc, dc) in first sc; *skip next sc, (sc, dc) in next sc; rep from * across to last 2 sc; skip next sc, sc in last sc; ch 1, turn.

**Rows 4 through 12:** Rep Rows 2 and 3 four times more, then rep Row 2 once more, changing to white in last sc. With white, ch 1, turn. Finish off lime.

**Row 13:** With white, sc in first sc and in each sc across; ch 1, turn.

**Rows 14 through 18:** Rep Rows 14 through 18 on Left Front.

**Row 19:** With med pink, rep Row 13. At end of row, do not ch 1. Finish off; weave in ends.

### Armhole Shaping

**Row 1:** With wrong side facing, skip first 2 sc on Row 19 of Right Front, join lt pink with sl st in next sc, ch 1, sc in same sc as joining and in each sc across: 17 sc; ch 1, turn.

**Rows 2 through 11:** Rep Rows 2 through 11 on Left Front Armhole Shaping. At end of Row 11, do not ch 1. Finish off; weave in ends.

### Neck Shaping

**Row 1:** With right side facing, skip first 7 sc on Row 11 of Armhole Shaping, join white with sl st in next sc, ch 1, sc in same sc as joining and in each sc across: 10 sc; ch 1, turn.

**Rows 2 through 9:** Sc in first sc and in each sc across; ch 1, turn. At end of Row, do not ch 1. Finish off; weave in ends.

## BACK

### Right Leg

Work same as Front Left Leg.

### Left Leg

Work same as Front Right Leg.

### Body

**Row 1 (wrong side):** Sc in first st and in each st across Left Leg, pick up Right Leg, with wrong side facing, sc dec in same st as last sc on Left Leg and in first st on Right Leg, sc in same st as last st on Right Leg and in each st across Right Leg: 39 sc; ch 1, turn.

**Rows 2 through 19:** Work same as Rows 2 through 19 on Front Body.

**Row 20:** Work (sc, dc) in first sc; *skip next sc, (sc, dc) in next sc; rep from * across to last 2 sc; skip next sc, sc in last sc: 43 sts; ch 1, turn.

**Row 21:** Sc in first st and in each st across: 43 sc; ch 1, turn.

**Rows 22 through 32:** Rep Rows 20 and 21 five times more, then rep Row 20 once more.

**Row 33:** Sc in first 20 sts, sc dec in next 2 sts, sc in last 21 sts, changing to white in last sc: 42 sc. With white, ch 1, turn. Finish off lime.

**Rows 34 through 37:** With white, sc in first sc and in each sc across; ch 1, turn. At end of Row 37, change to mint in last sc. With mint, ch 1, turn. Finish off white.

**Row 38:** With mint, sc in first sc and each sc across, changing to lime in last sc. With lime, ch 1, turn. Finish off mint.

**Row 39:** With lime, rep Row 38, changing to med pink in last sc. With med pink, ch 1, turn. Finish off lime.

**Row 40:** With med pink, rep Row 38. At end of row, do not ch 1. Finish off; weave in ends.

### Armhole Shaping

**Row 1:** With wrong side facing, skip first 2 sc on Row 40 of Back Body, join white with sl st in next sc, ch 1, sc in same sc as joining and in each sc across to last 2 sc: 38 sc; ch 1, turn, leaving rem sts unworked.

**Rows 2 through 18:** Sc in first sc and in each sc across; ch 1, turn.

### Left Neck Shaping

**Row 1 (wrong side):** Sc in first 10 sc: 10 sc; ch 1, turn, leaving rem sts unworked.

**Row 2:** Sc in first sc and in each sc across. Finish off; weave in ends.

### Right Neck Shaping

**Row 1:** With wrong side facing, skip next 18 sc on Row 18 of Armhole Shaping, join white with sl st in next sc, ch 1, sc in same sc as joining and in each sc across: 10 sc; ch 1, turn.

**Row 2:** Sc in first sc and in each sc across. Finish off; weave in ends.

### Left Placket

**Row 1:** With wrong side facing, join lime with sl st in edge of last sc on Row 1 of Left Front, ch 1, sc in edge of same row, work 26 more sc evenly spaced in edge of rows on Left Front and Left Front Armhole Shaping, ending with sc in edge of Row 11 of Left Front Armhole Shaping: 27 sc; ch 1, turn.

**Row 2:** Sc in first sc and in each sc across; ch 1, turn.

**Row 3:** Sc in first 3 sc; *ch 2, skip next 2 sc, sc in next 5 sc; rep from * 2 times more; ch 2, skip next 2 sc, sc in last sc: 19 sc and 4 ch-2 sps; ch 1, turn.

**Row 4:** Sc in first sc; *2 sc in next ch-2 sp, sc in next 5 sc; rep from * 2 times more; 2 sc in next ch-2 sp, sc in last 3 sc: 27 sc; ch 1, turn.

**Row 5:** Sc in first sc and in each sc across. Finish off; weave in ends.

## Right Placket

**Row 1:** With wrong side facing, join lime with sl st in edge of last sc on Row 11 of Right Front Armhole Shaping, ch 1, sc in edge of same row, work 26 more sc evenly spaced in edge of rows on Right Front Armhole Shaping and Right Front, ending with sc in edge of Row 1 of Right Front: 27 sc; ch 1, turn.

**Rows 2 through 5:** Sc in first sc and in each sc across; ch 1, turn. At end of Row 5, do not ch 1. Finish off; weave in ends.

Sew shoulder seams.

## Neck Edging

**Row 1:** With right side facing, join lime with sl st in top edge of Row 5 on Right Placket, ch 1, sc in edge of same row, sc in edge of next 4 rows, sc in next 6 sc on Row 11 of Right Front Armhole Shaping, sc dec in next sc of Right Front Armhole Shaping and in edge of Row 1 of Right Front Neck Shaping, sc in edge of next 9 rows on Right Neck Shaping (Front and Back), sc dec in edge of Row 1 on Right Back Neck Shaping and in next sc on Row 18 of Back Armhole Shaping, sc in next 16 sc on Row 18, sc dec in next sc on Back Armhole Shaping and in edge of Row 1 on Left Back Neck Shaping, sc in edge of next 9 rows on Left Neck Shaping (Back and Front), sc dec in edge of Row 1 on Left Front Neck Shaping and in next sc on Row 11 of Left Front Armhole Shaping, sc in next 6 sc on Row 11, sc in edge of next 5 rows of Left Placket: 60 sc; ch 1, turn.

**Row 2:** Sc in first sc and in each sc around, working sc dec in sc before and after sc dec in each of 4 corners (skipping each sc dec): 52 sc. Finish off; weave in ends.

## Placket and Neck Edging

With right side facing, join lime with sl st in last sc on Row 5 of Right Placket, ch 1, sc in same sc as joining and in each sc across Row 5, sc in edge of Rows 1 and 2 of Neck Edging, sc in edge of last sc made, sc in each sc on Row 2 of Neck Edging, sc in edge of last sc made, sc in edge of Rows 2 and 1 of Neck Edging, sc in each sc on Row 5 of Left Placket: 112 sc. Finish off; weave in ends.

Sew bottom edge of Plackets to skipped sc on Row 21 of Front Body between Right Front and Left Front. Sew buttons onto Right Placket.

## SLEEVES (MAKE 2)

With white, ch 23.

**Row 1 (wrong side):** Sc in 2nd ch from hook and in each rem ch across: 22 sc; ch 1, turn.

**Row 2 (right side):** Work 2 sc in first sc, sc in each sc across to last sc, 2 sc in last sc: 24 sc; ch 1, turn.

**Row 3:** Sc in first sc and in each sc across; ch 1, turn.

**Row 4:** Rep Row 2: 26 sc.

**Rows 5 through 7:** Rep Row 3 three times more.

**Row 8:** Rep Row 2: 28 sc.

**Rows 9 and 10:** Rep Row 3 two times more.

**Rows 11 through 16:** Rep Rows 8 through 10 two times more. At end of Row 11: 30 sc. At end of Row 14: 32 sc.

**Rows 17 through 19:** Rep Rows 2 and 3, then rep Row 2 once more. At end of Row 17: 34 sc. At end of Row 19: 36 sc; do not ch 1. Finish off; weave in ends.

## Sleeve Ribbing

**Row 1:** With right side facing, join lime with sl st in free lp of first ch on Row 1 of Sleeve, ch 1, sc in same ch as joining, sc in free lp of each ch across: 22 sc; ch 1, turn.

**Row 2:** Sc in first sc and in each sc across; ch 1, turn.

**Row 3:** Sc in first sc, FPdc around next sc; *sc in next sc, FPdc around next sc; rep from * across to last 2 sc; sc in last 2 sc: 12 sc and 10 FPdc; ch 1, turn.

**Row 4:** Sc in first st and in each st across; ch 1, turn.

**Row 5:** Sc in first sc, FPdc around next FPdc; *sc in next sc, FPdc around next FPdc; rep from * across to last 2 sc; sc in last 2 sc; ch 1, turn.

**Row 6:** Rep Row 4. At end of row, do not ch 1. Finish off; weave in ends.

Rep Ribbing on other sleeve. Set in sleeves. Sew sleeve and side seams.

# Hat

**Size:** 3 to 6 months

**Materials**
Light worsted weight yarn
1 oz lt blue
small amount med blue (for pompons)
small amount lime (for pompons)
Size F (3.75 mm) crochet hook (or size required for gauge)

**GAUGE**
Rnds 1 through 8 = 3" diameter

## Instructions

### CROWN

Starting in center with lt blue, ch 3; join with sl st to form a ring.

**Rnd 1 (wrong side):** Ch 1, 6 sc in ring: 6 sc; join with sl st in first sc; ch 1, turn.

**Rnd 2 (right side):** 2 sc in first sc and in each sc around: 12 sc; join as before; ch 1, turn.

**Rnd 3:** Sc in first sc, 2 sc in next sc; *sc in next sc, 2 sc in next sc; rep from * around: 18 sc; join; ch 1, turn.

**Rnd 4:** Sc in first 2 sc, 2 sc in next sc; *sc in next 2 sc, 2 sc in next sc; rep from * around: 24 sc; join; ch 1, turn.

**Rnd 5:** Sc in first 3 sc, 2 sc in next sc; *sc in next 3 sc, 2 sc in next sc; rep from * around: 30 sc; join; ch 1, turn.

**Rnd 6:** Sc in first 4 sc, 2 sc in next sc; *sc in next 4 sc, 2 sc in next sc; rep from * around: 36 sc; join; ch 1, turn.

**Rnd 7:** Sc in first 5 sc, 2 sc in next sc; *sc in next 5 sc, 2 sc in next sc; rep from * around: 42 sc; join; ch 1, turn.

**Rnd 8:** Sc in first 6 sc, 2 sc in next sc; *sc in next 6 sc, 2 sc in next sc; rep from * around: 48 sc; join; ch 1, turn.

**Rnd 9:** Sc in first 7 sc, 2 sc in next sc; *sc in next 7 sc, 2 sc in next sc; rep from * around: 54 sc; join; ch 1, turn.

**Rnd 10:** Sc in first 8 sc, 2 sc in next sc; *sc in next 8 sc, 2 sc in next sc; rep from * around: 60 sc; join; ch 1, turn.

**Rnd 11:** Sc in first 9 sc, 2 sc in next sc; *sc in next 9 sc, 2 sc in next sc; rep from * around: 66 sc; join; ch 1, turn.

**Rnd 12:** Sc in first sc and in each sc around; join; ch 1, turn.

**Rnds 13 through 18:** Rep Rnd 12 six times more. At end of Rnd 18, ch 1. Do not turn.

**Rnd 19 (right side):** Sc in back lp of first sc and in back lp of each sc around; join; ch 1, turn.

**Rnds 20 through 22:** Rep Rnd 12 three times more. At end of Rnd 22, do not ch 1. Finish off; weave in ends.

### EAR FLAPS

#### Left Flap

**Row 1:** With wrong side facing, skip first 8 sc on Rnd 22, join lt blue with sl st in next sc, ch 1, sc in same sc as joining, sc in next 9 sc: 10 sc; ch 1, turn.

**Row 2:** Sc in first sc and in each sc across; ch 1, turn.

**Row 3:** Sc dec in first 2 sc, sc in each sc across to last 2 sc, sc dec in last 2 sc: 8 sc; ch 1, turn.

**Rows 4 through 8:** Rep Rows 2 and 3 two times more, then rep Row 2 once more. At end of Row 5: 6 sc. At end of Row 7: 4 sc.

**Row 9:** Sc in first 2 sc, sc dec in last 2 sc: 3 sc; ch 1, turn.

**Row 10:** Rep Row 2.

**Row 11:** Skip first sc, sc dec in last 2 sc: 1 sc. Finish off; weave in ends.

#### Right Flap

**Row 1:** With wrong side facing, skip next 29 sc on Rnd 22, join lt blue with sl st in next sc, ch 1, sc in same sc as joining, sc in next 9 sc: 10 sc; ch 1, turn.

**Rows 2 through 11:** Rep Rows 2 through 11 on Left Flap.

#### Edging

With wrong side facing, join lt blue with sl st in 2nd sc on Rnd 22, ch 1, (sc, dc) in same sc as joining; *skip next sc, (sc, dc) in next sc*; rep from * to * 2 times more; ***(sc, dc) in edge of Row 1 of flap, **skip next row, (sc, dc) in edge of next row**; rep from ** to ** 3 times more on same edge of flap, (sc, dc) in ch-1 sp and in sc dec on Row 11 of flap; rep from ** to ** 5 times more on other edge of same flap***; rep from * to * 14 times more across Rnd 22; rep from *** to *** on edges of other flap; (sc, dc) in next sc on Rnd 22; rep from * to * 4 times more: 94 sts; join with sl st in first sc. Finish off; weave in ends.

### TIES

Cut a piece of lt blue yarn 9 feet long. Fold piece in half and draw fold through bottom of ear flap. Insert hook in fold. With both strands of yarn held together, ch 38. Finish off. Cut a piece of lt blue yarn 10 feet long. Fold piece in half and draw fold through bottom of other ear flap. Insert hook in fold. With both strands of yarn held together, ch 48. Finish off.

### POMPONS

Make 2 pompons with lt blue, med blue and lime according to pompon instructions on page 80. Attach pompons to free end of ties.

# Bonnet

**Size:** 3 to 6 months

**Materials**

Light worsted weight yarn
   1 oz lt pink
     small amount mint (for pompons)
Size F (3.75 mm) crochet hook (or size required for gauge)

**Gauge**

In pattern, 18 sts = 4"; 18 rows = 4"

## Instructions

### CROWN

Starting at bottom with lt pink, ch 17.

**Row 1 (wrong side):** Sc in 2nd ch from hook and in each rem ch across: 16 sc; ch 1, turn.

**Row 2 (right side):** Work (sc, dc) in first sc; *skip next sc, (sc, dc) in next sc; rep from * across to last 3 sc; skip next sc, sc in last 2 sc: 16 sts; ch 1, turn.

**Row 3:** Work 2 sc in first sc, sc in each st across to last sc, 2 sc in last sc: 18 sc; ch 1, turn.

**Row 4:** Sc in first sc, (sc, dc) in next sc; *skip next sc, (sc, dc) in next sc; rep from * across to last 2 sc; skip next sc, sc in last sc: 18 sts; ch 1, turn.

**Row 5:** Rep Row 3: 20 sc.

**Row 6:** Rep Row 2.

**Row 7:** Sc in first st and in each st across: 20 sc; ch 1, turn.

**Rows 8 through 46:** Rep Rows 6 and 7 nineteen times more, then rep Row 6 once more.

**Row 47:** Sc dec in first 2 sts, sc in each st across to last 2 sts, sc dec in last 2 sts: 18 sc; ch 1, turn.

**Row 48:** Rep Row 4.

**Row 49:** Rep Row 47: 16 sc.

**Rows 50 and 51:** Rep Rows 6 and 7. At end of Row 51, do not ch 1. Finish off; weave in ends.

### Back Edging

With wrong side facing, join lt pink with sl st in edge of first sc on Row 1, sc in edge of next 21 rows; sc dec in edge of next 2 rows, sc dec in edge of next row and in edge of row after next (skipping row in between), sc dec in edge of next 2 rows, sc in edge of next 21 rows, sl st in edge of last row: 45 sc and 2 sl sts. Finish off; weave in ends.

Fold crown in half with wrong side together and short ends matching. Sew back seam along Back Edging.

### Front Edging

**Row 1:** With right side facing, join lt pink with sl st in edge of last sc on Row 1, ch 1, sc in edge of same row and in edge of each row across: 51 sc; ch 1, turn.

**Row 2:** Sc in first sc and in each sc across; ch 1, turn.

**Row 3:** Work (sc, dc) in first sc; *skip next sc, (sc, dc) in next sc; rep from * across to last 2 sc; skip next sc, sc in last sc; 51 sts. Do not ch 1 or turn.

### Neck Edging

**Row 1:** Working across bottom of crown, sc in edge of last sc made, work 35 more sc evenly spaced across bottom edge of Crown, working in edge of Front and Back Edgings, in last row of Crown and in free lps of foundation ch, ending with sc in edge of Row 3 of Front Edging: 36 sc; ch 1, turn.

**Row 2:** Sc in first sc and in each sc across. Finish off; weave in ends.

### TIES

Cut a piece of lt pink yarn 9 feet long. Fold piece in half and draw fold through corner of bonnet (first sc on Row 2 of Neck Edging). Insert hook in fold. With both strands of yarn held together, ch 38. Finish off. Cut a piece of lt pink yarn 10 feet long. Fold piece in half and draw fold through other corner of bonnet (last sc on Row 2 of Neck Edging). Insert hook in fold. With both strands of yarn held together, ch 48. Finish off.

### POMPONS

Make 2 pompons with mint according to pompon instructions on page 80. Attach pompons to free end of ties.

# Booties

**Size:** 3 to 6 months

**Materials**
Light worsted weight yarn
 1/2 oz lt blue
 small amount med blue (for pompons)
 small amount lime (for pompons)
Size F (3.75 mm) crochet hook (or size required for gauge)
Stitch markers

**Gauge**
In sc, 19 sts = 4"; 19 rows = 4"

## Instructions (make 2)

### Instep

With lt blue, ch 7. Place marker in first ch.

**Row 1 (right side):** Sc in 2nd ch from hook and in each rem ch across: 6 sc; ch 1, turn.

**Rows 2 through 7:** Sc in first sc and in each sc across; ch 1, turn. At end of Row 7, do not ch 1 and do not turn.

### Sides

**Rnd 1 (right side):** Ch 18, being careful not to twist ch, join with sl st in free lp of marked ch (move marker to 9th ch of ch-18), ch 1, sc in same ch, sc in free lp of next 5 chs, work 6 sc evenly spaced across edge of rows, sc in each sc in Row 7 of Instep, sc in each ch around: 36 sc; join with sl st in first sc; ch 1, turn.

**Rnds 2 through 5:** Sc in first sc and in each sc around; join as before; ch 1, turn. At end of Rnd 5, do not turn.

### Sole

**Rnd 1 (right side):** Sc in same sc as joining and in next 5 sc, sc dec in next 2 sc, sc in next 4 sc, sc dec in next 2 sc, sc in next 11 sc, sc dec in next 2 sc, sc in next 2 sc, sc dec in next 2 sc, sc in next 5 sc: 32 sc; join with sl st in first sc.

Rnd 2: Ch 1, sc in same sc as joining and in next 5 sc, sc dec in next 2 sc, sc in next 2 sc, sc dec in next 2 sc, sc in next 11 sc, (sc dec in next 2 sc) 2 times, sc in last 5 sc: 28 sc; join as before

**Rnd 3:** Ch 1, sc in same sc as joining and in next 4 sc, (sc dec in next 2 sc) 2 times, sc in next 10 sc, (sc dec in next 2 sc) 2 times, sc in last 5 sc: 24 sc; join. Finish off.

Sew bottom seam on Sole.

### Cuff

**Row 1:** With right side facing, join lt blue with sl st in free lp of marked ch on Rnd 1 of Sides, ch 1, sc in same ch, sc in free lp of next 6 chs, sc dec in free lp of next ch and in edge of last row on Instep (skipping last ch on Rnd 1 of Sides), sc in edge of next 5 rows, sc dec in edge of last row on Instep and in free lp of 2nd ch on Rnd 1 of Sides (skipping first ch), sc in free lp of last 7 chs: 21 sc; ch 1, turn.

**Row 2:** Sc in first sc; *ch 1, skip next sc, sc in next sc; rep from * across: 11 sc and 10 ch-1 sps; ch 1, turn.

**Row 3:** Work (sc, dc) in first sc; *skip next ch-1 sp, (sc, dc) in next sc; rep from * across to last 2 sts; skip next ch-1 sp, sc in next sc: 21 sts; ch 1, turn.

**Row 4:** Sc in first st and in each st across: 21 sc; ch 1, turn.

**Row 5:** Work (sc, dc) in first sc; *skip next sc, (sc, dc) in next sc; rep from * across to last 2 sc; skip next sc, sc in last sc; ch 1, turn.

**Rows 6 and 7:** Rep Rows 4 and 5. At end of Row 7, do not ch 1. Finish off.

Sew back seam of Cuff. Weave in all ends.

### TIES (MAKE 2)

Cut two 8 foot long pieces of lt blue. With both pieces held together, ch 75. Finish off.

Weave tie through ch-1 sps on Row 2 of Cuff.

### POMPONS

Make 4 pompons with lt blue, med blue and lime according to pompon instructions on page 80. Attach pompons to each end of ties.

# Tiny Togs

"I'm just so cute and warm as toast in my pretty new togs."

## SPECIAL STITCHES

**Cluster (CL):** *YO, insert hook in specified st and draw up a lp, YO and draw through 2 lps on hook; rep from * once more; YO and draw through all 3 lps on hook: CL made.

**Beginning cluster (beg CL):** Ch 2, dc in st at base of ch-2: beg CL made.

**Cross stitch (cross st):** Skip next st, CL in next st, dc in skipped st, working dc around CL: cross st made.

**To change color:** Work st until 2 lps rem on hook, drop old color, pick up new color and draw through both lps on hook, cut dropped color.

**Sc decrease (sc dec):** Insert hook in first specified st and draw up a lp, insert hook in second specified st and draw up a lp; YO and draw through all 3 lps on hook: sc dec made.

# Blanket

**Size:** 37" x 45½"

**Materials**
Light worsted weight yarn
    14 oz lime
    8 oz white
    5 oz med pink
Size F (3.75 mm) crochet hook (or size required for gauge)

**Gauge**
18 sc = 4"; 9 cross sts = 4"; 13 rows in pattern = 4"

## Instructions

### CENTER

With lime ch 193.

**Row 1 (wrong side):** Sc in 2nd ch from hook and in each rem ch across: 192 sc; ch 3 (counts as dc on next row now and throughout), turn.

**Row 2 (right side):** *Cross st in next 2 sc; rep from * across to last sc; dc in last sc: 95 cross sts and 2 dc; ch 1, turn.

**Row 3:** Sc in each cross st (in CL and dc) and dc across, sc in 3rd ch of turning ch-3: 192 sc; ch 3, turn.

**Row 4:** Rep Row 2, changing to white in last dc. With white, ch 1, turn. Finish off lime.

**Row 5:** With white, rep Row 3.

**Row 6:** With white, rep Row 2, changing to lime in last dc. With lime, ch 1, turn. Finish off white.

**Row 7:** With lime, rep Row 3, changing to pink in last sc. With pink, ch 3, turn. Finish off lime.

**Row 8:** With pink, rep Row 2, changing to lime in last dc. With lime, ch 1, turn. Finish off pink.

**Row 9:** With lime, rep Row 3, changing to white in last sc. With white, ch 3, turn. Finish off lime.

**Row 10:** With white, rep Row 2.

**Rows 11 through 16:** Rep Rows 5 though 10.

**Row 17:** With white, rep Row 3, changing to lime in last sc. With lime, ch 3, turn. Finish off white.

**Rows 18 through 23:** With lime, rep Rows 2 and 3 three times more.

**Rows 24 through 89:** Rep Rows 2 through 23 three times more.

**Rows 90 through 109:** Rep Rows 2 through 21. At end of Row 109, do not ch 3. Finish off; weave in ends.

### RIGHT EDGING

**Row 1:** With right side facing, join lime with sl st in edge of last sc on Row 1, ch 1, sc in edge of same row, work 162 more sc evenly spaced across right edges of rows: 163 sc; ch 1, turn.

**Row 2:** Sc in first sc and in each sc across; ch 3, turn.

**Row 3:** *Cross st in next 2 sc; rep from * across to last 2 sc; CL in next sc, dc in last sc: 80 cross sts, 1 CL and 2 dc; ch 1, turn.

**Row 4:** Sc in each cross st (in CL and dc), CL and dc across, sc in 3rd ch of turning ch-3: 163 sc; ch 3, turn.

**Rows 5 and 6:** Rep Rows 3 and 4. At end of Row 6, do not ch 3. Finish off; weave in ends.

### LEFT EDGING

**Row 1:** With right side facing, join lime with sl st in edge of first sc on Row 109 of Center, ch 1, sc in edge of same row, work 162 more sc evenly spaced across left edges of rows: 163 sc; ch 1, turn.

**Rows 2 through 6:** Rep Rows 2 through 6 on Right Edging. At end of Row 6, change to pink in last sc. With pink, ch 1, turn. Finish off lime.

## BORDER

**Rnd 1 (right side):** With right side facing and pink, work 2 sc in first sc on Row 6 of Left Edging (corner started), sc in each sc across Row 6 to last sc, 3 sc in last sc (corner made), 6 sc across edge of rows on Left Edging, work 191 sc evenly spaced in free lps of foundation ch of Center, 6 sc across edge of rows on Right Edging, 3 sc in first sc on Row 6 of Right Edging (corner made), sc in each sc across Row 6 to last sc, 3 sc in last sc (corner made), 6 sc across edge of rows on Right Edging, work 191 sc evenly spaced across Row 109 of Center, 6 sc across edge of rows on Left Edging, sc in same sc as first 2 sc (corner completed): 740 sc; join with sl st in first sc.

**Rnd 2:** Ch 1, (sc, dc) in same sc as joining (center sc of corner), (sc, dc) in next sc; *skip next sc, (sc, dc) in next sc; rep from * across each side, working (sc, dc) in each of 3 sc in each corner and ending with (sc, dc) in first sc of first corner; join. Finish off; weave in ends.

# Little Boy's Cardigan

**Size:** 3 to 6 months

## Materials
Light worsted weight yarn
    4 oz med blue
    1 oz white
    1/4 oz variegated
    1/8 oz lime

**3 LIGHT**

Size F (3.75 mm) crochet hook (or size required for gauge)
Five 5/8" diameter buttons
Matching sewing thread
Sewing needle

## Gauge
18 sc = 4"; 9 cross sts = 4"; 13 rows in pattern = 4"

## Instructions

### BACK

Starting at bottom with blue, ch 49.

**Row 1 (wrong side):** Sc in 2nd ch from hook and in each

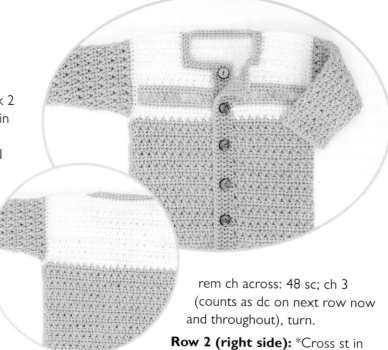

rem ch across: 48 sc; ch 3 (counts as dc on next row now and throughout), turn.

**Row 2 (right side):** *Cross st in next 2 sc; rep from * across to last sc; dc in last sc: 23 cross sts and 2 dc; ch 1, turn.

**Row 3:** Sc in each cross st (in CL and dc) and dc across, sc in 3rd ch of turning ch-3: 48 sc; ch 3, turn.

**Rows 4 through 23:** Rep Rows 2 and 3 ten times more. At end of Row 23, do not ch 3. Finish off; weave in ends.

#### Armhole Shaping

**Row 1:** With right side facing, skip first 2 sc on Row 23, join white with sl st in next sc, work beg CL; *cross st in next 2 sc; rep from * across to last 3 sc; CL in next sc: 21 cross sts, 1 CL and 1 beg CL: ch 1, turn, leaving rem sts unworked.

**Row 2:** Sc in each cross st (in CL and dc), CL and beg CL across: 44 sc; turn.

**Row 3:** Work beg CL; *cross st in next 2 sc; rep from * across to last sc; CL in last sc: 21 cross sts, 1 CL and 1 beg CL; ch 1, turn.

**Rows 4 through 11:** Rep Rows 2 and 3 four times more.

**Row 12:** Rep Row 2. At end of row, ch 1, turn.

**Rows 13 and 14:** Sc in first sc and in each sc across; ch 1, turn.

#### Right Neck Shaping

**Row 1 (right side):** Sc in first 12 sc: 12 sc; ch 1, turn, leaving rem sts unworked.

**Row 2:** Sc in first sc and in each sc across. Finish off; weave in ends.

#### Left Neck Shaping

**Row 1:** With right side facing, skip next 20 sc on Row 14 of Armhole Shaping, join white with sl st in next sc, ch 1, sc in same sc as joining and in each sc across: 12 sc; ch 1, turn.

**Row 2:** Sc in first sc and in each sc across. Finish off; weave in ends.

## LEFT FRONT

Starting at bottom with blue, ch 23.

**Row 1 (wrong side):** Sc in 2nd ch from hook and in each rem ch across: 22 sc; ch 3, turn.

**Row 2 (right side):** *Cross st in next 2 sc; rep from * across to last sc; dc in last sc: 10 cross sts and 2 dc; ch 1, turn.

**Row 3:** Sc in each cross st (in CL and dc) and dc across, sc in 3rd ch of turning ch-3: 22 sc; ch 3, turn.

**Rows 4 through 23:** Rep Rows 2 and 3 ten times more. At end of Row 23, do not ch 3. Finish off; weave in ends.

### Armhole Shaping

**Row 1:** With right side facing, skip first 2 sc on Row 23, join white with sl st in next sc, work beg CL; *cross st in next 2 sc; rep from * across to last sc; dc in last sc: 9 cross sts, 1 beg CL and 1 dc; ch 1, turn.

**Row 2:** Sc in each cross st (in CL and dc), beg CL and dc across, changing to lime in last sc: 20 sc. With lime, ch 1, turn. Finish off white.

**Row 3:** With lime, sc in first sc and in each sc across, changing to blue in last sc. With blue, ch 1, turn. Finish off lime.

**Row 4:** With blue, sc in first sc and in each sc across, changing to variegated in last sc. Finish off blue.

**Row 5:** With variegated, work beg CL; *cross st in next 2 sc; rep from * across to last sc; dc in last sc, changing to blue: 9 cross sts, 1 beg CL and 1 dc. With blue, ch 1, turn. Finish off variegated.

**Row 6:** With blue, rep Row 2, changing to lime in last sc. With lime, ch 1, turn. Finish off blue.

**Row 7:** With lime, rep Row 3, changing to white in last sc. With white, ch 1, turn. Finish off lime.

**Rows 8 through 10:** With white, rep Rows 4 and 5, then rep Row 4 once more. Do not change colors.

### Neck Shaping

**Row 1 (right side):** Work beg CL; *cross st in next 2 sc; rep from * 4 times more; CL in next sc: 5 cross sts, 1 CL and 1 beg CL; ch 1, turn, leaving rem sts unworked.

**Row 2:** Sc in each cross st (in CL and dc), CL and beg CL across: 12 sc; turn.

**Row 3:** Work beg CL; *cross st in next 2 sc; rep from * 4

times more; CL in next sc: 5 cross sts, 1 CL and 1 beg CL; ch 1, turn.

**Rows 4 through 6:** Rep Rows 2 and 3 once, then rep Row 2 once more. At end of Row 6, finish off; weave in ends.

## RIGHT FRONT

Starting at bottom with blue, ch 23.

**Rows 1 through 23:** Rep Rows 1 through 23 on Left Front. At end of Row 23, ch 3, turn.

### Armhole Shaping

**Row 1 (right side):** *Cross st in next 2 sc; rep from * 8 times more; CL in next sc: 9 cross sts, 1 CL and 1 dc; ch 1, turn, leaving rem sts unworked.

**Row 2:** Sc in each cross st (in CL and dc) and CL across, sc in 3rd ch of turning ch-3, changing to lime: 20 sc. With lime, ch 1, turn. Finish off white.

**Row 3:** With lime, sc in first sc and in each sc across, changing to blue in last sc. With blue, ch 1, turn. Finish off lime.

**Row 4:** With blue, sc in first sc and in each sc across, changing to variegated in last sc. With variegated, ch 3, turn. Finish off blue.

**Row 5:** With variegated, *cross st in next 2 sc; rep from * across to last sc; CL in last sc, changing to blue: 9 cross sts, 1 CL and 1 dc. With blue, ch 1, turn. Finish off variegated.

**Row 6:** With blue, rep Row 2, changing to lime in last sc. With lime, ch 1, turn. Finish off blue.

**Row 7:** With lime, rep Row 3, changing to white in last sc. With white, ch 1, turn. Finish off lime.

**Rows 8 through 10:** With white, rep Rows 4 and 5, then rep Row 4 once more. At end of Row 10, do not ch 3. Finish off; weave in ends.

### Neck Shaping

**Row 1:** With right side facing, skip first 8 sc on Row 10 of Armhole Shaping, join white with sl st in next sc, work beg CL; *cross st in next 2 sc; rep from * across to last sc; CL in last sc: 5 cross sts, 1 CL and 1 beg CL; ch 1, turn.

**Row 2:** Sc in each cross st (in CL and dc), CL and beg CL across: 12 sc; turn.

**Row 3:** Work beg CL; *cross st in next 2 sc; rep from * across to last sc; CL in last sc: 5 cross sts, 1 CL and 1 beg CL; ch 1, turn.

**Rows 4 through 6:** Repeat Rows 2 and 3 once more, then rep Row 2 once more. At end of Row 6, finish off; weave in ends.

## Left Placket

**Row 1:** With wrong side facing, join blue with sl st in edge of last sc on Row 1 of Left Front, ch 1, sc in edge of same row, work 44 more sc evenly spaced in edge of rows on Left Front and Left Front Armhole Shaping, ending with sc in edge of Row 10 of Left Front Armhole Shaping: 45 sc; ch 1, turn.

**Row 2:** Sc in first sc and in each sc across; ch 1, turn.

**Row 3:** Sc in first 6 sc; *ch 2, skip next 2 sc, sc in next 7 sc; rep from * 3 times more; ch 2, skip next 2 sc, sc in last sc: 35 sc and 5 ch-2 sps; ch 1, turn.

**Row 4:** Sc in first sc; *2 sc in next ch-2 sp, sc in next 7 sc; rep from * 3 times more; 2 sc in next ch-2 sp, sc in next 6 sc: 45 sc; ch 1, turn.

**Row 5:** Sc in first sc and in each sc across. Finish off; weave in ends.

## Right Placket

**Row 1:** With wrong side facing, join blue with sl st in edge of last sc on Row 10 of Right Front Armhole Shaping, ch 1, sc in edge of same row, work 44 more sc evenly spaced in edge of rows on Right Front Armhole Shaping and Right Front, ending with sc in edge of Row 1 of Right Front: 45 sc; ch 1, turn.

**Rows 2 through 5:** Sc in first sc and in each sc across; ch 1, turn. At end of Row 5, do not ch 1. Finish off; weave in ends.

Sew shoulder seams.

## Neck Edging

**Row 1:** With right side facing, join blue with sl st in top edge of Row 5 on Right Placket, ch 1, sc in edge of same row, sc in edge of next 4 rows, sc in next 7 sc on Row 10 of Front Right Armhole Shaping, sc dec in next sc of Right Front Armhole Shaping and in edge of Row 1 of Right Front Neck Shaping, work 9 sc evenly spaced in edge of rows on Right Neck Shaping (Front and Back), sc dec in edge of Row 1 on Back Right Neck Shaping and in next sc on Row 14 of Back Armhole Shaping, sc in next 18 sc on Row 14, sc dec in next sc on Back Armhole Shaping and in edge of Row 1 on Left Back Neck Shaping, work 9 sc evenly spaced in edge of rows on Left Neck Shaping (Back and Front), sc dec in edge of Row 1 on Left Front Neck Shaping and in next sc on Row 10 of Left Front Armhole Shaping, sc in next 7 sc on Row 10, sc in edge of next 5 rows of Left Placket: 64 sc; ch 1, turn.

**Row 2:** Sc in first sc and in each sc around, working sc dec in sc before and after sc dec in each of 4 corners (skipping each sc dec): 56 sc. Finish off; weave in ends.

## Placket and Neck Edging

With right side facing, join blue with sl st in last sc on Row 5 of Right Placket, ch 1, sc in same sc as joining, sc in each sc across Row 5, sc in edge of Rows 1 and 2 of Neck Edging, sc in edge of last sc made, sc in each st on Row 2 of Neck Edging, sc in edge of last sc made, sc in edge of Rows 2 and 1 of Neck Edging, sc in each sc on Row 5 of Left Placket: 152 sc. Finish off; weave in ends.

Sew buttons onto Right Placket.

## SLEEVES (MAKE 2)

With blue, ch 27.

**Row 1 (wrong side):** Sc in 2nd ch from hook and in each rem ch across: 26 sc; ch 3, turn.

**Row 2 (right side):** *Cross st in next 2 sc; rep from * across to last sc; dc in last sc: 12 cross sts and 2 dc; ch 1, turn.

**Row 3:** Sc in each cross st (in CL and dc) and dc across, sc in 3rd ch of turning ch-3: 26 sc; ch 3, turn.

**Row 4:** Rep Row 2.

**Row 5:** Work 2 sc in first dc, sc in each cross st (in CL and dc) and dc across to turning ch, 2 sc in 3rd ch of turning ch-3: 28 sc; ch 3, turn.

**Row 6:** Dc in next sc; *cross st in next 2 sc; rep from * across to last 2 sc; dc in last 2 sc: 12 cross sts and 4 dc; ch 1, turn.

**Row 7:** Rep Row 3.

**Row 8:** Rep Row 6.

**Row 9:** Rep Row 5: 30 sc.

**Row 10:** Rep Row 2.

**Rows 11 and 12:** Rep Rows 5 and 6. At end of Row 11: 32 sc.

**Row 13:** Rep Row 5: 34 sc.

**Rows 14 and 15:** Rep Rows 2 and 3.

**Rows 16 through 19:** Rep Rows 10 through 13. At end of Row 17: 36 sc. At end of Row 19: 38 sc.

**Row 20:** Rep Row 2, changing to white in last dc. With white, ch 1, turn. Finish off blue.

**Row 21:** With white, rep Row 5: 40 sc. At end of row, do not ch 3. Finish off; weave in ends.

Set in sleeves. Sew sleeve and side seams.

# Little Girl's Cardigan

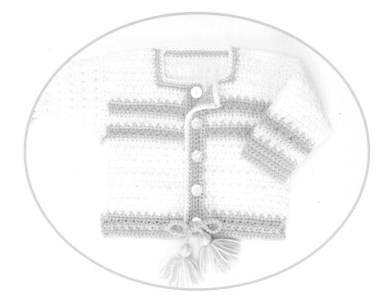

**Size:** 3 to 6 months

## Materials

Light worsted weight yarn
- 4 ¼ oz white
- ½ oz lime
- ¼ oz med pink

Five ⅝" diameter buttons
Matching sewing thread
Sewing needle

## Gauge

18 sc = 4"; 9 cross sts = 4"; 12 rows in pattern = 4"

## Instructions

### BACK

Starting at bottom with lime, ch 49.

**Row 1 (wrong side):** Sc in 2nd ch from hook and in each rem ch across: 48 sc; ch 1, turn.

**Row 2 (right side):** Sc in first sc and in each sc across; ch 3 (counts as dc on next row now and throughout), turn.

**Row 3:** Dc in next sc and in each sc across: 48 dc; ch 1, turn.

**Row 4:** Sc in first dc and in each dc across, sc in 3rd ch of turning ch-3: 48 sc; ch 3, turn.

**Row 5:** Rep Row 2, changing to white in last sc. With white, ch 3, turn. Finish off lime.

**Row 6:** With white, *cross st in next 2 sc; rep from * across to last sc; dc in last sc: 23 cross sts and 2 dc; ch 1, turn.

**Row 7:** Sc in each cross st (in CL and dc) and dc across, sc in 3rd ch of turning ch-3; ch 3, turn.

**Rows 8 through 17:** Rep Rows 6 and 7 five 5 times more. At end of Row 17, do not ch 3. Turn.

### Armhole Shaping

**Row 1 (right side):** Sl st in first 3 sc, work beg CL, *cross st in next 2 sc; rep from * across to last 3 sc, CL in next sc: 21 cross sts, 1 CL and 1 beg CL; ch 1, turn, leaving rem sts unworked.

**Row 2:** Sc in each cross st (in CL and dc) and CL across: 44 sc; turn.

**Row 3:** Work beg CL; *cross st in next 2 sc; rep from * across to last sc; CL in last sc: 21 cross sts, 1 CL and 1 beg CL; ch 1, turn.

**Rows 4 through 11:** Rep Rows 2 and 3 four times more.

**Row 12:** Rep Row 2. At end of row, ch 1, turn.

**Rows 13 and 14:** Sc in first sc and in each sc across; ch 1, turn.

### Right Neck Shaping

**Row 1 (right side):** Sc in first 12 sc: 12 sc; ch 1, turn, leaving rem sts unworked.

**Row 2:** Sc in first sc and in each sc across. Finish off; weave in ends.

### Left Neck Shaping

**Row 1:** With right side facing, skip next 20 sc on Row 14 of Armhole Shaping, join white with sl st in next sc, ch 1, sc in same sc as joining and in each sc across: 12 sc; ch 1, turn.

**Row 2:** Sc in first sc and in each sc across. Finish off; weave in ends.

### LEFT FRONT

Starting at bottom with lime, ch 23.

**Row 1 (wrong side):** Sc in 2nd ch from hook and in each rem ch across: 22 sc; ch 1, turn.

**Row 2 (right side):** Sc in first sc and in each sc across; ch 3, turn.

**Row 3:** Dc in next sc and in each sc across: 22 dc; ch 1, turn.

**Row 4:** Sc in first dc and in each dc across, sc in 3rd ch of turning ch-3: 22 sc; ch 1, turn.

**Row 5:** Rep Row 2, changing to white in last sc. With white, ch 3, turn. Finish off lime.

**Row 6:** With white, *cross st in next 2 sc; rep from * across to last sc; dc in last sc: 10 cross sts and 2 dc; ch 1, turn.

**Row 7:** Sc in each cross st (in CL and dc) and dc across, sc in 3rd ch of turning ch-3: 22 sc; ch 3, turn.

**Rows 8 through 16:** Rep Rows 6 and 7 four times more, then rep Row 6 once more, changing to lime in last sc. With lime, ch 1, turn. Finish off white.

**Row 17:** With lime, rep Row 7. At end of row, do not ch 1. Finish off; weave in ends.

## Armhole Shaping

**Row 1:** With right side facing, skip first 2 sc on Row 17, join pink with sl st in next sc, work beg CL; *cross st in next 2 sc; rep from * across to last sc; dc in last sc, changing to lime: 9 cross sts, 1 beg CL and 1 dc. With lime, ch 1, turn. Finish off pink.

**Row 2:** With lime, sc in each cross st (in CL and dc), beg CL and dc across, changing to white in last sc: 20 sc. With white, turn. Finish off lime.

**Row 3:** With white, work beg CL; *cross st in next 2 sc; rep from * across to last sc; dc in last sc, changing to lime: 9 cross sts, 1 beg CL and 1 dc. With lime, ch 1, turn. Finish off white.

**Row 4:** With lime, rep Row 2, changing to pink in last sc. With pink, turn. Finish off lime.

**Row 5:** With pink, rep Row 3, changing to lime in last dc. With lime, ch 1, turn. Finish off pink.

**Rows 6 and 7:** Rep Rows 2 and 3. At end of Row 7, do not change colors.

**Row 8:** With white, sc in each cross st (in CL and dc), beg CL and dc across; turn.

## Neck Shaping

**Row 1 (right side):** Work beg CL; *cross st in next 2 sc; rep from * 4 times more; CL in next sc: 5 cross sts, 1 CL and 1 beg CL; ch 1, turn, leaving rem sts unworked.

**Row 2:** Sc in each cross st (in CL and dc), CL and beg CL across: 12 sc; turn.

**Row 3:** Work beg CL; *cross st in next 2 sc; rep from * across to last sc; CL in last sc; ch 1, turn.

**Rows 4 through 6:** Rep Rows 2 and 3, then rep Row 2 once more. At end of Row 6, finish off; weave in ends.

## RIGHT FRONT

Starting at bottom with lime, ch 23.

**Rows 1 through 17:** Rep Rows 1 through 17 on Left Front. At end of Row 17, change to pink in last sc. With pink, ch 3, turn. Finish off lime.

## Armhole Shaping

**Row 1 (right side):** With pink, *cross st in next 2 sc; rep from * 8 times more; CL in next sc, changing to lime: 9 cross sts, 1 CL and 1 dc. With lime, ch 1, turn, leaving rem sts unworked. Finish off pink.

**Row 2:** With lime, sc in each cross st (in CL and dc) and CL across, sc in 3rd ch of turning ch-3, changing to white: 20 sc. With white, ch 3, turn. Finish off lime.

**Row 3:** With white, *cross st in next 2 sc; rep from * across to last sc; CL in last sc, changing to lime. With lime, ch 1, turn. Finish off white.

**Row 4:** With lime, rep Row 2, changing to pink in last sc. With pink, ch 3, turn. Finish off lime.

**Row 5:** With pink, rep Row 3, changing to lime in last st. With lime ch 1, turn. Finish off pink.

**Rows 6 and 7:** Rep Rows 2 and 3. At end of Row 7, do not change colors.

**Row 8:** With white, sc in each cross st (in CL and dc) and CL across, sc in 3rd ch of turning ch-3. Finish off.

## Neck Shaping

**Row 1:** With right side facing, skip first 8 sc on Row 8 of Armhole Shaping, join white with sl st in next sc, work beg CL; *cross st in next 2 sc; rep from * across to last sc; CL in last sc: 5 cross sts, 1 CL and 1 beg CL; ch 1, turn.

**Row 2:** Sc in each cross st (in CL and dc), CL and beg CL across: 12 sc; turn.

**Row 3:** Work beg CL; *cross st in next 2 sc; rep from * across to last sc; CL in last sc; ch 1, turn.

**Rows 4 through 6:** Rep Rows 2 and 3, then rep Row 2 once more. At end of Row 6, finish off; weave in ends.

## Left Placket

**Row 1:** With wrong side facing, join lime with sl st in edge of last sc on Row 1 of Left Front, ch 1, sc in edge of same row, work 35 more sc evenly spaced in edge of rows on Left Front and Left Front Armhole Shaping, ending with sc in edge of Row 8 of Left Front Armhole Shaping, changing to pink: 36 sc. With pink, ch 1, turn. Finish off lime.

**Row 2:** With pink, sc in first sc and in each sc across; ch l, turn.

**Row 3:** Sc in first sc; *ch 2, skip next 2 sc, sc in next 6 sc; rep from * 3 times more; ch 2, skip next 2 sc, sc in last sc: 26 sc and 5 ch-2 sps; ch l, turn.

**Row 4:** Sc in first sc; *2 sc in next ch-2 sp, sc in next 6 sc; rep from * 3 times more; 2 sc in next ch-2 sp, sc in next sc: 36 sc. Finish off; weave in ends.

**Right Placket**

**Row 1:** With wrong side facing, join lime with sl st in edge of last sc on Row 8 of Right Front Armhole Shaping, ch l, sc in edge of same row, work 35 more sc evenly spaced in edge of rows on Right Front Armhole Shaping and Right Front, ending with sc in edge of Row l of Right Front, changing to pink: 36 sc. With pink, ch l, turn. Finish off lime.

**Rows 2 through 4:** With pink, sc in first sc and in each sc across; ch l, turn. At end of Row 4, do not ch l. Finish off; weave in ends.

Sew shoulder seams.

**Neck Edging**

**Row 1:** With right side facing, join pink with sl st in top edge of Row 4 on Right Placket, ch l, sc in edge of same row, sc in edge of next 3 rows, sc in next 7 sc on Row 8 of Right Front Armhole Shaping, sc dec in next sc of Right Front Armhole Shaping and in edge of Row l of Right Front Neck Shaping, work 9 sc evenly spaced in edge of rows on Right Neck Shaping (Front and Back), sc dec in edge of Row l on Right Back Neck Shaping and in next sc on Row 14 of Back Armhole Shaping, sc in next 18 sc on Row 14, sc dec in next sc on Back Armhole Shaping and in edge of Row l on Left Back Neck Shaping, work 9 sc evenly spaced in edge of rows on Left Neck Shaping (Back and Front), sc dec in edge of Row l on Left Front Neck Shaping and in next sc on Row 8 of Left Front Armhole Shaping, sc in next 7 sc on Row 8, sc in edge of next 4 rows of Left Placket: 62 sc. Finish off; weave in ends.

**Placket and Neck Edging**

**Row 1:** With wrong side facing, join lime with sl st in last sc on Row 4 of Left Placket, ch l, sc in same sc and in each sc on Row 4, sc in edge of Row l of Neck Edging, sc in edge of last sc made, sc in each sc on Row l of Neck Edging, working sc dec in sc before and after sc dec in each of 4 corners (skipping each sc dec), sc in edge of last sc made, sc in edge of Row l of Neck Edging, sc in each sc on Row 4 of

Right Placket, changing to white in last sc: 130 sc. With white, ch l, turn. Finish off lime.

**Row 2 (right side):** With white, sc in first 38 sc across Right Placket, sc in edge of last sc made, sc in next 56 sc around neck, sc in edge of last sc made, sc in last 38 sc across Left Placket: 134 sc. Finish off; weave in ends.

Sew buttons onto Right Placket.

**SLEEVES (MAKE 2)**

With lime, ch 27.

**Row 1 (wrong side):** Sc in 2nd ch from hook and in each rem ch across: 26 sc; ch l, turn.

**Rows 2 through 6:** Sc in first sc and in each sc across; ch l, turn.

**Row 7:** Work 2 sc in first sc, sc in each sc across to last sc, 2 sc in last sc, changing to white in last sc: 28 sc. With white, ch 3, turn. Finish off lime.

**Row 8:** With white, *cross st in next 2 sc; rep from * across to last sc; dc in last sc, changing to lime: 13 cross sts and 2 dc. With lime, ch l, turn. Finish off white.

**Row 9:** With lime, work 2 sc in first dc, sc in each cross st (in CL and dc) across to turning ch, 2 sc in 3rd ch of turning ch-3, changing to pink: 30 sc. With pink, ch 3, turn. Finish off lime.

**Row 10:** With pink, dc in next sc; *cross st in next 2 sc; rep from * across to last 2 sc; dc in last 2 sc, changing to lime in last sc: 13 cross sts and 4 dc. With lime, ch l, turn. Finish off pink.

**Row 11:** With lime, sc in each cross st (in CL and dc) and dc across, sc in 3rd ch of turning ch-3, changing to white. With white, ch 3, turn. Finish off lime.

**Row 12:** With white, rep Row 10. Do not change colors.

**Row 13:** With white, rep Row 9: 32 sc. Do not change colors.

**Rows 14 through 17:** With white, rep Rows 8 through 11. Do not change colors. At end of Row 15: 34 sc.

**Rows 18 through 22:** Rep Rows 12 through 16. At end of Row 19: 36 sc. At end of Row 21: 38 sc.

**Row 23:** With white, rep Row 9: 40 sc. Do not change colors. At end of row, do not ch l. Finish off; weave in ends.

Set in sleeves. Sew sleeve and side seams.

### Drawstring

Cut a piece of lime yarn 14 feet long. Fold yarn in half. Insert hook in fold and ch 140 with both strands held together. Finish off. Weave drawstring between dc sts on Row 3 of Front and Back.

### Tassels

Make 2 tassels with white, lime and pink according to tassel instructions on page 80. Attach top of tassels to ends of drawstring.

# Shirt

**Size:** 3 to 6 months

**Materials**

Light worsted weight yarn

3 ¼ oz white

¼ oz med blue

¼ oz variegated

⅛ oz lime

Size F (3.75 mm) crochet hook

(or size required for gauge)

Two ⅝" diameter buttons

Matching sewing thread

Sewing needle

**Gauge**

In sc, 18 sts = 4"; 21 rows = 4"

## Instructions

### FRONT

Starting at bottom with white, ch 43.

**Row 1 (wrong side):** Sc in 2nd ch from hook and in each rem ch across: 42 sc; ch 1, turn.

**Row 2 (right side):** Sc in first sc and in each sc across; ch 1, turn.

**Rows 3 through 17:** Rep Row 2 fifteen times more. At end of Row 17, change to lime in last sc. With lime, ch 1, turn. Finish off white.

**Row 18:** With lime, rep Row 2, changing to blue in last sc. With blue, ch 1, turn. Finish off lime.

**Row 19:** With blue, sc in first sc and in each sc across, changing to variegated in last sc; ch 3 (counts as dc on next row now and throughout), turn.

**Row 20:** With variegated, *cross st in next 2 sc; rep from * across to last sc; dc in last sc, changing to blue: 20 cross sts and 2 dc. With blue, ch 1, turn. Finish off variegated.

**Row 21:** With blue, sc in each cross st (in CL and dc) and dc across, sc in 3rd ch of turning ch-3, changing to lime: 42 sc. With lime, ch 1, turn. Finish off blue.

**Row 22:** With lime, rep Row 2, changing to white in last sc. With white, ch 1, turn. Finish off lime.

**Rows 23 through 27:** With white, rep Row 2 five times more.

**Rows 28 and 29:** Rep Rows 18 and 19. At end of Row 29, do not change color and do not ch 3. Finish off. Turn.

### Armhole Shaping

**Row 1:** With right side facing, skip first 2 sc on Row 29, join variegated with sl st in next sc, ch 3; *cross st in next 2 sc; rep from * across to last 3 sc; dc in next sc, changing to blue: 18 cross sts and 2 dc. With blue, ch 1, turn, leaving rem sts unworked.

**Row 2:** With blue, sc in each cross st (in CL and dc) and dc across, sc in 3rd ch of beg ch-3, changing to lime: 38 sc. With lime, ch 1, turn. Finish off blue.

**Row 3:** With lime, sc in first sc and in each sc across, changing to white in last sc. With white, ch 1, turn. Finish off lime.

**Rows 4 through 10:** With white, sc in first sc and in each sc across; ch 1, turn.

### Left Neck Shaping

**Row 1 (right side):** Sc in first 10 sc: 10 sc; ch 1, turn, leaving rem sts unworked.

**Rows 2 through 9:** Sc in first sc and in each sc across; ch 1, turn. At end of Row 9, do not ch 1. Finish off; weave in ends.

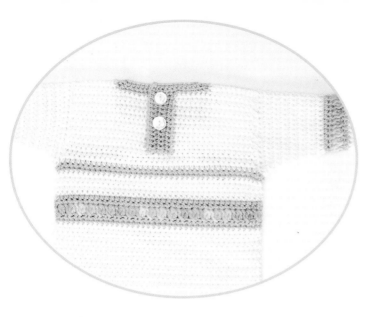

### Right Neck Shaping

**Row 1:** With right side facing, skip next 18 sc on Row 10 of Armhole Shaping, join white with sl st in next sc, ch 1, sc in same sc as joining and in each sc across: 10 sc; ch 1, turn.

**Rows 2 through 9:** Rep Rows 2 through 9 on Left Neck Shaping.

### BACK

Starting at bottom with white, ch 43.

**Rows 1 through 29:** Rep Rows 1 through 29 on Front.

### Armhole Shaping

**Row 1:** With right side facing, skip first 2 sc on Row 29, join white with sl st in next sc, ch 1, sc in same sc as joining and in each sc across to last 2 sc: 38 sc; ch 1, turn, leaving rem sts unworked.

**Rows 2 through 4:** Sc in first sc and in each sc across; ch 1, turn.

### Right Back

**Row 1 (right side):** Sc in first 17 sc: 17 sc; ch 1, turn, leaving rem sts unworked.

**Rows 2 through 14:** Sc in first sc and in each sc across; ch 1, turn.

### Neck Shaping

**Row 1 (right side):** Sc in first 10 sc: 10 sc; ch 1, turn, leaving rem sts unworked.

**Row 2:** Sc in first sc and in each sc across. Finish off; weave in ends.

### Left Back

**Row 1:** With right side facing, skip next 4 sc on Row 4 of Armhole Shaping, join white with sl st in next sc, ch 1, sc in same sc as joining and in each sc across: 17 sc; ch 1, turn.

**Rows 2 through 14:** Sc in first sc and in each sc across; ch 1, turn. At end of Row 14, do not ch 1. Finish off. Turn.

### Neck Shaping

**Row 1:** With right side facing, skip next 7 sc on Row 14 of Left Back, join white with sl st in next sc, ch 1, sc in same sc as joining and in each sc across: 10 sc; ch 1, turn.

**Row 2:** Sc in first sc and in each sc across. Finish off; weave in ends.

### Right Placket

**Row 1:** With wrong side facing, join blue with sl st in edge of first sc on Row 1 of Right Back, ch 1, sc in edge of same row, work 12 more sc evenly spaced in edge of rows on Right Back, ending with sc in edge of Row 14 of Right Back: 13 sc; ch 1, turn.

**Rows 2 and 3:** Sc in first sc and in each sc across; ch 1, turn.

**Row 4:** Sc in first sc; *ch 2, skip next 2 sc, sc in next 4 sc; rep from * once more: 9 sc and 2 ch-2 sps. Finish off.

### Left Placket

**Row 1:** With wrong side facing, join blue with sl st in edge of last sc on Row 14 of Left Back, ch 1, sc in edge of same row, work 12 more sc evenly spaced in edge of rows on Left Back, ending with sc in edge of Row 1 of Left Back: 13 sc; ch 1, turn.

**Rows 2 through 4:** Sc in first sc and in each sc across; ch 1, turn. At end of Row 4, do not ch 1. Finish off.

Sew shoulder seams.

### Neck Edging

With right side facing, join blue with sl st in top edge of Row 4 on Left Placket, ch 1, sc in edge of same row, sc in edge of next 3 rows, sc in next 6 sc on Row 14 of Left Back, sc dec in next sc of Left Back and in edge of Row 1 of Neck Shaping, sc in edge of next 9 rows on Left Neck Shaping (Back and Front), sc dec in edge of Row 1 of Front Left Neck Shaping and in next sc on Row 10 of Front Armhole Shaping, sc in next 16 sc on Row 10, sc dec in next sc on Row 10 of Front Armhole Shaping and in edge of Row 1 of Front Right Neck Shaping, sc in edge of next 9 rows on Right Neck Shaping (Front and Back), sc dec in edge of Row 1 of Back Right Neck Shaping and in next sc on Row 14 of Right Back, sc in next 6 sc on Row 14, sc in edge of next 4 rows on Right Placket: 58 sc. Finish off.

### Placket and Neck Edging

**Row 1:** With wrong side facing, join blue with sl st in last sc on Row 4 of Right Placket, ch 1, sc in same sc as joining, sc in next 3 sc, 2 sc in next ch-2 sp, sc in next 4 sc, 2 sc in next ch-2 sp, sc in next sc, sc in edge of Neck Edging, sc in edge of last sc made, sc in each sc of Neck Edging, working sc dec in sc before and after sc dec in each of 4 corners (skipping each sc dec), sc in edge of last sc made, sc in edge of Neck Edging, sc in each sc on Row 4 of Left Placket: 80 sc; ch 1, turn.

**Row 2 (right side):** Sc in first 15 sc, sc in edge of last sc, sc in next 52 sc, sc in edge of last sc, sc in next 15 sc: 84 sc. Finish off; weave in ends.

Sew bottom edges of Plackets to skipped sc on Row 4 of Back Armhole Shaping between Left Back and Right Back. Sew buttons onto left Placket.

### SLEEVES (MAKE 2)

With white, ch 23.

**Row 1 (wrong side):** Sc in 2nd ch from hook and in each rem ch across: 22 sc; ch 1, turn.

**Rows 2 and 3:** Sc in first sc and in each sc across; ch 1, turn. At end of Row 3, change to lime in last sc. With lime, ch 1, turn. Finish off white.

**Row 4:** With lime, work 2 sc in first sc, sc in each sc across to last sc, 2 sc in last sc, changing to blue in last sc: 24 sc. With blue, ch 1, turn. Finish off lime.

**Row 5:** With blue, sc in first sc and in each sc across, changing to variegated in last sc. With variegated, ch 3, turn. Finish off blue.

**Row 6:** With variegated, *cross st in next 2 sc; rep from * across to last sc; dc in last sc, changing to blue: 11 cross sts and 2 dc. With blue, ch 1, turn. Finish off variegated.

**Row 7:** With blue, sc in each cross st (in CL and dc) and dc across, sc in 3rd ch of turning ch-3, changing to lime. With lime, ch 1, turn. Finish off blue.

**Row 8:** With lime, rep Row 4, changing to white in last sc: 26 sc. With white, ch 1, turn. Finish off lime.

**Row 9:** With white, sc in first sc and in each sc across; ch 1, turn.

**Row 10:** Work 2 sc in first sc, sc in each sc across to last sc, 2 sc in last sc: 28 sc; ch 1, turn.

**Rows 11 through 13:** Rep Row 9 three times more.

**Row 14:** Rep Row 10: 30 sc.

**Rows 15 through 18:** Rep Rows 11 through 14. At end of Row 18: 32 sc.

**Row 19:** Rep Row 9.

**Rows 20 through 23:** Rep Rows 9 and 10 two times more. At end of Row 21: 34 sc. At end of Row 23: 36 sc; do not ch 1. Finish off; weave in ends.

Set in sleeves. Sew sleeve and side seams.

# Pants

**Size:** 3 to 6 months

**Materials**
Light worsted weight yarn
   3 oz med blue
Size F (3.75 mm) crochet hook (or size required for gauge)
1/2" wide elastic, 17" long

**Gauge**

18 sc = 4"; 9 cross sts = 4"; 13 rows in pattern = 4"

## Instructions

### PANTS FRONT

#### Right Leg

Starting at bottom of leg, ch 13.

**Row 1 (wrong side):** Sc in 2nd ch from hook and in each rem ch across: 12 sc; ch 3 (counts as dc on next row now and throughout), turn.

**Row 2 (right side):** *Cross st in next 2 sc; rep from * across to last sc; dc in last sc: 5 cross sts and 2 dc; ch 1, turn.

**Row 3:** Sc in each cross st (in CL and dc) and dc across, sc in 3rd ch of turning ch-3: 12 sc; ch 1, turn.

**Row 4:** Rep Row 2.

**Row 5:** Sc in each cross st (in CL and dc) and dc across, 2 sc in 3rd ch of turning ch-3: 13 sc; ch 3, turn.

**Row 6:** Dc in next sc; *cross st in next 2 sc; rep from * across to last sc; dc in last sc: 5 cross sts and 3 dc; ch 1, turn.

**Row 7:** Rep Row 5: 14 sc.

**Rows 8 through 10:** Rep Rows 4 though 6. At end of Row 9: 15 sc.

**Rows 11 through 18:** Rep Rows 7 through 10 two times more. At end of Row 11: 16 sc. At end of Row 13: 17 sc. At end of Row 15: 18 sc. At end of Row 17: 19 sc.

**Row 19:** Rep Row 5: 20 sc. At end of row, do not ch 3. Finish off; weave in ends.

## Left Leg

Starting at bottom of leg, ch 13.

**Row 1 (wrong side):** Sc in 2nd ch from hook and in each rem ch across: 12 sc; ch 3, turn.

**Row 2 (right side):** *Cross st in next 2 sc; rep from * across to last sc; dc in last sc: 5 cross sts and 2 dc; ch 1, turn.

**Row 3:** Sc in each cross st (in CL and dc) and dc across, sc in 3rd ch of turning ch-3: 12 sc; ch 3, turn.

**Row 4:** Rep Row 2.

**Row 5:** Work 2 sc in first dc, sc in each cross st (in CL and dc) across, sc in 3rd ch of turning ch-3: 13 sc; ch 3, turn.

**Row 6:** *Cross st in next 2 sc; rep from * across to last 2 sc; dc in last 2 sc: 5 cross sts and 3 dc; ch 1, turn.

**Row 7:** Rep Row 5: 14 sc.

**Rows 8 through 10:** Rep Rows 4 through 6. At end of Row 9: 15 sc.

**Rows 11 through 18:** Rep Rows 7 through 10 two times more. At end of Row 11: 16 sc. At end of Rows 13: 17 sc. At end of Row 15: 18 sc. At end of Row 17: 19 sc.

**Row 19:** Rep Row 5: 20 sc. At end of row, ch 3, turn.

### Body

**Row 1 (right side):** *Cross st in next 2 sc*; rep from * to * across to last sc on Left Leg; pick up Right Leg, with right side facing, cross st in last sc of Left Leg and in first sc of Right Leg; rep from * to * across to last sc on Right Leg; dc in last sc: 19 cross sts and 2 dc; ch 1, turn.

**Row 2:** Sc in each cross st (in CL and dc) and dc across, sc in 3rd ch of turning ch-3: 40 sc; ch 3, turn.

**Row 3:** *Cross st in next 2 sc; rep from * across to last sc; dc in last sc: 19 cross sts and 2 dc; ch 1, turn.

**Rows 4 through 13:** Rep Rows 2 and 3 five times more.

**Row 14:** Sc dec in first 2 sts, sc in each cross st (in CL and dc) across to last 2 sts, sc dec in last 2 sts: 38 sc; ch 1, turn.

**Rows 15 and 16:** Sc in first sc and in each sc across; ch 1, turn.

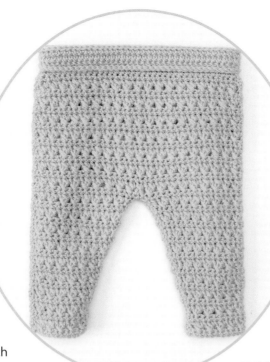

## Waistband

**Row 1 (right side):** Sl st in front lp of each sc across: 38 sl sts; ch 1, turn.

**Row 2:** Sc in back lp of each sc on Row 16 of Body: 38 sc; ch 1, turn.

**Rows 3 and 4:** Sc in first sc and in each sc across; ch 1, turn.

**Rows 5 through 8:** Rep Rows 1 through 4, working sc in Row 6 in back lp of each sc on Row 4 of Waistband. At end of Row 8, do not ch 1. Finish off; weave in ends.

## PANTS BACK

### Left Leg

Work same as Front Right Leg.

### Right Leg

Work same as Front Left Leg.

### Body

**Row 1 (right side):** *Cross st in next 2 sc*; rep from * to * across to last sc on Right Leg; pick up Left Leg, with right side facing, cross st in last sc of Right Leg and in first sc of Left Leg; rep from * to * across to last sc on Left Leg; dc in last sc: 19 cross sts and 2 dc; ch 1, turn.

**Rows 2 through 16:** Work same as Rows 2 through 16 on Front Body.

### Waistband

Work same as Front Waistband.

### Assembly

With wrong sides facing, joining front and back together, sew side and crotch seams. Sew ends of elastic together. Fold Row 8 of Waistband back over elastic to wrong side and sew Waistband seam.

# Romper with Booties

**Size:** 3 to 6 months

**Materials**

Light worsted weight yarn
   6 oz white
   $^1/_2$ oz med pink
Size F (3.75 mm) crochet hook (or size required for gauge)
Four $^5/_8$" diameter buttons
Matching sewing thread
Sewing needle
Stitch markers

**Gauge**

18 sc = 4"; 9 cross sts = 4"; 15 rows in pattern = 4"

# Instructions

### BACK

#### Left Leg

Starting at bottom of leg with white, ch 13.

**Row 1 (wrong side):** Sc in 2nd ch from hook and in each rem ch across: 12 sc; ch 1, turn.

**Row 2 (right side):** Sc in first sc and in each sc across; ch 1, turn.

**Row 3:** Sc in first sc and in each sc across; ch 3 (counts as dc on next row now and throughout), turn.

**Row 4:** *Cross st in next 2 sc; rep from * across to last sc; dc in last sc: 5 cross sts and 2 dc; ch 1, turn.

**Row 5:** Sc in each cross st (in CL and dc) and dc across to turning ch, 2 sc in 3rd ch of turning ch-3: 13 sc; ch 1, turn.

**Row 6:** Rep Row 2.

**Row 7:** Sc in first sc and in each sc across to last sc, 2 sc in last sc: 14 sc; ch 3, turn.

**Rows 8 through 11:** Rep Rows 4 through 7. At end of Row 9: 15 sc. At end of Row 11: 16 sc.

**Row 12:** Rep Row 4.

**Row 13:** Sc in each cross st (in CL and dc) and dc across, sc in 3rd ch of turning ch-3; ch 1, turn.

**Row 14:** Rep Row 2.

**Row 15:** Rep Row 7: 17 sc.

**Row 16:** Dc in next sc; *cross st in next 2 sc; rep from * across to last sc; dc in last sc: 7 cross sts and 3 dc; ch 1, turn.

**Rows 17 through 19:** Rep Rows 5 through 7. At end of Row 17: 18 sc. At end of Row 19: 19 sc.

**Row 20:** Rep Row 16.

**Rows 21 through 23:** Rep Rows 13 through 15. At end of Row 23: 20 sc; do not ch 3. Finish off.

#### Right Leg

Starting at bottom of leg with white, ch 13.

**Rows 1 through 3:** Rep Rows 1 through 3 on Left Leg.

**Row 4:** *Cross st in next 2 sc; rep from * across to last sc; dc in last sc: 5 cross sts and 2 dc; ch 1, turn.

**Row 5:** Work 2 sc in first dc, sc in each cross st (in CL and dc) and dc across, sc in 3rd ch of turning ch-3: 13 sc; ch 1, turn.

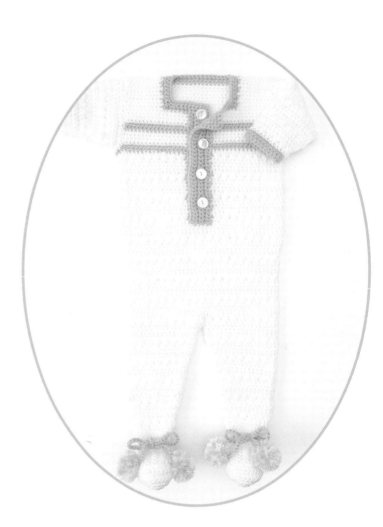

**Row 6:** Sc in first sc and in each sc across; ch 1, turn.

**Row 7:** Work 2 sc in first sc, sc in each sc across: 14 sc; ch 3, turn.

**Rows 8 through 11:** Rep Rows 4 through 7. At end of Row 9: 15 sc. At end of Row 11: 16 sc.

**Row 12:** Rep Row 4.

**Row 13:** Sc in each cross st (in CL and dc) and dc across, sc in 3rd ch of turning ch-3; ch 1, turn.

**Row 14:** Rep Row 6.

**Row 15:** Rep Row 7: 17 sc.

**Row 16:** *Cross st in next 2 sc; rep from * across to last 2 sc; dc in last 2 sc: 7 cross sts and 3 dc; ch 1, turn.

**Rows 17 through 19:** Rep Rows 5 through 7. At end of Row 17: 18 sc. At end of Row 19: 19 sc.

**Row 20:** Rep Row 16.

**Rows 21 through 23:** Rep Rows 13 through 15. At end of Row 23: 20 sc. Do not finish off.

## Body

**Row 1 (right side):** *Cross st in next 2 sc*; rep from * to * across to last sc on Right Leg; pick up Left Leg, with right side facing, cross st in last sc of Right Leg and in first sc of Left Leg; rep from * to * across to last sc on Left Leg; dc in last sc: 19 cross sts and 2 dc; ch 1, turn.

**Row 2:** Sc in each cross st (in CL and dc) and dc across, sc in 3rd ch of turning ch-3: 40 sc; ch 1, turn.

**Row 3:** Sc in first sc and in each sc across; ch 1, turn.

**Row 4:** Sc in first sc and in each sc across; ch 3, turn.

**Row 5:** *Cross st in next 2 sc; rep from * across to last sc; dc in last sc: 19 cross sts and 2 dc; ch 1, turn.

**Rows 6 through 15:** Rep Rows 2 through 5 two times more, then rep Rows 2 and 3 once more.

**Row 16:** Work 2 sc in first sc, sc in each sc across to last sc, 2 sc in last sc: 42 sc; ch 1, turn.

**Row 17:** Dc in next sc; *cross st in next 2 sc; rep from * across to last 2 sc; dc in last 2 sc: 19 cross sts and 4 dc; ch 1, turn.

**Rows 18 through 20:** Rep Rows 2 through 4.

**Row 21:** Rep Row 17.

**Rows 22 through 33:** Rep Rows 18 through 21 three times more.

**Row 34:** Sc in first sc and in each sc across. Turn.

## Armhole Shaping

**Row 1 (right side):** Sl st in first 3 sc, ch 1, sc in same sc and in each sc across to last 2 sc: 38 sc; ch 1, turn, leaving rem sts unworked.

**Rows 2 through 18:** Sc in first sc and in each sc across; ch 1, turn.

## Right Neck Shaping

**Row 1 (right side):** Sc in first 10 sc: 10 sc; ch 1, turn, leaving rem sts unworked.

**Row 2:** Sc in first sc and in each sc across. Finish off; weave in ends.

## Left Neck Shaping

**Row 1:** With right side facing, skip next 18 sc on Row 18 of Armhole Shaping, join white with sl st in next sc, ch 1, sc in same sc as joining and in each sc across: 10 sc; ch 1, turn.

**Row 2:** Sc in first sc and in each sc across. Finish off; weave in ends.

## FRONT

### Right Leg

Work same as Back Left Leg.

### Left Leg

Work same as Back Right Leg.

### Body

**Row 1 (right side):** *Cross st in next 2 sc*; rep from * to * across to last sc on Left Leg; pick up Right Leg, with right side facing, cross st in last sc of Left Leg and in first sc of Right Leg; rep from * to * across to last sc on Right Leg; dc in last sc: 19 cross sts and 2 dc; ch 1, turn.

**Rows 2 through 19:** Work same as Rows 2 through 19 on Back Body.

### Right Front

**Row 1 (wrong side):** Sc in first 19 sc: 19 sc; ch 3, turn, leaving rem sts unworked.

**Row 2 (right side):** *Cross st in next 2 sc; rep from * across to last 2 sc; dc in last 2 sc: 8 cross sts and 3 dc; ch 1, turn.

**Row 3:** Sc in each cross st (in CL and dc) and dc across, sc in 3rd ch of turning ch-3: 19 sc; ch 1, turn.

**Row 4:** Sc in first sc and in each sc across; ch 1, turn.

**Row 5:** Sc in first sc and in each sc across; ch 3, turn.

**Rows 6 through 13:** Rep Rows 2 through 5 two times more.

**Row 14:** Rep Row 2, changing to pink in last dc.

**Row 15:** With pink, rep Row 3.

### Armhole Shaping

**Row 1 (right side):** Sc in first 17 sc, changing to white in last sc: 17 sc. With white, ch 1, turn, leaving rem sts unworked. Finish off pink.

**Rows 2 through 5:** With white, sc in first sc and in each sc across; ch 1, turn. At end of Row 5, change to pink in last sc. With pink, ch 1, turn. Finish off white.

**Rows 6 and 7:** With pink, sc in first sc and in each sc across; ch 1, turn. At end of Row 7, change to white in last sc. With white, ch 1, turn. Finish off pink.

**Rows 8 through 11:** Rep Rows 2 through 5. At end of Row 11, do not change color.

### Neck Shaping

**Row 1 (wrong side):** Sc in first 10 sc: 10 sc; ch 1, turn, leaving rem sts unworked.

**Rows 2 through 9:** Sc in first sc and in each sc across; ch 1, turn. At end of Row 9, do not ch 1. Finish off; weave in ends.

### Left Front

**Row 1:** With wrong side facing, skip next 4 sc on Row 19 of Front Body, join white with sl st in next sc, ch 1, sc in same sc as joining and in each sc across: 19 sc; ch 3, turn.

**Row 2:** Dc in next sc; *cross st in next 2 sc; rep from * across to last sc; dc in last sc: 8 cross sts and 3 dc; ch 1, turn.

**Row 3:** Sc in each cross st (in CL and dc) and dc across, sc in 3rd ch of turning ch-3: 19 sc; ch 1, turn.

**Row 4:** Sc in first sc and in each sc across; ch 1, turn.

**Row 5:** Sc in first sc and in each sc across; ch 3, turn.

**Rows 6 through 13:** Rep Rows 2 through 5 two times more.

**Row 14:** Rep Row 2, changing to pink in last dc. With pink, ch 1, turn. Finish off white.

**Row 15:** With pink, rep Row 3. At end of row, do not ch 1. Turn. Do not finish off.

### Armhole Shaping

**Row 1 (right side):** Sl st in first 3 sc, ch 1, sc in same sc and in each sc across, changing to white in last sc: 17 sc. With white, ch 1, turn. Finish off pink.

**Rows 2 through 11:** Rep Rows 2 through 11 on Right Front Armhole Shaping. At end of Row 11, do not ch 1. Finish off; weave in ends.

### Neck Shaping

**Row 1:** With wrong side facing, skip first 7 sc on Row 11 of Armhole Shaping, join white with sl st in next sc, ch 1, sc in same sc as joining and in each sc across: 10 sc; ch 1, turn.

**Rows 2 through 9:** Rep Rows 2 through 9 on Right Front Neck Shaping.

### Left Placket

**Row 1:** With wrong side facing, join pink with sl st in edge of first sc on Row 1 of Left Front, ch 1, sc in edge of same row, work 29 more sc evenly spaced in edge of rows on Left Front and Left Front Armhole Shaping, ending with sc in edge of Row 11 of Left Front Armhole Shaping: 30 sc; ch 1, turn.

**Row 2:** Sc in first sc and in each sc across; ch 1, turn.

**Row 3:** Sc in first 3 sc; *ch 2, skip next 2 sc, sc in next 6 sc; rep from * 2 times more; ch 2, skip next 2 sc, sc in last sc: 22 sc and 4 ch-2 sps; ch 1, turn.

**Row 4:** Sc in first sc; *2 sc in next ch-2 sp, sc in next 6 sc; rep from * 2 times more; 2 sc in next ch-2 sp, sc in last 3 sc: 30 sc; ch 1, turn.

**Row 5:** Sc in first sc and in each sc across. Finish off; weave in ends.

### Right Placket

**Row 1:** With wrong side facing, join pink with sl st in edge of first sc on Row 11 of Right Front Armhole Shaping, ch 1, sc in edge of same row, work 29 more sc evenly spaced in edge of rows on Right Front Armhole Shaping and Right Front, ending with sc in edge of Row 1 of Right Front: 30 sc; ch 1, turn.

**Rows 2 through 5:** Sc in first sc and in each sc across; ch 1, turn. At end of Row 5, do not ch 1. Finish off; weave in ends.

Sew shoulder seams.

### Neck Edging

**Row 1:** With right side facing, join pink with sl st in top edge of Row 5 on Right Placket, ch 1, sc in edge of same row, sc in edge of next 4 rows, sc in next 6 sc on Row 11 of Right Front Armhole Shaping, sc dec in next sc of Right Front Armhole Shaping and in edge of Row 1 of Right Front Neck Shaping, sc in edge of next 9 rows on Right Neck Shaping (Front and Back), sc dec in edge of Row 1 on Right Back Neck Shaping and in next sc on Row 18 of Back Armhole Shaping, sc in next 16 sc on Row 18 of Back Armhole Shaping, sc dec in next sc on Back Armhole Shaping and in edge of Row 1 on Left Back Neck Shaping, sc in edge of next 9 rows on Left Neck Shaping (Back and Front), sc dec in edge of Row 1 on Left Front Neck Shaping and in next sc on Row 11 of Left Front Armhole Shaping, sc in next 6 sc on Row 11, sc in edge of next 5 rows of Left Placket: 60 sc; ch 1, turn.

**Row 2:** Sc in first sc and in each sc around, working sc dec in sc before and after sc dec in each of 4 corners: 52 sc. Finish off; weave in ends.

### Placket and Neck Edging

With right side facing, join pink with sl st in last sc on Row 5 of Right Placket, ch 1, sc in same sc as joining and in each sc across Row 5, sc in edge of Rows 1 and 2 of Neck Edging, sc in edge of last sc made, sc in each sc on Row 2 of Neck Edging, sc in edge of last sc made, sc in edge of Rows 2 and 1 of Neck Edging, sc in each sc on Row 5 of Left Placket: 118 sc. Finish off; weave in ends.

Sew bottom edge of Plackets to skipped sc on Row 19 of Front Body between Right Front and Left Front. Sew buttons onto Right Placket.

### SLEEVES (MAKE 2)

With pink, ch 23.

**Row 1 (wrong side):** Sc in 2nd ch from hook and in each rem ch across: 22 sc; ch 1, turn.

**Row 2 (right side):** Sc in first sc and in each sc across, changing to white in last sc. With white, ch 1, turn. Finish off pink.

**Row 3:** Work 2 sc in first sc, sc in each sc across to last sc, 2 sc in last sc: 24 sc; ch 3, turn.

**Row 4:** *Cross st in next 2 sc; rep from * across to last sc; dc in last sc: 11 cross sts and 2 dc; ch 3, turn.

**Row 5:** Work 2 sc in first dc, sc in each cross st (in CL and dc) and dc across to turning ch, 2 sc in 3rd ch of turning ch-3: 26 sc; ch 1, turn.

**Rows 6 and 7:** Rep Rows 2 and 3. At end of Row 7: 28 sc.

**Row 8:** Dc in first sc; *cross st in next 2 sc; rep from * across to last 2 sc; dc in last 2 sc: 12 cross sts and 4 dc; ch 1, turn.

**Row 9:** Sc in each cross st (in CL and dc) and dc across, sc in 3rd ch of turning ch-3; ch 1, turn.

**Rows 10 through 13:** Rep Rows 2 through 5. At end of Row 11: 30 sc. At end of Row 13: 32 sc.

**Rows 14 and 15:** Rep Row 2 two times more.

**Row 16:** Rep Row 8.

**Row 17:** Rep Row 5: 34 sc.

**Rows 18 and 19:** Rep Rows 2 and 3. At end of Row 19: 36 sc; do not ch 3. Finish off; weave in ends.

### BOOTIES (MAKE 2)

#### Instep

With white, ch 7. Place marker in first ch.

**Row 1 (right side):** Sc in 2nd ch from hook and in each rem ch across: 6 sc; ch 1, turn.

**Rows 2 through 7:** Sc in first sc and in each sc across; ch 1, turn. At end of Row 7, do not ch 1 and do not turn.

#### Sides

**Rnd 1 (right side):** Ch 18, being careful not to twist ch, join with sl st in free lp of marked ch (move marker to 9th ch of ch-18), ch 1, sc in same ch, sc in free lp of next 5 chs, work 6 sc evenly spaced across edge of rows, sc in each sc in Row 7 of Instep, sc in each ch around: 36 sc; join with sl st in first sc; ch 1, turn.

**Rnds 2 through 5:** Sc in first sc and in each sc around; join as before; ch 1, turn. At end of Rnd 5, do not turn.

#### Sole

**Rnd 1 (right side):** Sc in same sc as joining and in next 5 sc, sc dec in next 2 sc, sc in next 4 sc, sc dec in next 2 sc, sc in next 11 sc, sc dec in next 2 sc, sc in next 2 sc, sc dec in next 2 sc, sc in next 5 sc: 32 sc; join with sl st in first sc.

**Rnd 2:** Ch 1, sc in same sc as joining and in next 5 sc, sc dec in next 2 sc, sc in next 2 sc, sc dec in next 2 sc, sc in next 11 sc, (sc dec in next 2 sc) 2 times, sc in last 5 sc: 28 sc; join as before.

**Rnd 3:** Ch 1, sc in same sc as joining and in next 4 sc, (sc dec in next 2 sc) 2 times, sc in next 10 sc, (sc dec in next 2 sc) 2 times, sc in last 5 sc: 24 sc; join. Finish off.

Sew bottom seam on Sole.

#### Cuff

**Row 1:** With right side facing, join white with sl st in free lp of marked ch on Rnd 1 of Sides, ch 1, sc in same ch, sc in free lp of next 8 chs, work 6 sc evenly spaced across edge of Instep rows, sc in free lp of next 9 chs: 24 sc; ch 1, turn.

**Row 2:** Sc in first sc and in each sc across; ch 1, turn.

**Row 3:** Sc in first sc; *ch 1, skip next sc, sc in next sc; rep from * across to last sc; sc in last sc: 13 sc and 11 ch-1 sps; ch 1, turn.

**Row 4:** Sc in each sc and in each ch-1 sp across: 24 sc. Finish off; weave in ends.

Sew back seam on Cuff. Sew bootie to romper leg. Weave in all ends.

## TIES (MAKE 2)

Cut two 8 foot long pieces of pink. With both pieces held together, ch 75. Finish off.

Weave ties through ch-1 sps on Row 3 of each Cuff.

## POMPONS

Make 4 pompons with pink and white according to pompon instructions on page 80. Attach pompons to each end of ties.

# Hat

**Size:** 3 to 6 months

**Materials**

Light worsted weight yarn
1 3/4 oz med blue
    small amount variegated (for pompons)
Size F (3.75 mm) crochet hook (or size required for gauge)

**3 LIGHT**

**Gauge**

Rnds 1 through 8 = 3" diameter

## Instructions

### CROWN

Starting in center with blue ch 3; join with sl st to form a ring.

**Rnd 1 (wrong side):** Ch 1, 6 sc in ring: 6 sc; join with sl st in first sc; ch 1, turn.

**Rnd 2 (right side):** 2 sc in first sc and in each sc around: 12 sc; join as before; ch 1, turn.

**Rnd 3:** Sc in first sc, 2 sc in next sc; *sc in next sc, 2 sc in next sc; rep from * around: 18 sc; join; ch 1, turn.

**Rnd 4:** Sc in first 2 sc, 2 sc in next sc; *sc in next 2 sc, 2 sc in next sc; rep from * around: 24 sc; join; ch 1, turn.

**Rnd 5:** Sc in first 3 sc, 2 sc in next sc; *sc in next 3 sc, 2 sc in next sc; rep from * around: 30 sc; join; ch 1, turn.

**Rnd 6:** Sc in first 4 sc, 2 sc in next sc; *sc in next 4 sc, 2 sc in next sc; rep from * around: 36 sc; join; ch 1, turn.

**Rnd 7:** Sc in first 5 sc, 2 sc in next sc; *sc in next 5 sc, 2 sc in next sc; rep from * around: 42 sc; join; ch 1, turn.

**Rnd 8:** Sc in first 6 sc, 2 sc in next sc; *sc in next 6 sc, 2 sc in next sc; rep from * around: 48 sc; join; ch 1, turn.

**Rnd 9:** Sc in first 7 sc, 2 sc in next sc; *sc in next 7 sc, 2 sc in next sc; rep from * around: 54 sc; join; ch 1, turn.

**Rnd 10:** Sc in first 8 sc, 2 sc in next sc; *sc in next 8 sc, 2 sc in next sc; rep from * around: 60 sc; join; ch 1, turn.

**Rnd 11:** Sc in first 9 sc, 2 sc in next sc; *sc in next 9 sc, 2 sc in next sc; rep from * around: 66 sc; join; ch 1, turn.

**Rnd 12:** Sc in first sc and in each sc around; join; ch 1, turn.

**Rnds 13 through 18:** Rep Rnd 12 six times more. At end of Rnd 18, ch 1. Do not turn.

**Rnd 19 (right side):** Sc in back lp of first sc and in back lp of each sc around; join; ch 1, turn.

**Rnds 20 through 24:** Rep Rnd 12 five times more. At end of Rnd 24, do not ch 1. Finish off; weave in ends.

### EAR FLAPS

#### Left Flap

**Row 1:** With wrong side facing, skip first 8 sc on Rnd 24, join blue with sl st in next sc, ch 1, sc in same sc as joining, sc in next 9 sc: 10 sc; ch 1, turn.

**Row 2:** Sc in first sc and in each sc across; ch 1, turn.

**Row 3:** Sc dec in first 2 sc, sc in each sc across to last 2 sc, sc dec in last 2 sc: 8 sc; ch 1, turn.

**Rows 4 through 8:** Rep Rows 2 and 3 two times more, then rep Row 2 once more. At end of Row 5: 6 sc. At end of Row 7: 4 sc.

**Row 9:** Sc in first 2 sc, sc dec in last 2 sc: 3 sc; ch 1, turn.

**Row 10:** Rep Row 2.

**Row 11:** Skip first sc, sc dec in last 2 sc: 1 sc. Finish off; weave in ends.

## Right Flap

**Row 1:** With wrong side facing, skip next 29 sc on Rnd 24, join blue with sl st in next sc, ch 1, sc in same sc as joining, sc in next 9 sc: 10 sc; ch 1, turn.

**Rows 2 through 11:** Rep Rows 2 through 11 on Left Flap.

### Edging

With wrong side facing, join blue with sl st in 2nd sc on Rnd 24, ch 1, (sc, dc) in same sc as joining; *skip next sc, (sc, dc) in next sc*; rep from * to * 2 times more; ***(sc, dc) in edge of Row 1 of flap, **skip next row, (sc, dc) in edge of next row**; rep from ** to ** 3 times more on same edge of flap, (sc, dc) in sc dec and in ch-1 sp on Row 11 of flap; rep from ** to ** 5 times more on other edge of same flap***; rep from * to * 14 times more across Rnd 24; rep from *** to *** on edges of other flap; (sc, dc) in next sc on Rnd 24; rep from * to * 4 times more: 94 sts; join with sl st in first sc. Finish off; weave in ends.

### BRIM

**Row 1:** With right side facing and flaps at bottom, join blue with sl st in front lp of first sc on Rnd 18, ch 1, sc in front lp of same sc and in next 7 sc; *2 sc in front lp of next sc, sc in front lp of next 9 sc, 2 sc in front lp of next sc, sc in front lp of next 8 sc; rep from * 2 times more; 2 sc in front lp of last sc: 73 sc; ch 1, turn.

**Rows 2 through 5:** Sc in first sc and in each sc across; ch 1, turn.

**Row 6:** Sc in first sc and in each sc across; ch 3 (counts as dc on next row now and throughout), turn.

**Row 7:** *Cross st in next 2 sc; rep from * across to last 2 sc; dc in last 2 sc: 35 cross sts and 3 dc; ch 1, turn.

**Row 8:** Sc in each cross st (in CL and dc) and dc across, sc in 3rd ch of turning ch-3: 73 sc; ch 3, turn.

**Rows 9 through 14:** Rep Rows 7 and 8 three times more. At end of Row 14, do not ch 3. Finish off; weave in ends.

Sew back seam of Brim. Fold first 7 rows of Brim down and last 7 rows of Brim up.

### TIES

Cut a piece of blue yarn 9 feet long. Fold piece in half and draw fold through bottom of ear flap. Insert hook in fold. With both strands of yarn held together, ch 38. Finish off. Cut a piece of blue yarn 10 feet long. Fold piece in half and draw fold through bottom of other ear flap. Insert hook in fold. With both strands of yarn held together, ch 48. Finish off.

### POMPONS

Make 2 pompons with variegated according to pompon instructions on page 80. Attach pompons to free end of ties.

# Bonnet

**Size:** 3 to 6 months

**Materials**
Light worsted weight yarn
  1 3/4 oz white
  1/4 oz med pink
  1/4 oz lime
Size F (3.75 mm) crochet hook (or size required for gauge)

**Gauge**
18 sc = 4"; 9 cross sts = 4"; 12 rows in pattern = 4"

## Instructions

### CROWN

Starting at back with lime, ch 23.

**Row 1 (right side):** Sc in 2nd ch from hook and in next 19 chs, 2 sc in next ch, 5 sc in last ch, working in free lps on opposite side of ch, 2 sc in next ch, sc in last 20 chs: 49 sc; ch 1, turn.

**Row 2:** Sc in first 23 sc, 2 sc in each of next 3 sc, sc in last 23 sc, changing to white in last sc: 52 sc. With white, ch 2

41

(counts as hdc on next row now and throughout), turn. Finish off lime.

**Row 3:** With white, *cross st in next 2 sc*; rep from * to * 10 times more; (cross st in next 2 sc, ch 1) 2 times; rep from * to * 12 times more; hdc in last sc: 25 cross sts, 2 chs and 2 hdc: ch 1, turn.

**Row 4:** Sc in each cross st (in CL and dc), hdc and ch across, sc in 2nd ch of turning ch-2: 54 sc; ch 2, turn.

**Row 5:** *Cross st in next 2 sc; rep from * across to last sc; hdc in last sc: 26 cross sts and 2 hdc: ch 1, turn.

**Row 6:** Sc in each cross st (in CL and dc) and hdc across, sc in 2nd ch of turning ch-2: 54 sc; ch 2, turn.

**Rows 7 through 9:** Rep Rows 5 and 6, then rep Row 5 once more. At end of Row 9, change to lime in last st. With lime, ch 1, turn. Finish off white.

**Row 10:** With lime, rep Row 6, changing to pink in last sc. With pink, ch 2, turn. Finish off lime.

**Row 11:** With pink, rep Row 5, changing to lime in last st. With lime, ch 1, turn. Finish off pink.

**Row 12:** With lime, rep Row 6, changing to white in last sc. With white, ch 2, turn. Finish off lime.

**Row 13:** With white, rep Row 5, changing to lime in last st. With lime, ch 1, turn. Finish off white.

**Rows 14 through 16:** Rep Rows 10 through 12. At end of Row 16, change to white in last sc. With white, ch 1, turn. Finish off lime.

### Front Edging

**Row 1 (right side):** With white, sc in first sc and in each sc across: 54 sc; ch 1, turn.

**Row 2 (wrong side):** Sc in first sc and in each sc across. Do not turn and do not finish off.

### Neck Edging

**Row 1 (wrong side):** Working across bottom of crown, sc in edge of last sc made, work 17 more sc evenly spaced across edge of rows to center, work 18 more sc evenly spaced across edge of rows, ending with sc in edge of Row 2 of Front Edging: 36 sc; ch 1, turn.

**Row 2 (right side):** Sc in first sc and in each sc across. Finish off; weave in ends.

### TIES

Cut a piece of white yarn 9 feet long. Fold piece in half and draw fold through corner of bonnet (last sc on Row 2 of Neck Edging). Insert hook in fold. With both strands of yarn held together, ch 38. Finish off. Cut a piece of white yarn 10 feet long. Fold piece in half and draw fold through other corner of bonnet (first sc on Row 2 of Neck Edging). Insert hook in fold. With both strands of yarn held together, ch 48. Finish off.

### TASSELS

Make 2 tassels with white, lime and pink according to tassel instructions on page 80. Attach top of tassels to free end of ties.

# Booties

**Size:** 3 to 6 months

**Materials**

Light worsted weight yarn

¾ oz med blue

    small amount variegated (for pompons)

Size F (3.75 mm) crochet hook (or size required for gauge)

Stitch markers

**Gauge**

In sc, 19 sts = 4"; 19 rows = 4"

## Instructions (make 2)

### INSTEP

With blue, ch 7. Place marker in first ch.

**Row 1 (right side):** Sc in 2nd ch from hook and in each rem ch across: 6 sc; ch 1, turn.

**Rows 2 through 7:** Sc in first sc and in each sc across; ch 1, turn. At end of Row 7, do not ch 1 and do not turn.

### SIDES

**Rnd 1 (right side):** Ch 18, being careful not to twist ch, join with sl st in free lp of marked ch (move marker to 9th ch of ch-18), ch 1, sc in same ch, sc in free lp of next 5 chs, work 6 sc evenly spaced across edge of rows, sc in each sc in Row 7 of Instep, sc in each ch around: 36 sc; join with sl st in first sc; ch 1, turn.

**Rnds 2 through 5:** Sc in first sc and in each sc around; join as before; ch 1, turn. At end of Rnd 5, do not turn.

### Sole

**Rnd 1 (right side):** Sc in same sc as joining and in next 5 sc, sc dec in next 2 sc, sc in next 4 sc, sc dec in next 2 sc, sc in next 11 sc, sc dec in next 2 sc, sc in next 2 sc, sc dec in next 2 sc, sc in next 5 sc: 32 sc; join with sl st in first sc.

**Rnd 2:** Ch 1, sc in same sc as joining and in next 5 sc, sc dec in next 2 sc, sc in next 2 sc, sc dec in next 2 sc, sc in next 11 sc, (sc dec in next 2 sc) 2 times, sc in last 5 sc: 28 sc; join as before

**Rnd 3:** Ch 1, sc in same sc as joining and in next 4 sc, (sc dec in next 2 sc) 2 times, sc in next 10 sc, (sc dec in next 2 sc) 2 times, sc in last 5 sc: 24 sc; join. Finish off.

Sew bottom seam on Sole.

### CUFF

**Row 1:** With right side facing, join blue with sl st in free lp of marked ch on Rnd 1 of Sides, ch 1, sc in same ch, sc in free lp of next 6 chs, sc dec in free lp of next ch and in edge of last row on Instep (skipping last ch on Rnd 1 of Sides), sc in edge of next 5 rows, sc dec in edge of last row on Instep and in free lp of 2nd ch on Rnd 1 of Sides (skipping first ch), sc in free lp of last 7 chs: 21 sc; ch 1, turn.

**Row 2:** Sc in first sc and in each sc across; ch 1, turn.

**Row 3:** Sc in first sc; *ch 1, skip next sc, sc in next sc; rep from * across: 11 sc and 10 ch-1 sps; ch 1, turn.

**Row 4:** Sc in each sc and in each ch-1 sp across: 21 sc; ch 3 (counts as dc on next row now and throughout), turn.

**Row 5:** *Cross st in next 2 sc; rep from * across to last 2 sc; dc in last 2 sc: 9 cross sts and 3 dc; ch 1, turn.

**Row 6:** Sc in each cross st (in CL and dc) and dc across, sc in 3rd ch of turning ch-3: 21 sc; ch 3, turn.

**Row 7:** Rep Row 5. At end of row, do not ch 1. Finish off.

Sew back seam of Cuff. Weave in all ends.

### TIES (MAKE 2)

Cut two 8 foot long pieces of blue. With both pieces held together, ch 75. Finish off.

Weave tie through ch-1 sps on Row 3 of Cuff.

### POMPONS

Make 4 pompons with variegated according to pompon instructions on page 80. Attach pompons to each end of ties.

# Just so Adorable

"I'm just all smiles and so adorable in my tickle-me-pink outfit."

## SPECIAL STITCHES

**Cluster (CL):** *YO, insert hook in specified st and draw up a lp, YO and draw through 2 lps on hook; rep from * 2 times more; YO and draw through all 4 lps on hook: CL made.

**To change color:** Work st until 2 lps rem on hook, drop old color, pick up new color and draw through both lps on hook, cut dropped color.

**Sc decrease (sc dec):** Insert hook in first specified st and draw up a lp, insert hook in second specified st and draw up a lp; YO and draw through all 3 lps on hook: sc dec made.

# Blanket

**Size:** 37" x 41"

**Materials**
Light worsted weight yarn
14 oz med pink
7 oz white
2 1/2 oz med blue
2 1/2 oz lime
Size F (3.75 mm) crochet hook (or size required for gauge)

**Gauge**
In pattern: 19 sts = 4"; 13 rows = 4"

## Instructions

### CENTER

With pink, ch 182.

**Row 1 (wrong side):** Sc in 2nd ch from hook and in each rem ch across: 181 sc; ch 3 (counts as dc on next row now and throughout), turn.

**Row 2 (right side):** CL in next sc; *ch 1, skip next sc, CL in next sc; rep from * across to last sc; dc in last sc: 90 CL, 89 chs and 2 dc; ch 1, turn.

**Row 3:** Sc in each CL, dc and ch across, sc in 3rd ch of turning ch-3: 181 sc; ch 3, turn.

**Row 4:** Rep Row 2, changing to white in last st. With white, ch 1, turn. Finish off pink.

**Row 5:** With white, rep Row 3.

**Row 6:** With white, rep Row 2, changing to pink in last st. With pink, ch 1, turn Finish off white.

**Row 7:** With pink, rep Row 3, changing to blue in last st. With blue, ch 1, turn. Finish off pink.

**Row 8:** With blue, sc in first sc and in each sc across, changing to lime in last sc. With lime, ch 1, turn. Finish off blue.

**Row 9:** With lime, sc in first sc and in each sc across, changing to white in last sc. With white, ch 3, turn. Finish 7off lime.

**Row 10:** With white, rep Row 2, changing to lime in last st. With lime, ch 1, turn. Finish off white.

**Row 11:** With lime, rep Row 3, changing to blue in last sc. With blue, ch 1, turn. Finish off lime.

**Row 12:** With blue, rep Row 8, changing to pink in last sc. With pink, ch 1, turn. Finish off blue.

**Row 13:** With pink, rep Row 9, changing to white in last sc. With white, ch 3, turn. Finish off pink.

**Rows 14 and 15:** With white, rep Rows 2 and 3, changing to pink in last sc on Row 15. With pink, ch 3, turn. Finish off white.

**Rows 16 through 19:** With pink, rep Rows 2 and 3 two times more.

**Rows 20 through 127:** Rep Rows 2 through 19 six times more. At end of Row 127, do not ch 3. Finish off; weave in ends.

### RIGHT EDGING

**Row 1:** With right side facing, join pink with sl st in edge of last sc on Row 1, ch 1, sc in edge of same row, work 160 more sc evenly spaced across right edge of rows: 161 sc; ch 1, turn.

**Row 2:** Sc in first sc and in each sc across; ch 3, turn.

**Row 3:** CL in next sc; *ch 1, skip next sc, CL in next sc; rep from * across to last sc; dc in last sc: 80 CL, 79 chs and 2 dc; ch 1, turn.

**Row 4:** Sc in each CL, dc and ch across, sc in 3rd ch of turning ch-3: 161 sc; ch 3, turn.

**Rows 5 and 6:** Rep Rows 3 and 4. At end of Row 6, do not ch 3. Finish off; weave in ends.

### LEFT EDGING

**Row 1:** With right side facing, join pink with sl st in edge of first sc on Row 127, ch 1, sc in edge of same sc, work 160 more sc evenly spaced across left edge of rows: 161 sc; ch 1, turn.

**Rows 2 through 6:** Rep Rows 2 through 6 on Right Edging. At end of Row 6, ch 1, turn. Do not finish off.

### BORDER

**Rnd 1 (right side):** Work 2 sc in first sc on Row 6 of Left Edging (first corner started), sc in each rem sc on Row 6 of Left Edging across to last sc, 3 sc in last sc (corner made), work 6 sc across edge of rows on Left Edging, sc in free lp of each foundation ch at base of each sc on Row 1 of Center, work 6 sc across edge of rows on Right Edging, 3 sc in first sc on Row 6 of Right Edging (corner made), sc in each rem sc on Row 6 of Right Edging across to last sc, 3 sc in last sc (corner made), work 6 sc across edge of rows on Right Edging, sc in each sc on Row 127 of Center, work 6 sc across edge of rows on Left Edging, sc in same sc as first 2 sc (first corner completed): 716 sc; join with sl st in first sc.

**Rnd 2:** Ch 1, work 2 sc in same sc as joining (center sc of corner), *sc in each sc across to center sc in next corner, 3 sc in center sc of corner; rep from * 2 times more; sc in each sc across to first 2 sc, sc in same sc as first 2 sc: 724 sc; join as before.

**Rnd 3:** Ch 1, (sc, dc) in same sc as joining (center sc of corner), (sc, dc) in next sc; *skip next sc, (sc, dc) in next sc; rep from * across each side, working (sc, dc) in each of 3 sc in each corner and ending with (sc, dc) in first sc of first corner; join. Finish off; weave in ends.

# Cardigan

**Size:** 3 to 6 months

**Materials**
Light worsted weight yarn
   2¹/₂ oz med pink
   3 oz white
   ¹/₈ oz med blue
   ¹/₈ oz lime

Size F (3.75 mm) crochet hook (or size required for gauge)
Five ⁵/₈" diameter buttons
Matching sewing thread
Sewing needle

**Gauge**
In pattern, 19 sts = 4"; 15 rows = 4"

## Instructions

### BACK

Starting at bottom with pink, ch 49.

**Row 1 (wrong side):** Sc in 2nd ch from hook and in each rem ch across: 48 sc; ch 3 (counts as dc on next row now and throughout), turn.

**Row 2 (right side):** CL in next sc; *ch 1, skip next sc, CL in next sc; rep from * across to last 2 sc; dc in last 2 sc: 23 CL, 22 chs and 3 dc; ch 1, turn.

**Row 3:** Sc in each CL, dc and ch across, sc in 3rd ch of turning ch-3: 48 sc; ch 1, turn.

**Row 4:** Sc in first sc and in each sc across; ch 1, turn.

**Row 5:** Sc in first sc and in each sc across; ch 3, turn.

**Rows 6 through 25:** Rep Rows 2 through 5 five times more.

**Rows 26 and 27:** Rep Rows 2 and 3. At end of Row 27, do not ch 1. Turn.

#### Armhole Shaping

**Row 1 (right side):** Sl st in first 3 sc, ch 1, sc in same sc and in each sc across to last 2 sc, changing to white in last sc: 44 sc. With white, ch 1, turn, leaving rem sts unworked. Finish off pink.

**Row 2:** With white, sc in first sc and in each sc across; ch 3, turn.

**Row 3:** CL in next sc; *ch 1, skip next sc, CL in next.sc; rep

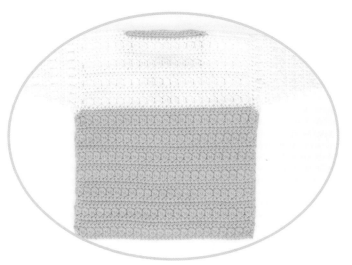

from * across to last 2 sc; dc in last 2 sc: 21 CL, 20 chs and 3 dc; ch 1, turn.

**Row 4:** Sc in each CL, dc and ch across, sc in 3rd ch of turning ch-3: 44 sc; ch 1, turn.

**Row 5:** Sc in first sc and in each sc across; ch 1, turn.

**Rows 6 through 13:** Rep Rows 2 through 5 two times more.

**Rows 14 through 16:** Rep Rows 2 through 4.

### Right Neck Shaping

**Row 1 (right side):** Sc in first 12 sc: 12 sc; ch 1, turn, leaving rem sts unworked.

**Row 2:** Sc in first sc and in each sc across. Finish off; weave in ends.

### Left Neck Shaping

**Row 1:** With right side facing, skip next 20 sc on Row 16 of Armhole Shaping, join white with sl st in next sc, ch 1, sc in same sc as joining and in each sc across: 12 sc; ch 1, turn.

**Row 2:** Sc in first sc and in each sc across. Finish off; weave in ends.

## LEFT FRONT

Starting at bottom with pink, ch 23.

**Row 1 (wrong side):** Sc in 2nd ch from hook and in each rem ch across: 22 sc; ch 3, turn.

**Row 2 (right side):** CL in next sc; *ch 1, skip next sc, CL in next sc; rep from * across to last 2 sc; dc in last 2 sc: 10 CL, 9 chs and 3 dc; ch 1, turn.

**Row 3:** Sc in each CL, dc and ch across, sc in 3rd ch of turning ch-3: 22 sc; ch 1, turn.

**Row 4:** Sc in first sc and in each sc across; ch 1, turn.

**Row 5:** Sc in first sc and in each sc across; ch 3, turn.

**Rows 6 through 25:** Rep Rows 2 through 5 five times more.

**Rows 26 and 27:** Rep Rows 2 and 3. At end of Row 27, do not ch 1. Turn.

### Armhole Shaping

**Row 1 (right side):** Sl st in first 3 sc, ch 1, sc in same sc and in each sc across, changing to white in last sc: 20 sc. With white, ch 1, turn. Finish off pink.

**Row 2:** With white, sc in first sc and in each sc across; ch 3, turn.

**Row 3:** CL in next sc; *ch 1, skip next sc, CL in next sc; rep from * across to last 2 sc; dc in last 2 sc, changing to pink in last dc: 9 CL, 8 chs and 3 dc. With pink, ch 1, turn. Finish off white.

**Row 4:** With pink, sc in each CL, dc and ch across, sc in 3rd ch of turning ch-3, changing to blue: 20 sc. With blue, ch 1, turn. Finish off pink.

**Row 5:** With blue, sc in first sc and in each sc across, changing to lime in last sc. With lime, ch 1, turn. Finish off blue.

**Row 6:** With lime, rep Row 2, changing to white in last sc. With white, ch 3, turn. Finish off lime.

**Row 7:** With white, rep Row 3, changing to lime in last dc. With lime, ch 1, turn. Finish off white.

**Row 8:** With lime, rep Row 4, changing to blue in last sc. With blue, ch 1, turn. Finish off lime.

**Row 9:** With blue, rep Row 5, changing to pink in last sc. With pink, ch 1, turn. Finish off blue.

**Row 10:** With pink, rep Row 2, changing to white in last sc. With white, ch 3, turn. Finish off pink.

**47**

## Neck Shaping

**Row 1 (right side):** With white, CL in next sc; *ch 1, skip next sc, CL in next sc; rep from * 3 times more; dc in next 2 sc: 5 CL, 4 chs and 3 dc; ch 1, turn, leaving rem sts unworked.

**Row 2:** Sc in each CL, dc and ch across, sc in 3rd ch of turning ch-3: 12 sc; ch 1, turn.

**Row 3:** Sc in first sc and in each sc across; ch 1, turn.

**Row 4:** Sc in first sc and in each sc across; ch 3, turn.

**Row 5:** CL in next sc; *ch 1, skip next sc, CL in next sc; rep from * across to last 2 sc; dc in last 2 sc: 5 CL, 4 chs and 3 dc; ch 1, turn.

**Rows 6 through 8:** Rep Rows 2 through 4. At end of Row 8, do not ch 3. Finish off; weave in ends.

## RIGHT FRONT

Starting at bottom with pink, ch 23.

**Row 1 (wrong side):** Sc in 2nd ch from hook and in each rem ch across: 22 sc; ch 3, turn.

**Row 2 (right side):** Dc in next sc, CL in next sc; *ch 1, skip next sc, CL in next sc; rep from * across to last sc; dc in last sc: 10 CL, 9 chs and 3 dc; ch 1, turn.

**Row 3:** Sc in each CL, dc and ch across, sc in 3rd ch of turning ch-3: 22 sc; ch 1, turn.

**Row 4:** Sc in first sc and in each sc across; ch 1, turn.

**Row 5:** Sc in first sc and in each sc across; ch 3, turn.

**Rows 6 through 25:** Rep Rows 2 through 5 five times more.

**Rows 26 and 27:** Rep Rows 2 and 3.

### Armhole Shaping

**Row 1 (right side):** Sc in first 20 sc, changing to white in last sc: 20 sc. With white, ch 1, turn, leaving rem sts unworked. Finish off pink.

**Row 2:** With white, sc in first sc and in each sc across; ch 3, turn.

**Row 3:** Dc in next sc, CL in next sc; *ch 1, skip next sc, CL in next sc; rep from * across to last sc; dc in last sc, changing to pink: 9 CL, 8 chs and 3 dc. With pink, ch 1, turn. Finish off white.

**Row 4:** With pink, sc in each CL, dc and ch across, sc in 3rd ch of turning ch-3, changing to blue: 20 sc. With blue, ch 1, turn. Finish off pink.

**Row 5:** With blue, sc in first sc and in each sc across,

changing to lime in last sc. With lime, ch 1, turn. Finish off blue.

**Row 6:** With lime, rep Row 2, changing to white in last sc. With white, ch 3, turn. Finish off lime.

**Row 7:** With white, rep Row 3, changing to lime in last dc. With lime, ch 1, turn. Finish off white.

**Row 8:** With lime, rep Row 4, changing to blue in last sc. With blue, ch 1, turn. Finish off lime.

**Row 9:** With blue, rep Row 5, changing to pink in last sc. With pink, ch 1, turn. Finish off blue.

**Row 10:** With pink, sc in first sc and in each sc across. Finish off; weave in ends.

### Neck Shaping

**Row 1:** With right side facing, skip first 8 sc on Row 10 of Armhole Shaping, join white with sl st in next sc, ch 3 (counts as dc), dc in next sc, CL in next sc; *ch 1, skip next sc, CL in next sc; rep from * across to last sc; dc in last sc: 5 CL, 4 chs and 3 dc; ch 1, turn.

**Row 2:** Sc in each CL, dc and ch across, sc in 3rd ch of turning ch-3: 12 sc; ch 1, turn.

**Row 3:** Sc in first sc and in each sc across; ch 1, turn.

**Row 4:** Sc in first sc and in each sc across; ch 3, turn.

**Row 5:** Dc in next sc, CL in next sc; *ch 1, skip next sc, CL in next sc; rep from * across to last sc; dc in last sc: 5 CL, 4 chs and 3 dc; ch 1, turn.

**Rows 6 through 8:** Rep Rows 2 through 4. At end of Row 8, do not ch 3. Finish off; weave in ends.

### Left Placket

**Row 1:** With wrong side facing, join pink with sl st in edge of last sc on Row 1 of Left Front, ch 1, sc in edge of same row, work 44 more sc evenly spaced in edge of rows on Left Front and Left Front Armhole Shaping, ending with sc in edge of Row 10 of Left Front Armhole Shaping: 45 sc; ch 1, turn.

**Row 2:** Sc in first sc and in each sc across; ch 1, turn.

**Row 3:** Sc in first 6 sc; *ch 2, skip next 2 sc, sc in next 7 sc; rep from * 3 times more; ch 2, skip next 2 sc, sc in last sc: 35 sc and 5 ch-2 sps; ch 1, turn.

**Row 4:** Sc in first sc; *2 sc in next ch-2 sp, sc in next 7 sc; rep from * 3 times more; 2 sc in next ch-2 sp, sc in next 6 sc: 45 sc; ch 1, turn.

**Row 5:** Sc in first sc and in each sc across. Finish off; weave in ends.

## Right Placket

**Row 1:** With wrong side facing, join pink with sl st in edge of last sc on Row 10 of Right Front Armhole Shaping, ch 1, sc in edge of same row, work 44 more sc evenly spaced in edge of rows on Right Front Armhole Shaping and Right Front, ending with sc in edge of Row 1 of Right Front: 45 sc; ch 1, turn.

**Rows 2 through 5:** Sc in first sc and in each sc across; ch 1, turn. At end of Row 5, do not ch 1. Finish off; weave in ends.

Sew shoulder seams.

## Neck Edging

**Row 1:** With right side facing, join pink with sl st in top edge of Row 5 on Right Placket, ch 1, sc in edge of same row, sc in edge of next 4 rows, sc in next 7 sc on Row 10 of Right Front Armhole Shaping, sc dec in next sc of Right Front Armhole Shaping and in edge of Row 1 of Right Front Neck Shaping, work 9 sc evenly spaced in edge of rows on Right Neck Shaping (Front and Back), sc dec in edge of Row 1 on Right Back Neck Shaping and in next sc on Row 16 of Back Armhole Shaping, sc in next 18 sc on Row 16, sc dec in next sc on Back Armhole Shaping and in edge of Row 1 on Left Back Neck Shaping, work 9 sc evenly spaced in edge of rows on Left Neck Shaping (Back and Front), sc dec in edge of Row 1 on Left Front Neck Shaping and in next sc on Row 10 of Left Front Armhole Shaping, sc in next 7 sc on Row 10, sc in edge of next 5 rows of Left Placket: 64 sc; ch 1, turn.

**Row 2:** Sc in first sc and in each sc around, working sc dec in sc before and after sc dec in each of 4 corners (skipping each sc dec): 56 sc. Finish off; weave in ends.

## Placket and Neck Edging

With right side facing, join pink with sl st in last sc on Row 5 of Right Placket, ch 1, sc in same sc as joining, sc in each sc across Row 5, sc in edge of Rows 1 and 2 of Neck Edging, sc in edge of last sc made, sc in each st on Row 2 of Neck Edging, sc in edge of last sc made, sc in edge of Rows 2 and 1 of Neck Edging, sc in each sc on Row 5 of Left Placket: 152 sc. Finish off; weave in ends.

Sew buttons onto Right Placket.

## SLEEVES (MAKE 2)

With pink, ch 27.

**Row 1 (wrong side):** Sc in 2nd ch from hook and in each rem ch across, changing to blue in last sc: 26 sc. With blue, ch 1, turn. Finish off pink.

**Row 2 (right side):** With blue, sc in first sc and in each sc across, changing to lime in last sc. With lime, ch 1, turn. Finish off blue.

**Row 3:** With lime, sc in first sc and in each sc across, changing to white in last sc. With white, ch 3, turn. Finish off lime.

**Row 4:** With white, CL in next sc; *ch 1, skip next sc, CL in next sc; rep from * across to last 2 sc; dc in last 2 sc, changing to lime in last dc: 12 CL, 11 chs and 3 dc. With lime, ch 1, turn. Finish off white.

**Row 5:** With lime, sc in each CL, dc and ch across, sc in 3rd ch of turning ch-3, changing to blue: 26 sc. With blue, ch 1, turn. Finish off lime.

**Row 6:** With blue, rep Row 2, changing to pink in last sc. With pink, ch 1, turn. Finish off blue.

**Row 7:** With pink, work 2 sc in first sc, sc in each sc across to last sc, 2 sc in last sc, changing to white in last sc: 28 sc. With white, ch 3, turn. Finish off pink.

**Row 8:** With white, dc in next sc, CL in next sc; *ch 1, skip next sc, CL in next sc; rep from * across to last sc; dc in last sc: 13 CL, 12 chs and 3 dc; ch 1, turn.

**Row 9:** Sc in each CL, dc and ch across, sc in 3rd ch of turning ch-3: 28 sc; ch 1, turn.

**Row 10:** Sc in first sc and in each sc across; ch 1, turn.

**Row 11:** Work 2 sc in first sc, sc in each sc across to last sc, 2 sc in last sc: 30 sc; ch 3, turn.

**Row 12:** CL in next sc; *ch 1, skip next sc, CL in next sc; rep from * across to last 2 sc; dc in last 2 sc: 14 CL, 13 chs and 3 dc; ch 1, turn.

**Row 13:** Work 2 sc in first dc, sc in each CL, dc and ch across to turning ch-3, 2 sc in 3rd ch of turning ch-3: 32 sc; ch 1, turn.

**Row 14:** Rep Row 10.

**Row 15:** Sc in first sc and in each sc across; ch 3, turn.

**Row 16:** Rep Row 8: 15 CL, 14 chs and 3 dc.

**Row 17:** Rep Row 13: 34 sc; ch 1, turn.

**Rows 18 and 19:** Rep Rows 10 and 11. At end of Row 19: 36 sc.

**Row 20:** Rep Row 8: 17 CL, 16 chs and 3 dc.

**Row 21:** Rep Row 13: 38 sc.

**Row 22:** Rep Row 10.

**Row 23:** Rep Row 15.

**Row 24:** Rep Row 12: 18 CL, 17 chs and 3 dc.

**Row 25:** Rep Row 13: 40 sc. At end of row, do not ch 1. Finish off; weave in ends.

Set in sleeves. Sew sleeve and side seams.

# Shirt

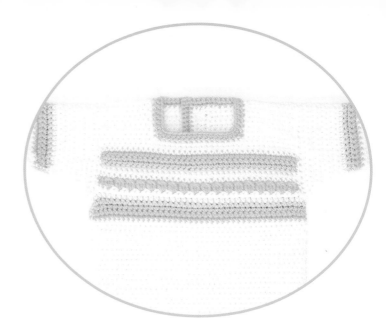

**Size:** 3 to 6 months

**Materials**
Light worsted weight yarn
   3 oz white
   1/4 oz med pink
   1/8 oz med blue
   1/8 oz lime
Size F (3.75 mm) crochet hook
   (or size required for gauge)
Two 5/8" diameter buttons
Matching sewing thread
Sewing needle

**Gauge**
In sc, 18 sts = 4"; 20 rows = 4"

## Instructions

### FRONT

Starting at bottom with white, ch 43.

**Row 1 (wrong side):** Sc in 2nd ch from hook and in each rem ch across: 42 sc; ch 1, turn.

**Row 2 (right side):** Sc in first sc and in each sc across; ch 1, turn.

**Rows 3 through 25:** Rep Row 2 twenty three times more. At end of Row 25, change to pink in last sc. With pink, ch 1, turn. Finish off white.

**Rows 26 and 27:** With pink, rep Row 2 two times more. At end of Row 27, change to blue in last sc. With blue, ch 1, turn. Finish off pink.

**Row 28:** With blue, rep Row 2, changing to lime in last sc. With lime, ch 1, turn. Finish off blue.

**Row 29:** With lime, rep Row 2, changing to white in last sc. With white, ch 1, turn. Finish off lime.

**Row 30:** With white, sc in first sc and in each sc across. Turn.

### Armhole Shaping

**Row 1 (wrong side):** Sl st in first 3 sc, ch 1, sc in same sc, sc in each sc across to last 2 sc, changing to pink in last sc: 38 sc. With pink, ch 3 (counts as dc on next row), turn, leaving rem sts unworked.

**Row 2 (right side):** CL in next sc; *ch 1, skip next sc, CL in next sc; rep from * across to last 2 sc; dc in last 2 sc, changing to white in last dc: 18 CL, 17 chs and 3 dc. With white, ch 1, turn. Finish off pink.

**Row 3:** With white, sc in each CL, dc and ch across, sc in 3rd ch of turning ch-3: 38 sc; ch 1, turn.

**Row 4:** Sc in first sc and in each sc across, changing to lime in last sc. With lime, ch 1, turn. Finish off white.

**Row 5:** With lime, rep Row 4, changing to blue in last sc. With blue, ch 1, turn. Finish off lime.

**Row 6:** With blue, rep Row 4, changing to pink in last sc. With pink, ch 1, turn. Finish off blue.

**Row 7:** With pink, sc in first sc and in each sc across; ch 1, turn.

**Row 8:** With pink, rep Row 4, changing to white in last sc. With white, ch 1, turn. Finish off pink.

**Rows 9 and 10:** With white, rep Row 7; ch 1, turn.

### Right Neck Shaping

**Row 1 (wrong side):** Sc in first 10 sc: 10 sc; ch 1, turn, leaving rem sts unworked.

**Rows 2 through 9:** Sc in first sc and in each sc across; ch 1, turn. At end of Row 9, do not ch 1. Finish off; weave in ends.

### Left Neck Shaping

**Row 1:** With wrong side facing, skip next 18 sc on Row 10

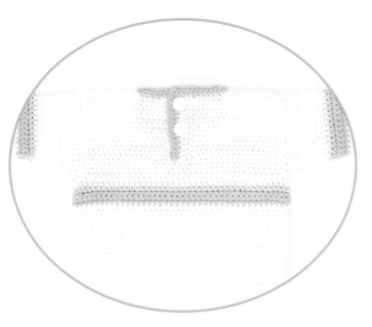

of Armhole Shaping, join white with sl st in next sc, ch 1, sc in same sc as joining and in each sc across: 10 sc; ch 1, turn.

**Rows 2 through 9:** Rep Rows 2 through 9 of Right Neck Shaping. At end of Row 9, do not ch 1. Finish off; weave in ends.

## BACK

Starting at bottom with white, ch 43.

**Rows 1 through 30:** Rep Rows 1 through 30 on Front.

### Armhole Shaping

**Row 1 (wrong side):** Sl st in first 3 sc, ch 1, sc in same sc, sc in each sc across to last 2 sc: 38 sc; ch 1, turn, leaving rem sts unworked.

**Rows 2 through 4:** Sc in first sc and in each sc across; ch 1, turn.

### Left Back

**Row 1 (wrong side):** Sc in first 17 sc: 17 sc; ch 1, turn, leaving rem sts unworked.

**Rows 2 through 14:** Sc in first sc and in each sc across; ch 1, turn.

### Neck Shaping

**Row 1 (wrong side):** Sc in first 10 sc: 10 sc; ch 1, turn, leaving rem sts unworked.

**Row 2 (right side):** Sc in first sc and in each sc across. Finish off; weave in ends.

### Right Back

**Row 1:** With wrong side facing, skip next 4 sc on Row 4 of Armhole Shaping, join white with sl st in next sc, ch 1, sc in same sc and in each sc across: 17 sc; ch 1, turn.

**Rows 2 through 14:** Sc in first sc and in each sc across; ch 1, turn. At end of Row 14, do not ch 1. Finish off; weave in ends.

### Neck Shaping

**Row 1:** With wrong side facing, skip next 7 sc on Row 14 of Right Back, join white with sl st in next sc, ch 1, sc in same sc and in each sc across: 10 sc; ch 1, turn.

**Row 2 (right side):** Sc in first sc and in each sc across. Finish off; weave in ends.

### Right Placket

**Row 1:** With wrong side facing, join white with sl st in edge of first sc on Row 1 of Right Back, ch 1, sc in edge of same row, work 12 more sc evenly spaced in edge of rows on Right Back, ending with sc in edge of Row 14 of Right Back: 13 sc; ch 1, turn.

**Rows 2 and 3:** Sc in first sc and in each sc across; ch 1, turn.

**Row 4:** Sc in first sc; *ch 2, skip next 2 sc, sc in next 4 sc; rep from * once more: 9 sc and 2 ch-2 sps. Finish off.

### Left Placket

**Row 1:** With wrong side facing, join white with sl st in edge of first sc on Row 14 of Left Back, ch 1, sc in edge of same row, work 12 more sc evenly spaced in edge of rows on Left Back, ending with sc in edge of Row 1 of Left Back: 13 sc; ch 1, turn.

**Rows 2 through 4:** Sc in first sc and in each sc across; ch 1, turn. At end of Row 4, do not ch 1. Finish off.

Sew shoulder seams.

### Neck Edging

With right side facing, join white with sl st in top edge of Row 4 on Left Placket, ch 1, sc in edge of same row, sc in edge of next 3 rows, sc in next 6 sc on Row 14 of Left Back, sc dec in next sc of Left Back and in edge of Row 1 of Neck Shaping, sc in edge of next 9 rows on Left Neck Shaping (Back and Front), sc dec in edge of Row 1 of Left Neck Shaping and in next sc on Row 10 of Front Armhole Shaping, sc in next 16 sc on Row 10, sc dec in next sc on Front Armhole Shaping and in edge of Row 1 of Right Front Neck Shaping, sc in edge of next 9 rows on Right Neck Shaping (Front and Back), sc dec in edge of Row 1 of Back Right Neck Shaping and in next sc on Row 14 of Right Back, sc in next 6 sc on Row 14, sc in edge of next 4 rows on Right Placket: 58 sc. Finish off.

### Placket and Neck Edging

**Row 1:** With wrong side facing, join pink with sl st in last sc on Row 4 of Right Placket, ch 1, sc in same sc as joining, sc in next 3 sc, 2 sc in next ch-2 sp, sc in next 4 sc, 2 sc in next ch-2 sp, sc in next sc, sc in edge of Neck Edging, sc in edge of last sc made, sc in each sc of Neck Edging, working sc dec in sc before and after sc dec in each of 4 corners (skipping each sc dec), sc in edge of last sc made, sc in edge of Neck Edging, sc in each sc on Row 4 of Left Placket: 80 sc; ch 1, turn.

**Row 2 (right side):** Sc in first 15 sc, sc in edge of last sc, sc in next 52 sc, sc in edge of last sc, sc n next 15 sc: 84 sc. Finish off; weave in ends.

Sew bottom edges of Plackets to skipped sc on Row 4 of Back Armhole Shaping between Left Back and Right Back. Sew buttons onto left Placket.

## SLEEVES (MAKE 2)

With white, ch 27.

**Row 1 (wrong side):** Sc in 2nd ch from hook and in each rem ch across, changing to pink in last sc: 26 sc. With pink, ch 1, turn. Finish off white.

**Row 2 (right side):** With pink, sc in first sc and in each sc across; ch 1, turn.

**Row 3:** Rep Row 2, changing to blue in last sc. With blue, ch 1, turn. Finish off pink.

**Row 4:** With blue, work 2 sc in first sc, sc in each sc across to last sc, 2 sc in last sc, changing to lime in last sc: 28 sc. With lime, ch 1, turn. Finish off blue.

**Row 5:** With lime, rep Row 2, changing to white in last sc. With white, ch 1, turn. Finish off lime.

**Rows 6 and 7:** With white, rep Row 2 two times more.

**Row 8:** With white, work 2 sc in first sc, sc in each sc across to last sc, 2 sc in last sc: 30 sc; ch 1, turn.

**Rows 9 through 11:** Rep Rows 6 through 8. At end of Row 11: 32 sc.

**Row 12:** With white, rep Row 2.

**Row 13:** Rep Row 8: 34 sc.

**Rows 14 and 15:** Rep Rows 12 and 13. At end of Row 15: 36 sc; do not ch 1. Finish off; weave in ends.

Set in sleeves. Sew sleeve and side seams.

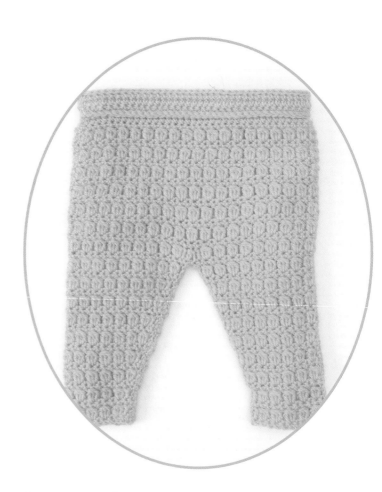

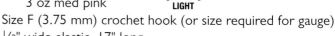

**Size:** 3 to 6 months

**Materials**
Light worsted weight yarn
   3 oz med pink
Size F (3.75 mm) crochet hook (or size required for gauge)
1/2" wide elastic, 17" long

**Gauge**
In pattern, 18 sts = 4"; 13 rows = 4"

## Instructions

### PANTS FRONT

#### Right Leg

Starting at bottom of leg, ch 13.

**Row 1 (wrong side):** Sc in 2nd ch from hook and in each rem ch across: 12 sc; ch 3 (counts as dc on next row now and throughout), turn.

**Row 2 (right side):** Dc in next sc, CL in next sc; *ch 1, skip next sc, CL in next sc; rep from * across to last sc; dc in last sc: 5 CL, 4 chs and 3 dc; ch 1, turn.

**Row 3:** Sc in each CL, dc and ch across, sc in 3rd ch of turning ch-3: 12 sc; ch 3, turn.

**Row 4:** Rep Row 2.

**Row 5:** Sc in each CL, dc and ch across, 2 sc in 3rd ch of turning ch-3: 13 sc; ch 3, turn.

**Row 6:** CL in next sc; *ch 1, skip next sc, CL in next sc; rep from * across to last sc; dc in last sc: 6 CL, 5 chs and 2 dc; ch 1, turn.

**Row 7:** Rep Row 5: 14 sc.

**Rows 8 through 10:** Rep Rows 4 through 6. At end of Row 9: 15 sc.

**Rows 11 through 18:** Rep Rows 7 through 10 two times more. At end of Row 11: 16 sc. At end of Row 13: 17 sc. At end of Row 15: 18 sc. At end of Row 17: 19 sc.

**Row 19:** Rep Row 5: 20 sc. At end of row, do not ch 3. Finish off; weave in ends.

### Left Leg

Starting at bottom of leg, ch 13.

**Row 1 (wrong side):** Sc in 2nd ch from hook and in each rem ch across: 12 sc; ch 3, turn.

**Row 2 (right side):** CL in next sc; *ch 1, skip next sc, CL in next sc; rep from * across to last 2 sc; dc in last 2 sc: 5 CL, 4 chs and 3 dc; ch 1, turn.

**Row 3:** Sc in each CL, dc and ch across, sc in 3rd ch of turning ch-3: 12 sc; ch 3, turn.

**Row 4:** Rep Row 2.

**Row 5:** Work 2 sc in first dc, sc in each rem CL, dc and ch across, sc in 3rd ch of turning ch-3: 13 sc; ch 3, turn.

**Row 6:** CL in next sc; *ch 1, skip next sc, CL in next sc; rep from * across to last sc; dc in last sc: 6 CL, 5 chs and 2 dc; ch 1, turn.

**Row 7:** Rep Row 5: 14 sc.

**Rows 8 through 10:** Rep Rows 4 through 6. At end of Row 9: 15 sc.

**Rows 11 through 18:** Rep Rows 7 through 10 two times more. At end of Row 11: 16 sc. At end of Row 13: 17 sc. At end of Row 15: 18 sc. At end of Row 17: 19 sc.

**Row 19:** Rep Row 5: 20 sc. Do not finish off.

### Body

**Row 1 (right side):** CL in next sc; *ch 1, skip next sc, CL in next sc*; rep from * to * across to last 2 sc of Left Leg; dc in next sc, pick up Right Leg, with right side facing, work CL in

last sc of Left Leg and in first sc of Right Leg (working first dc of CL in last sc on Left Leg and last 2 dc of CL in first sc on Right Leg), dc in next sc on Right Leg, CL in next sc; rep from * to * across to last sc; ch 1, dc in last sc: 19 CL, 17 chs and 4 dc; ch 1, turn.

**Row 2:** Sc in each CL, dc and ch across, sc in 3rd ch of turning ch-3: 40 sc; ch 3, turn.

**Row 3:** CL in next sc; *ch 1, skip next sc, CL in next sc; rep from * across to last 2 sc; dc in last 2 sc: 19 CL, 17 chs and 4 dc; ch 1, turn.

**Rows 4 through 13:** Rep Rows 2 and 3 five times more.

**Row 14:** Work sc dec in first 2 sts, sc in each st across to last 2 sts; work sc dec in last 2 sts: 38 sc; ch 1, turn.

**Rows 15 and 16:** Sc in first sc and in each sc across; ch 1, turn. Do not finish off.

### Waistband

**Row 1 (right side):** Sl st in front lp of each sc across: 38 sl sts; ch 1, turn.

**Row 2:** Sc in back lp of each sc on Row 16 of Body: 38 sc; ch 1, turn.

**Rows 3 and 4:** Sc in first sc and in each sc across; ch 1, turn.

**Rows 5 through 8:** Rep Rows 1 through 4, working sc in Row 6 in back lp of each sc on Row 4 of Waistband. At end of Row 8, do not ch 1. Finish off; weave in ends.

## PANTS BACK

### Left Leg

Work same as Front Right Leg.

### Right Leg

Work same as Front Left Leg.

### Body

**Row 1 (right side):** CL in next sc; *ch 1, skip next sc, CL in next sc*; rep from * to * across to last 2 sc of Right Leg; dc in next sc, pick up Left Leg, with right side facing, work CL in last sc of Right Leg and in first sc of Left Leg (working first dc of CL in last sc on Right Leg and last 2 dc of CL in first sc on Left Leg), dc in next sc on Left Leg, CL in next sc; rep from * to * across to last sc; ch 1, dc in last sc: 19 CL, 17 chs and 4 dc; ch 1, turn.

**Rows 2 through 16:** Work same as Rows 2 through 16 on Front Body.

**Waistband**

Work same as Front Waistband.

**Assembly**

With wrong sides facing, joining front and back together, sew side and crotch seams. Sew ends of elastic together. Fold Row 8 of Waistband back over elastic to wrong side and sew Waistband seam.

# Romper

**Size:** 3 to 6 months

**Materials**

Light worsted weight yarn
    5 oz lime
    1 oz white
    small amount med blue
Size F (3.75 mm) crochet hook (or size required for gauge)
Four 5/8" diameter buttons
Matching sewing thread
Sewing needle

**Gauge**

In pattern, 19 sts = 4"; 15 rows = 4"

## Instructions

### PANTS BACK

**Left Leg**

Starting at bottom of leg with lime, ch 13.

**Row 1 (wrong side):** Sc in 2nd ch from hook and in each rem ch across: 12 sc; ch 1, turn.

**Row 2 (right side):** Sc in first sc and in each sc across; ch 1, turn.

**Row 3:** Sc in first sc and in each sc across; ch 3 (counts as first dc on next row now and throughout), turn.

**Row 4:** Dc in next sc, CL in next sc; *ch 1, skip next sc, CL in next sc; rep from * across to last sc; dc in last sc: 5 CL, 4 chs and 3 dc; ch 1, turn.

**Row 5:** Sc in each CL, dc and ch across, 2 sc in 3rd ch of turning ch-3: 13 sc; ch 1, turn.

**Row 6:** Rep Row 2.

**Row 7:** Sc in first sc and in each sc across to last sc, 2 sc in last sc: 14 sc; ch 3, turn.

**Rows 8 through 11:** Rep Rows 4 through 7. At end of Row 9: 15 sc. At end of Row 11: 16 sc.

**Row 12:** Rep Row 4.

**Row 13:** Sc in each CL, dc and ch across, sc in 3rd ch of turning ch-3; ch 1, turn.

**Row 14:** Rep Row 2.

**Row 15:** Rep Row 7: 17 sc.

**Rows 16 through 23:** Rep Rows 4 through 7 two times more. At end of Row 17: 18 sc. At end of Row 19: 19 sc. At end of Row 21: 20 sc. At end of Row 23, do not ch 1. Finish off; weave in ends.

**Right Leg**

Starting at bottom with lime, ch 13.

**Row 1 (wrong side):** Sc in 2nd ch from hook and in each rem ch across: 12 sc; ch 1, turn.

**Row 2 (right side):** Sc in first sc and in each sc across; ch 1, turn.

**Row 3:** Sc in first sc and in each sc across; ch 3, turn.

**Row 4:** CL in next sc; *ch 1, skip next sc, CL in next sc; rep from * across to last 2 sc; dc in last 2 sc: 5 CL, 4 chs and 3 dc; ch 1, turn.

**Row 5:** Work 2 sc in first dc, sc in each CL, dc and ch across, sc in 3rd ch of turning ch-3: 13 sc; ch 1, turn.

**Row 6:** Rep Row 2.

**Row 7:** Work 2 sc in first sc, sc in each sc across: 14 sc; ch 3, turn.

**Rows 8 through 11:** Rep Rows 4 through 7. At end of Row 9: 15 sc. At end of Row 11: 16 sc.

**Row 12:** Rep Row 4.

**Row 13:** Sc in each CL, dc and ch across, sc in 3rd ch of turning ch-3; ch 1, turn.

**Row 14:** Rep Row 2.

**Row 15:** Rep Row 7: 17 sc.

**Rows 16 through 23:** Rep Rows 4 through 7 two times more. At end of Row 17: 18 sc. At end of Row 19: 19 sc. At end of Row 21: 20 sc. At end of Row 23, do not finish off.

## Body

**Row 1 (right side):** CL in next sc; *ch 1, skip next sc, CL in next sc*; rep from * to * across to last 2 sc on Right Leg; dc in next sc, pick up Left Leg, with right side facing, work CL in last sc on Right Leg and in first sc on Left Leg (working first dc of CL in last sc on Right Leg and last 2 dc of CL in first sc on Left Leg), dc in next sc on Left Leg, CL in next sc; rep from * to * across to last sc; ch 1, dc in last sc: 19 CL, 17 chs and 4 dc; ch 1, turn.

**Row 2:** Sc in each CL, dc and ch across, sc in 3rd ch of turning ch-3: 40 sc; ch 1, turn.

**Row 3:** Sc in first sc and in each sc across: ch 1, turn.

**Row 4:** Sc in first sc and in each sc across: ch 3, turn.

**Row 5:** CL in next sc; *ch 1, skip next sc, CL in next sc; rep from * across to last 2 sc; dc in last 2 sc: 19 CL, 18 chs and 3 dc; ch 1, turn.

**Rows 6 through 13:** Rep Rows 2 through 5 two times more.

**Rows 14 and 15:** Rep Rows 2 and 3.

**Row 16:** Work 2 sc in first sc, sc in each sc across to last sc, 2 sc in last sc: 42 sc; ch 3, turn.

**Row 17:** Dc in next sc, CL in next sc; *ch 1, skip next sc, CL in next sc; rep from * across to last sc; dc in last sc: 20 CL, 19 chs and 3 dc; ch 1, turn.

**Rows 18 through 20:** Rep Rows 2 through 4.

**Row 21:** Rep Row 17.

**Rows 22 through 33:** Rep Rows 18 through 21 three times more.

**Row 34:** Rep Row 2. At end of row, do not ch 1. Finish off; weave in ends.

### Armhole Shaping

**Row 1:** With right side facing, skip first 2 sc on Row 34 of Body, join white with sl st in next sc, ch 1, sc in same sc as joining, sc in each sc across to last 2 sc: 38 sc; ch 1, turn, leaving rem sts unworked.

**Rows 2 through 18:** Sc in first sc and in each sc across; ch 1, turn.

### Right Neck Shaping

**Row 1 (right side):** Sc in first 10 sc: 10 sc; ch 1, turn, leaving rem sts unworked.

**Row 2:** Sc in first sc and in each sc across. Finish off; weave in ends.

### Left Neck Shaping

**Row 1:** With right side facing, skip next 18 sc on Row 18 of Armhole Shaping, join white with sl st in next sc, ch 1, sc in same sc as joining, sc in each sc across: 10 sc; ch 1, turn.

**Row 2:** Sc in first sc and in each sc across. Finish off; weave in ends.

## FRONT

### Right Leg

Work same as Back Left Leg.

### Left Leg

Work same as Back Right Leg.

### Body

**Row 1 (right side):** CL in next sc; *ch 1, skip next sc, CL in next sc*; rep from * to * across to last 2 sc on Left Leg; dc in next sc, pick up Right Leg, with right side facing, work CL in last sc on Left Leg and in first sc on Right Leg (working first dc of CL in last sc on Left Leg and last 2 dc of CL in first sc on Right Leg), dc in next sc on Right Leg, CL in next sc; rep from * to * across to last sc; ch 1, dc in last sc: 19 CL, 17 chs and 4 dc; ch 1, turn.

**Rows 2 through 19:** Rep Rows 2 through 19 on Back Body.

### Right Front

**Row 1 (wrong side):** Sc in first 19 sc: 19 sc; ch 3, turn, leaving rem sts unworked.

**Row 2 (right side):** CL in next sc; *ch 1, skip next sc, CL in next sc; rep from * across to last sc; dc in last sc: 9 CL, 8 chs and 2 dc; ch 1, turn.

**Row 3:** Sc in each CL, dc and ch across, sc in 3rd ch of turning ch-3: 19 sc; ch 1, turn.

**Row 4:** Sc in first sc and in each sc across; ch 1, turn.

**Row 5:** Sc in first sc and in each sc across; ch 3, turn.

**Rows 6 through 13:** Rep Rows 2 through 5 two times more.

**Rows 14 and 15:** Rep Rows 2 and 3, changing to white in last sc on Row 15. With white, ch 1, turn. Finish off lime.

## Armhole Shaping

**Row 1 (right side):** With white, sc in first 17 sc, changing to blue in last sc: 17 sc. With blue, ch 1, turn, leaving rem sts unworked. Finish off white.

**Row 2:** With blue, sc in first sc and in each sc across, changing to lime in last sc. With lime, ch 1, turn. Finish off blue.

**Row 3:** With lime, rep Row 2, changing to blue in last sc. With blue, ch 1, turn. Finish off lime.

**Row 4:** With blue, rep Row 2, changing to white in last sc. With white, ch 1, turn. Finish off blue.

**Rows 5 through 7:** With white, sc in first sc and in each sc across; ch 1, turn. At end of Row 7, change to blue in last sc. With blue, ch 1, turn. Finish off white.

**Rows 8 through 11:** Rep Rows 2 through 5.

## Neck Shaping

**Row 1 (wrong side):** Sc in first 10 sc: 10 sc; ch 1, turn, leaving rem sts unworked.

**Rows 2 through 9:** Sc in first sc and in each sc across; ch 1, turn. At end of Row 9, do not ch 1. Finish off; weave in ends.

## Left Front

**Row 1:** With wrong side facing, skip next 4 sc on Row 19 of Front Body, join lime with sl st in next sc, ch 1, sc in same sc as joining, sc in each sc across: 19 sc; ch 3, turn.

**Row 2 (right side):** Dc in next sc; *ch 1, skip next sc, CL in next sc; rep from * across to last 2 sc; dc in last 2 sc: 8 CL, 7 chs and 4 dc; ch 1, turn.

**Row 3:** Sc in each CL, dc and ch across, sc in 3rd ch of turning ch-3; ch 1, turn.

**Row 4:** Sc in first sc and in each sc across; ch 1, turn.

**Row 5:** Sc in first sc and in each sc across; ch 3, turn.

**Rows 6 through 13:** Rep Rows 2 through 5 two times more.

**Row 14:** Rep Row 2.

**Row 15:** Sc in each CL, dc and ch across, sc in 3rd ch of turning ch-3. Finish off; weave in ends.

## Armhole Shaping

**Row 1:** With right side facing, skip first 2 sc on Row 15 of Left Front, join white with sl st in next sc, ch 1, sc in same sc as joining, sc in each sc across, changing to blue in last sc: 17 sc; ch 1, turn.

**Rows 2 through 11:** Rep Rows 2 through 11 on Right Front Armhole Shaping. At end of Row 11, do not ch 1. Finish off; weave in ends.

## Neck Shaping

**Row 1:** With wrong side facing, skip first 7 sc on Row 11 of Armhole Shaping, join white with sl st in next sc, ch 1, sc in same sc as joining and in each sc across: 10 sc; ch 1, turn.

**Rows 2 through 9:** Rep Rows 2 through 9 on Right Front Neck Shaping.

## Left Placket

**Row 1:** With wrong side facing, join lime with sl st in edge of first sc on Row 1 of Left Front, ch 1, sc in edge of same row, work 29 more sc evenly spaced in edge of rows on Left Front and Left Front Armhole Shaping, ending with sc in edge of Row 11 of Left Front Armhole Shaping: 30 sc; ch 1, turn.

**Row 2:** Sc in first sc and in each sc across; ch 1, turn.

**Row 3:** Sc in first 3 sc; *ch 2, skip next 2 sc, sc in next 6 sc; rep from * 2 times more; ch 2, skip next 2 sc, sc in last sc: 22 sc and 4 ch-2 sps; ch 1, turn.

**Row 4:** Sc in first sc; *2 sc in next ch-2 sp, sc in next 6 sc; rep from * 2 times more; 2 sc in next ch-2 sp, sc in last 3 sc: 30 sc; ch 1, turn.

**Row 5:** Sc in first sc and in each sc across. Finish off; weave in ends.

## Right Placket

**Row 1:** With wrong side facing, join lime with sl st in edge of first sc on Row 11 of Right Front Armhole Shaping, ch 1, sc in edge of same row, work 29 more sc evenly spaced in edge of rows on Right Front Armhole Shaping and Right Front, ending with sc in edge of Row 1 of Right Front: 30 sc; ch 1, turn.

**Rows 2 through 5:** Sc in first sc and in each sc across; ch 1, turn. At end of Row 5, finish off; weave in ends.

Sew shoulder seams.

## Neck Edging

**Row 1:** With right side facing, join lime with sl st in top edge of Row 5 on Right Placket, ch 1, sc in edge of same row, sc in edge of next 4 rows, sc in next 6 sc on Row 11 of Right Front Armhole Shaping, sc dec in next sc of Right Front Armhole Shaping and in edge of Row 1 of Right Front Neck Shaping, sc in edge of next 9 rows on Right Neck Shaping (Front and Back), sc dec in edge of Row 1 on Right Back Neck Shaping and in next sc on Row 18 of Back Armhole Shaping, sc in next 16 sc on Row 18 of Back Armhole Shaping, sc dec in next sc on Back Armhole Shaping and in edge of Row 1 on Left Back Neck Shaping, sc in edge of next 9 rows on Left Neck Shaping (Back and Front), sc dec in edge of Row 1 on Left Front Neck Shaping and in next sc on Row 11 of Left Front Armhole Shaping, sc in next 6 sc on Row 11, sc in edge of next 5 rows of Left Placket: 60 sc; ch 1, turn.

**Row 2:** Sc in first sc and in each sc around, working sc dec in sc before and after sc dec in each of 4 corners: 52 sc. Finish off; weave in ends.

## Placket and Neck Edging

With right side facing, join lime with sl st in last sc on Row 5 of Right Placket, ch 1, sc in same sc as joining, sc in each sc across Row 5, sc in edge of Rows 1 and 2 of Neck Edging, sc in edge of last sc made, sc in each sc on Row 2 of Neck Edging, sc in edge of last sc made, sc in edge of Rows 2 and 1 of Neck Edging, sc in each sc on Row 5 of Left Placket: 118 sc. Finish off; weave in ends.

Sew bottom edge of Plackets to skipped sc on Row 19 of Front Body between Right Front and Left Front. Sew buttons onto Right Placket.

## SLEEVES (MAKE 2)

Starting at bottom of sleeve, ch 23.

**Row 1 (wrong side):** Sc in 2nd ch from hook and in each rem ch across: 22 sc; ch 1, turn.

**Row 2 (right side):** Sc in first sc and in each sc across; ch 1, turn.

**Row 3:** Work 2 sc in first sc, sc in each sc across to last sc, 2 sc in last sc: 24 sc; ch 3, turn.

**Row 4:** CL in next sc; *ch 1, skip next sc, CL in next sc; rep from * across to last 2 sc; dc in last 2 sc: 11 CL, 10 chs and 3 dc; ch 1, turn.

**Row 5:** Work 2 sc in first dc, sc in each CL, dc and ch across, 2 sc in 3rd ch of turning ch-3: 26 sc; ch 1, turn.

**Rows 6 through 8:** Rep Rows 2 through 4. At end of Row 7: 28 sc.

**Row 9:** Sc in each CL, dc and ch across, sc in 3rd ch of turning ch-3; ch 1, turn.

**Rows 10 and 11:** Rep Rows 2 and 3. At end of Row 11: 30 sc.

**Row 12:** Dc in next sc, CL in next sc; *ch 1, skip next sc, CL in next sc; rep from * across to last sc; dc in last sc: 14 CL, 13 chs and 3 dc; ch 1, turn.

**Row 13:** Rep Row 5: 32 sc.

**Row 14:** Rep Row 2.

**Row 15:** Sc in first sc and in each sc across; ch 3, turn.

**Rows 16 and 17:** Rep Rows 4 and 5. At end of Row 17: 34 sc.

**Rows 18 and 19:** Rep Rows 2 and 3. At end of Row 19: 36 sc. Finish off; weave in ends.

Set in sleeves. Sew sleeve, side and crotch seams.

# Pink Bonnet

**Size:** 3 to 6 months

**Materials**
Light worsted weight yarn
    1 oz med pink
      small amount white (for tassels)
      small amount med blue (for tassels)
      small amount lime (for tassels)
Size F (3.75 mm) crochet hook (or size required for gauge)

**3 LIGHT**

**Gauge**
In pattern, 19 sts = 4"; 17 rows = 4"

## Instructions

### CROWN

Starting at back with pink, ch 23.

**Row 1 (right side):** Sc in 2nd ch from hook and in next 19 chs, 2 sc in next ch , 5 sc in last ch, working in free lps on opposite side of ch, 2 sc in next ch, sc in last 20 chs: 49 sc; ch 1, turn.

**Row 2:** Sc in first 23 sc 2 sc in each of next 3 sc, sc in last 23 sc: 52 sc; ch 2 (counts as hdc on next row now and throughout), turn.

**Row 3:** CL in next sc; *ch 1, skip next sc, CL in next sc*; rep from * to * 11 times more; (ch 1, CL in next sc) 2 times; rep from * to * 11 times more; dc in next sc, hdc in last sc: 26 CL, 25 chs, 1 dc and 2 hdc; ch 1, turn.

**Row 4:** Sc in each CL, dc, hdc and ch across, sc in 2nd ch of turning ch-2: 54 sc; ch 1, turn.

**Rows 5 and 6:** Sc in first sc and in each sc across; ch 1, turn.

**Row 7:** CL in next sc; *ch 1, skip next sc, CL in next SC; rep from * to last 2 sc, hdc in next sc, sc in last sc: 26 CL, 25 chs, 1 hdc and 2 sc; ch 1, turn.

**Row 8:** Sc in each CL, hdc, sc and ch across, sc in turning ch-1: 54 sc; ch 1, turn.

**Rows 9 through 20:** Rep Rows 5 through 8 three times more.

**Row 21:** Rep Row 5. Do not finish off.

### Front Edging
With wrong side facing, (sc, dc) in first sc; *skip next sc, (sc, dc) in next sc; rep from * across to last 3 sc; skip next sc, sc in last 2 sc. Do not finish off.

### Neck Edging
**Row 1 (wrong side):** Working across bottom of crown, sc in edge of last sc made, work 17 more sc evenly spaced across edge of rows to center, work 18 more sc evenly spaced across edge of rows, ending with sc in edge of Front Edging: 36 sc; ch 1, turn.

**Row 2 (right side):** Sc in first sc and in each sc across. Finish off; weave in ends.

### TIES

Cut a piece of pink yarn 9 feet long. Fold piece in half and draw fold through corner of bonnet (last sc on Row 2 of Neck Edging). Insert hook in fold. With both strands of yarn held together, ch 38. Finish off. Cut a piece of pink yarn 10 feet long. Fold piece in half and draw fold through other corner of bonnet (first sc on Row 2 of Neck Edging). Insert hook in fold. With both strands of yarn held together, ch 48. Finish off.

### TASSELS

Make 2 tassels with pink, white, blue and lime according to tassel instructions on page 80. Attach top of tassels to free end of ties.

# Lime Bonnet

**Size:** 3 to 6 months

**Materials**

Light worsted weight yarn
   3/4 oz lime
   1/4 oz med blue
   small amount white (for pompons)
Size F (3.75 mm) crochet hook (or size required for gauge)

**Gauge**

In pattern, 19 sts = 4"; 13 rows = 4"

## Instructions

### CROWN

Starting at back with blue, ch 23.

**Row 1 (right side):** Sc in 2nd ch from hook and in next 19 chs, 2 sc in next ch, 5 sc in last ch, working in free lps on opposite side of ch, 2 sc in next ch, sc in last 20 chs: 49 sc; ch 1, turn.

**Row 2:** Sc in first 23 sc, 2 sc in each of next 3 sc, sc in last 23 sc, changing to lime in last sc: 52 sc. With lime, ch 2 (counts as hdc on next row now and throughout), turn. Finish off blue.

**Row 3:** With lime, CL in next sc; *ch 1, skip next sc, CL in next sc*; rep from * to * 11 times more; (ch 1, CL in next sc) 2 times; rep from * to * 11 times more; dc in next sc, hdc in last sc: 26 CL, 25 chs, 1 dc and 2 hdc: ch 1, turn.

**Row 4:** Sc in each CL, dc, hdc and ch across, sc in 2nd ch of turning ch-2: 54 sc; ch 2, turn.

**Row 5:** CL in next sc; *ch 1, skip next sc, CL in next sc; rep from * across to last 2 sc; dc in next sc, hdc in last sc: 26 CL, 25 chs, 1 dc and 2 hdc: ch 1, turn.

**Rows 6 through 15:** Rep Rows 4 and 5 five times more. At end of Row 15, change to blue in last st. With blue, ch 1, turn. Finish off lime.

### Front Edging

**Row 1 (wrong side):** With blue, sc in each CL, dc, hdc and ch across, sc in 2nd ch of turning ch-2: 54 sc; ch 1, turn.

**Row 2 (right side):** Sc in first sc and in each sc across; ch 1, turn.

**Row 3:** Sc in first sc and in each sc across. Do not finish off.

### Neck Edging

**Row 1 (wrong side):** Working across bottom of crown, sc in edge of last sc made, work 17 more sc evenly spaced across edge of rows to center, work 18 more sc evenly spaced across edge of rows, ending with sc in edge of Row 3 of Front Edging: 36 sc; ch 1, turn.

**Row 2 (right side):** Sc in first sc and in each sc across. Finish off; weave in ends.

### TIES

Cut a piece of blue yarn 9 feet long. Fold piece in half and draw fold through corner of bonnet (last sc on Row 2 of Neck Edging). Insert hook in fold. With both strands of yarn held together, ch 38. Finish off. Cut a piece of blue yarn 10 feet long. Fold piece in half and draw fold through other corner of bonnet (first sc on Row 2 of Neck Edging). Insert hook in fold. With both strands of yarn held together, ch 48. Finish off.

### POMPONS

Make 2 pompons with white, lime and blue according to pompon instructions on page 80. Attach pompons to free end of ties.

# Booties

**Size:** 3 to 6 months

**Materials**

Light worsted weight yarn
   3/4 oz med blue
   small amount lime (for pompons)
   small amount white (for pompons)
Size F (3.75 mm) crochet hook (or size required for gauge)
Stitch markers

**Gauge**

In sc, 19 sts = 4"; 19 rows = 4"

## Instructions (make 2)

### INSTEP

With blue, ch 7. Place marker in first ch.

**Row 1 (right side):** Sc in 2nd ch from hook and in each rem ch across: 6 sc; ch 1, turn.

**Rows 2 through 7:** Sc in first sc and in each sc across; ch 1, turn. At end of Row 7, do not ch 1 and do not turn.

### SIDES

**Rnd 1 (right side):** Ch 18, being careful not to twist ch, join with sl st in free lp of marked ch (move marker to 9th ch of ch-18), ch 1, sc in same ch, sc in free lp of next 5 chs, work 6 sc evenly spaced across edge of rows, sc in each sc in Row 7 of Instep, sc in each ch around: 36 sc; join with sl st in first sc; ch 1, turn.

**Rnds 2 through 5:** Sc in first sc and in each sc around; join as before; ch 1, turn. At end of Rnd 5, do not turn.

### SOLE

**Rnd 1 (right side):** Sc in same sc as joining and in next 5 sc, sc dec in next 2 sc, sc in next 4 sc, sc dec in next 2 sc, sc in next 11 sc, sc dec in next 2 sc, sc in next 2 sc, sc dec in next 2 sc, sc in next 5 sc: 32 sc; join with sl st in first sc.

**Rnd 2:** Ch 1, sc in same sc as joining and in next 5 sc, sc dec in next 2 sc, sc in next 2 sc, sc dec in next 2 sc, sc in next 11 sc, (sc dec in next 2 sc) 2 times, sc in last 5 sc: 28 sc; join as before.

**Rnd 3:** Ch 1, sc in same sc as joining and in next 4 sc, (sc dec in next 2 sc) 2 times, sc in next 10 sc, (sc dec in next 2 sc) 2 times, sc in last 5 sc: 24 sc; join. Finish off.

Sew bottom seam on Sole.

### CUFF

**Row 1:** With right side facing, join blue with sl st in free lp of marked ch on Rnd 1 of Sides, ch 1, sc in same ch, sc in free lp of next 6 chs, sc dec in free lp of next ch and in edge of last row on Instep (skipping last ch on Rnd 1 of Sides), sc in edge of next 5 rows of Instep, sc dec in edge of last row on Instep and in free lp of 2nd ch on Rnd 1 of Sides (skipping first ch), sc in free lp of last 7 chs: 21 sc; ch 1, turn.

**Row 2:** Sc in first sc; *ch 1, skip next sc, sc in next sc; rep from * across: 11 sc and 10 ch-1 sps; ch 3 (counts as dc on next row now and throughout), turn.

**Row 3:** CL in next ch-1 sp;*ch 1, skip next sc, CL in next ch-1 sp; rep from * 8 times more; dc in last sc: 10 CL, 9 chs and 2 dc; ch 1, turn.

**Row 4:** Sc in first dc, sc in each CL and in each ch across, sc in 3rd ch of turning ch-3: 21 sc; ch 3, turn.

**Row 5:** Rep Row 3. At end of row, do not ch 1. Finish off.

Sew back seam of Cuff. Weave in all ends.

## TIES (MAKE 2)

Cut two 8 foot long pieces of blue. With both pieces held together, ch 75. Finish off.

Weave tie through ch-1 sps on Row 2 of Cuff.

## POMPONS

Make 4 pompons with white, lime and blue according to pompon instructions on page 80. Attach pompons to each end of ties.

# Too Cute

"It's so cozy and comfy in my fabulous new clothes, I think I'll just doze off!"

## SPECIAL STITCHES

**To change color:** Work st until 2 lps rem on hook, drop old color, pick up new color and draw through both lps on hook, cut dropped color.

**Sc decrease (sc dec):** Insert hook in first specified st and draw up a lp, insert hook in second specified st and draw up a lp; YO and draw through all 3 lps on hook: sc dec made.

# Blanket

**Size:** 36" x 43"

**Materials**

Light worsted weight yarn
- 6 oz white
- 12 oz lime
- 15 oz mint

Size F (3.75 mm) crochet hook (or size required for gauge)

**Gauge**

In pattern, 20 sts = 4"; 20 rows = 4"

## Instructions

### CENTER

With lime, ch 182.

**Row 1 (right side):** Sc in 2nd ch from hook and in each rem ch across: 181 sc; ch 1, turn.

**Row 2:** Sc in first sc; *tr in next sc, sc in next sc; rep from * across: 181 sts; ch 1, turn.

**Row 3:** Sc in first st and in each st across: 181 sc; ch 1, turn.

**Rows 4 through 7:** Rep Rows 2 and 3 two times more, changing to mint in last sc of Row 7. With mint, ch 1, turn. Finish off lime.

**Rows 8 and 9:** With mint, rep Row 3 two times more, changing to white in last sc of Row 9. With white, ch 1, turn. Finish off mint.

**Rows 10 through 12:** With white, rep Rows 2 and 3, then rep Row 2 once more, changing to mint in last sc of Row 12. With mint, ch 1, turn. Finish off white.

**Row 13:** With mint, rep Row 3, changing to lime in last sc. With lime, ch 1, turn. Finish off mint.

**Row 14:** With lime, rep Row 2, changing to mint in last sc. With mint, ch 1, turn. Finish off lime.

**Row 15:** With mint, rep Row 3, changing to white in last sc. With white, ch 1, turn. Finish off mint.

**Rows 16 through 21:** Rep Rows 10 through 15.

**Rows 22 through 24:** Rep Rows 10 through 12.

**Rows 25 and 26:** With mint, rep Row 3 two times more, changing to lime in last sc of Row 26. With lime, ch 1, turn. Finish off mint.

**Rows 27 through 33:** With lime, rep Row 3, then rep Rows 2 and 3 three times more, changing to mint in last sc of Row 33. With mint, ch 1, turn. Finish off lime.

**Rows 34 through 42:** With mint, rep Rows 2 and 3 four times more, then rep Row 2 once more, changing to lime in last sc of Row 42. With lime, ch 1, turn. Finish off mint.

**Row 43:** With lime, rep Row 3.

**Rows 44 through 159:** Rep Rows 2 through 43 two times more, then rep Rows 2 through 33 once more. At end of Row 159, ch 1, do not change to mint and do not turn. Do not finish off.

### LEFT EDGING

**Row 1 (right side):** With lime, sc in edge of last sc on Row 159, work 154 more sc evenly spaced across left edge of rows: 155 sc; ch 1, turn.

**Row 2:** Sc in first sc; *tr in next sc, sc in next sc; rep from * across: 155 sts; ch 1, turn.

**Row 3:** Sc in first st and in each st across: 155 sc; ch 1, turn.

**Rows 4 through 7:** Rep Rows 2 and 3 two times more, changing to mint in last sc of Row 7. With mint, ch 1, turn. Finish off lime.

**Rows 8 through 15:** With mint, rep Rows 2 and 3 four times more. At end of Row 15, do not ch 1. Finish off mint.

## RIGHT EDGING

**Row 1:** With right side facing, join lime with sl st in edge of first sc in Row 1 of Center, ch 1, sc in edge of same sc, work 154 more sc evenly spaced across right edge of rows: 155 sc; ch 1, turn.

**Rows 2 through 15:** Rep Rows 2 through 15 on Left Edging. At end of Row 15, ch 1, do not turn. Do not finish off.

## TOP EDGING

**Row 1 (right side):** With mint, work 14 sc across edge of rows on Right Edging, sc in each sc across Row 159 of Center, work 14 sc across edge of rows on Left Edging: 209 sc; ch 1, turn.

**Row 2:** Sc in first sc; *tr in next sc, sc in next sc; rep from * across: 209 sts; ch 1, turn.

**Row 3:** Sc in first st and in each st across: 209 sc; ch 1, turn.

**Rows 4 through 9:** Rep Rows 2 and 3 three times more. At end of Row 9, do not ch 1. Finish off.

## BOTTOM EDGING

**Row 1:** With right side facing, join mint with sl st in edge of last sc on last row of Left Edging, ch 1, sc in edge of same sc, work 13 more sc across edge of rows on Left Edging, sc in free lp of each foundation ch at base of each sc on Row 1 of Center, work 14 sc across edge of rows on Right Edging: 209 sc; ch 1, turn.

**Rows 2 through 9:** Rep Rows 2 through 9 on Top Edging. At end of Row 9, ch 1, do not turn. Do not finish off.

## BORDER

**Rnd 1:** With right side facing and mint, work 2 more sc in same st as last sc on Row 9 of Bottom Edging (first corner started); work 7 sc across edge of rows on Bottom Edging, sc in each sc in last row of Right Edging, work 7 sc across edge of rows on Top Edging, 3 sc in first sc in Row 9 of Top edging (corner made), sc in each rem sc in Row 9 of Top Edging across to last sc, work 3 sc in last sc (corner made), work 7 sc across edge of rows on Top Edging, sc in each sc in last row of Left Edging, work 7 sc across edge of rows on Bottom Edging, 3 sc in first sc in Row 9 of Bottom Edging (corner made), sc in each rem sc in Row 9 of Bottom Edging across to last sc, sc in last sc (first corner completed): 764 sc; join with sl st in first sc.

**Rnd 2:** Ch 1, (sc, dc) in same sc as joining (center sc of corner); *skip next sc, (sc, dc) in next sc; rep from * around all 4 sides, working (sc, dc) 2 times in center sc of each of next 3 corners; (sc, dc) in same sc as first sc; join as before. Finish off. Weave in all ends.

**Size:** 3 to 6 months

**Materials**
Light worsted weight yarn
  2 $^1/_2$ oz white
  3 $^3/_4$ oz lime
  $^1/_8$ oz mint

Size F (3.75 mm) crochet hook (or size required for gauge)
Five $^5/_8$" diameter buttons
Matching sewing thread
Sewing needle

**Gauge**
In pattern, 18 sts = 4"; 20 rows = 4"

## Instructions

### BACK

Starting at bottom with lime, ch 49.

**Row 1 (right side):** Sc in 2nd ch from hook and in each rem ch across: 48 sc; ch 1, turn.

**Row 2:** Sc in first sc; *tr in next sc, sc in next sc; rep from * across to last sc; sc in last sc; 48 sts; ch 1, turn.

**Row 3:** Sc in first st and in each st across; 48 sc; ch 1, turn.

**Rows 4 through 34:** Rep Rows 2 and 3 fifteen times more, then rep Row 2 once more, changing to white in last sc of Row 34. With white, ch 1, turn. Finish off lime.

**Row 35:** With white, sc in first st and in each st across. Turn.

### Armhole Shaping

**Row 1 (wrong side):** Sl st in first 3 sc, ch 1, sc in same sc; *tr in next sc, sc in next sc; rep from * 20 times more; sc in next sc: 44 sts; ch 1, turn, leaving rem sts unworked

**Row 2:** Sc in first st and in each st across: 44 sc; ch 1, turn.

**Row 3:** Sc in first sc; *tr in next sc, sc in next sc; rep from * across to last sc; sc in last sc: 44 sts; ch 1, turn.

**Rows 4 through 19:** Rep Rows 2 and 3 eight times more.

**Row 20:** Rep Row 2.

## Left Neck Shaping

**Row 1 (wrong side):** Sc in first 12 sc: 12 sc; ch 1, turn, leaving rem sts unworked.

**Row 2:** Sc in first sc and in each sc across. Finish off; weave in ends.

## Right Neck Shaping

**Row 1:** With wrong side facing, skip next 20 sc on Row 20 of Armhole Shaping, join white with sl st in next sc, ch 1, sc in same sc as joining and in each sc across: 12 sc; ch 1, turn.

**Row 2:** Sc in first sc and in each sc across. Finish off; weave in ends.

## LEFT FRONT

Starting at bottom with lime, ch 23.

**Row 1 (right side):** Sc in 2nd ch from hook and in each rem sc across: 22 sc; ch 1, turn.

**Row 2:** Sc in first sc; *tr in next sc, sc in next sc; rep from * across to last sc; sc in last sc; 22 sts; ch 1, turn.

**Row 3:** Sc in first st and in each st across: 22 sc; ch 1, turn.

**Rows 4 through 34:** Rep Rows 2 and 3 fifteen times more, then rep Row 2 once more, changing to white in last sc of Row 34. With white, ch 1, turn. Finish off lime.

**Row 35:** With white, rep Row 3.

## Armhole Shaping

**Row 1 (wrong side):** Sc in first sc; *tr in next sc, sc in next sc; rep from * 8 times more; sc in next sc, changing to mint: 20 sts. With mint, ch 1, turn, leaving rem sts unworked. Finish off white.

**Row 2:** With mint, sc in first st and in each st across,

changing to lime in last sc: 20 sc. With lime, ch 1, turn. Finish off mint.

**Row 3:** With lime, sc in first sc; *tr in next sc, sc in next sc; rep from * across to last sc; sc in last sc, changing to mint: 20 sts. With mint, ch 1, turn. Finish off lime.

**Row 4:** With mint, sc in first st and in each st across, changing to white in last sc: 20 sc. With white, ch 1, turn. Finish off mint.

**Row 5:** With white, sc in first sc; *tr in next sc, sc in next sc; rep from * across to last sc; sc in last sc: 20 sts; ch 1, turn.

**Row 6:** Sc in first st and in each st across: 20 sc; ch 1, turn.

**Row 7:** Sc in first sc; *tr in next sc, sc in next sc; rep from * across to last sc; sc in last sc, changing to mint: 20 sts. With mint, ch 1, turn. Finish off white.

**Rows 8 through 12:** Rep Rows 2 through 6. At end of Row 12, do not ch 1. Finish off.

## Neck Shaping

**Row 1:** With wrong side facing, skip first 8 sc on Row 12 of Armhole Shaping, join white with sl st in next sc, ch 1, sc in same sc; *tr in next sc, sc in next sc; rep from * across to last sc; sc in last sc: 12 sts; ch 1, turn.

**Row 2:** Sc in first st and in each st across: 12 sc; ch 1, turn.

**Row 3:** Sc in first sc; *tr in next sc, sc in next sc; rep from * across to last sc; sc in last sc: 12 sts; ch 1, turn.

**Rows 4 through 9:** Rep Rows 2 and 3 three times more. At end of Row 9, do not ch 1. Finish off; weave in ends.

## RIGHT FRONT

Starting at bottom with lime, ch 23.

**Row 1 (right side):** Sc in 2nd ch from hook and in each rem ch across: 22 sc; ch 1, turn.

**Row 2:** Sc in first 2 sc; *tr in next sc, sc in next sc; rep from * across: 22 sts; ch l, turn.

**Row 3:** Sc in first st and in each st across: 22 sc; ch l, turn.

**Rows 4 through 34:** Rep Rows 2 and 3 fifteen times more, then rep Row 2 once more, changing to white in last sc on Row 34. With white, ch 1, turn. Finish off lime.

**Row 35:** With white, sc in first st and in each st across. Turn.

### Armhole Shaping

**Row I (wrong side):** Sl st in first 3 sc, ch l, sc in same sc; *sc in next sc, tr in next sc; rep from * across to last sc; sc in last sc, changing to mint: 20 sts. With mint, ch l, turn. Finish off white.

**Row 2:** With mint, sc in first st and in each st across, changing to lime in last sc: 20 sc. With lime, ch l, turn. Finish off mint.

**Row 3:** With lime, sc in first 2 sc; *tr in next sc, sc in next sc; rep from * across, changing to mint in last sc: 20 sts. With mint, ch l, turn. Finish off lime.

**Row 4:** With mint, sc in first st and in each st across, changing to white in last sc: 20 sc. With white, ch l, turn. Finish off mint.

**Row 5:** With white, sc in first 2 sc; *tr in next sc, sc in next sc; rep from * across: 20 sts; ch l, turn.

**Row 6:** Sc in first st and in each st across: 20 sc; ch l, turn.

**Row 7:** Sc in first 2 sc; *tr in next sc, sc in next sc; rep from * across, changing to mint in last sc: 20 sts. With mint, ch 1, turn. Finish off white.

**Rows 8 through 12:** Rep Rows 2 through 6.

### Neck Shaping

**Row I (wrong side):** Sc in first 2 sc; *tr in next sc, sc in next sc; rep from * 4 times more: 12 sts; ch l, turn, leaving rem sts unworked.

**Row 2:** Sc in first st and in each st across: 12 sc; ch l, turn.

**Row 3:** Sc in first 2 sc; *tr in next sc, sc in next sc; rep from * across: 12 sts; ch l, turn.

**Rows 4 through 9:** Rep Rows 2 and 3 three times more. At end of Row 9, do not ch l. Finish off; weave in ends.

### Left Placket

**Row I:** With wrong side facing, join lime with sl st in edge of last sc on Row 1 of Left Front, ch 1, sc in edge of same row, work 44 more sc evenly spaced in edge of rows on Left Front and Left Front Armhole Shaping, ending with sc in edge of Row 12 of Left Front Armhole Shaping: 45 sc; ch 1, turn.

**Row 2:** Sc in first sc and in each sc across; ch l, turn.

**Row 3:** Sc in first 6 sc; *ch 2, skip next 2 sc, sc in next 7 sc; rep from * 3 times more; ch 2, skip next 2 sc, sc in last sc: 35 sc and 5 ch-2 sps; ch l, turn.

**Row 4:** Sc in first sc; *2 sc in next ch-2 sp, sc in next 7 sc; rep from * 3 times more; 2 sc in next ch-2 sp, sc in next 6 sc: 45 sc; ch l, turn.

**Row 5:** Sc in first sc and in each sc across. Finish off; weave in ends.

### Right Placket

**Row I:** With wrong side facing, join lime with sl st in edge of first sc on Row 12 of Right Front Armhole Shaping, ch l, sc in edge of same row, work 44 more sc evenly spaced in edge of rows on Right Front Armhole Shaping and Right Front, ending with sc in edge of Row 1 of Right Front: 45 sc; ch l, turn.

**Rows 2 through 5:** Sc in first sc and in each sc across; ch l, turn. At end of Row 5, do not ch l. Finish off; weave in ends.

Sew shoulder seams.

### Neck Edging

**Row I:** With right side facing, join lime with sl st in top edge of Row 5 on Right Placket, ch l, sc in edge of same row, sc in edge of next 4 rows, sc in next 7 sc on Row 12 of Right Front Armhole Shaping, sc dec in next sc of Right Front Armhole Shaping and in edge of Row 1 of Right Front Neck Shaping, sc in edge of next 9 rows on Right Neck Shaping (Front and Back), sc dec in edge of Row 1 on Right Back Neck Shaping and in next sc on Row 20 of Back Armhole Shaping, sc in next 18 sc on Row 20, sc dec in next sc on Back Armhole Shaping and in edge of Row 1 on Left Back Neck Shaping, sc in edge of next 9 rows on Left Neck Shaping (Back and Front), sc dec in edge of Row 1 on Left Front Neck Shaping and in next sc on Row 12 of Left Front Armhole Shaping, sc in next 7 sc on Row 12, sc in edge of next 5 rows of Left Placket: 64 sc; ch l, turn.

**Row 2:** Sc in first sc and in each sc around, working sc dec in sc before and after sc dec in each of 4 corners (skipping each sc dec): 56 sc. Finish off; weave in ends.

### Placket and Neck Edging

With right side facing, join lime with sl st in last sc on Row 5 of Right Placket, ch l, sc in same sc as joining, sc in each sc across Row 5, sc in edge of Rows 1 and 2 of Neck Edging, sc in edge of last sc made, sc in each st on Row 2 of Neck Edging, sc in edge of last sc made, sc in edge of Rows 2 and 1 of Neck Edging, sc in each sc on Row 5 of Left Placket: 152 sc. Finish off; weave in ends.

Sew buttons onto Right Placket.

## SLEEVES (MAKE 2)

With lime, ch 27.

**Row 1 (right side):** Sc in 2nd ch from hook and in each rem ch across: 26 sc; ch 1, turn.

**Row 2:** Sc in first sc; *tr in next sc, sc in next sc; rep from * across to last sc; sc in last sc: 26 sts; ch 1, turn.

**Row 3:** Sc in first st and in each st across: 26 sc; ch 1, turn.

**Rows 4 through 6:** Rep Rows 2 and 3 once, then rep Row 2 once more.

**Row 7:** Work 2 sc in first sc, sc in each st across to last sc, 2 sc in last sc: 28 sc; ch 1, turn.

**Row 8:** Sc in first 2 sc; *tr in next sc, sc in next sc; rep from * across: 28 sts; ch 1, turn.

**Row 9:** Rep Row 3.

**Row 10:** Sc in first 2 sc; *tr in next sc, sc in next sc; rep from * across, changing to white in last sc: 28 sts. With white, ch 1, turn. Finish off lime.

**Row 11:** With white, rep Row 3: 28 sc.

**Row 12:** Sc in first 2 sc; *tr in next sc, sc in next sc; rep from * across, changing to mint in last sc: 28 sts. With mint, ch 1, turn. Finish off white.

**Row 13:** With mint, sc in first st and in each st across, changing to lime in last sc: 28 sc. With lime, ch 1, turn. Finish off mint.

**Row 14:** With lime, sc in first 2 sc; *tr in next sc, sc in next sc; rep from * across, changing to mint in last sc: 28 sts. With mint, ch 1, turn. Finish off lime.

**Row 15:** With white, rep Row 7: 30 sc.

**Rows 16 through 18:** Rep Rows 2 and 3 once, then rep Row 2 once more.

**Rows 19 and 20:** Rep Rows 7 and 8. At end of Row 19: 32 sc.

**Row 21:** Rep Row 3.

**Row 22:** Rep Row 8.

**Rows 23 through 28:** Rep Rows 15 through 20. At end of Row 23: 34 sc. At end of Row 27: 36 sc.

**Row 29:** Rep Row 7: 38 sc.

**Row 30:** Rep Row 2.

**Row 31:** Rep Row 7: 40 sc. At end of row, do not ch 1. Finish off; weave in ends.

Set in sleeves. Sew sleeve and side seams.

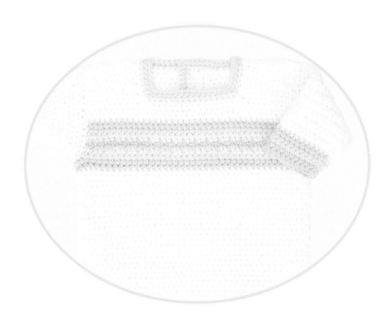

# Shirt

**Size:** 3 to 6 months

## Materials

Light worsted weight yarn
   3 1/2 oz white
   1/8 oz lime
   1/4 oz mint
Size F (3.75 mm) crochet hook (or size required for gauge)
Two 5/8" diameter buttons
Matching sewing thread
Sewing needle

## Gauge

In sc, 18 sts = 4"; 21 rows = 4"

## Instructions

### FRONT

Starting at bottom with white, ch 43.

**Row 1 (wrong side):** Sc in 2nd ch from hook and in each rem ch across: 42 sc; ch 1, turn.

**Row 2 (right side):** Sc in first sc and in each sc across; ch 1, turn.

**Rows 3 through 28:** Rep Row 2 twenty six times more. At end of Row 28, change to lime in last sc. With lime, ch 1, turn. Finish off white.

**Row 29:** With lime, rep Row 2, changing to mint in last sc. With mint, ch 1, turn. Finish off lime.

**Row 30:** With mint, sc in first sc and in each sc across. Turn.

### Armhole Shaping

**Row 1 (wrong side):** Sl st in first 3 sc, ch 1, sc in same sc, sc in each sc across to last 2 sc, changing to white in last sc: 38 sc. With white, ch 1, turn, leaving rem sts unworked. Finish off mint.

**Row 2:** With white, sc in first sc and in each sc across, changing to lime in last sc. With lime, ch 1, turn. Finish off white.

**Row 3:** With lime, sc in first sc; *tr in next sc, sc in next sc; rep from * across to last sc; sc in last sc, changing to white: 38 sts. With white, ch 1, turn. Finish off lime.

**Row 4:** With white, sc in first st and in each st across, changing to mint in last sc: 38 sc. With mint, ch 1, turn. Finish off white.

**Row 5:** With mint, sc in first sc and in each sc across; ch 1, turn.

**Row 6:** Sc in first sc and in each sc across, changing to lime in last sc. With lime, ch 1, turn. Finish off mint.

**Row 7:** With lime, sc in first sc and in each sc across, changing to white in last sc. With white, ch 1, turn. Finish off lime.

**Rows 8 through 11:** With white, sc in first sc and in each sc across; ch 1, turn.

### Left Neck Shaping

**Row 1 (right side):** Sc in first 10 sc: 10 sc; ch 1, turn, leaving rem sts unworked.

**Rows 2 through 9:** Sc in first sc and in each sc across, ch 1, turn. At end of Row 9, do not ch 1. Finish off.

### Right Neck Shaping

**Row 1:** With right side facing, skip next 18 sc on Row 11 of Armhole Shaping, join white with sl st in next sc, ch 1, sc in same sc and in each rem sc across: 10 sc, ch 1, turn.

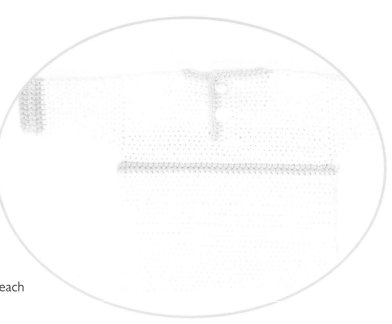

**Rows 2 through 9:** Rep Rows 2 through 9 of Left Neck Shaping.

### BACK

Starting at bottom with white, ch 43.

**Rows 1 through 29:** Rep Rows 1 through 29 on Front.

**Row 30:** With mint, sc in first sc and in each sc across. Finish off.

### Armhole Shaping

**Row 1:** With wrong side facing, skip first 2 sc, join white with sl st in next sc, ch 1, sc in same sc, sc in each sc across to last 2 sc: 38 sc; ch 1, turn.

**Rows 2 through 4:** Sc in first sc and in each sc across; ch 1, turn.

### Left Back

**Row 1 (wrong side):** Sc in first 17 sc: 17 sc; ch 1, turn, leaving rem sts unworked.

**Rows 2 through 14:** Sc in first sc and in each sc across; ch 1, turn.

### Neck Shaping

**Row 1 (wrong side):** Sc in first 10 sc: 10 sc; ch 1, turn, leaving rem sts unworked.

**Row 2:** Sc in first sc and in each sc across. Finish off; weave in ends.

### Right Back

**Row 1:** With wrong side facing, skip next 4 sc on Row 4 of Armhole Shaping, join white with sl st in next sc, ch 1, sc in same sc and in each rem sc across: 17 sc; ch 1, turn.

**Rows 2 through 14:** Sc in first sc and in each sc across; ch 1, turn. At end of Row 14, do not ch 1. Finish off.

## Neck Shaping

**Row 1:** With wrong side facing, skip next 7 sc on Row 14 of Right Back, join white with sl st in next sc, ch 1, sc in same sc and in each sc across: 10 sc; ch 1, turn.

**Row 2:** Sc in first sc and in each sc across. Finish off; weave in ends.

## Right Placket

**Row 1:** With wrong side facing, join white with sl st in edge of first sc on Row 1 of Right Back, ch 1, sc in edge of same row, work 12 more sc evenly spaced in edge of rows on Right Back, ending with sc in edge of Row 14 of Right Back: 13 sc; ch 1, turn.

**Rows 2 and 3:** Sc in first sc and in each sc across; ch 1, turn.

**Row 4:** Sc in first sc; *ch 2, skip next 2 sc, sc in next 4 sc; rep from * once more: 9 sc and 2 ch-2 sps. Finish off.

## Left Placket

**Row 1:** With wrong side facing, join white with sl st in edge of first sc on Row 14 of Left Back, ch 1, sc in edge of same row, work 12 more sc evenly spaced in edge of rows on Left Back, ending with sc in edge of Row 1 of Left Back: 13 sc; ch 1, turn.

**Rows 2 through 4:** Sc in first sc and in each sc across; ch 1, turn. At end of Row 4, do not ch 1. Finish off.

Sew shoulder seams.

## Neck Edging

With right side facing, join white with sl st in top edge of Row 4 on Left Placket, ch 1, sc in edge of same row, sc in edge of next 3 rows, sc in next 6 sc on Row 14 of Left Back, sc dec in next sc of Left Back and in edge of Row 1 of Neck Shaping, sc in edge of next 9 rows on Left Neck Shaping (Back and Front), sc dec in edge of Row 1 of Left Neck Shaping and in next sc on Row 11 of Front Armhole Shaping, sc in next 16 sc on Row 11, sc dec in next sc on Front Armhole Shaping and in edge of Row 1 of Right Front Neck Shaping, sc in edge of next 9 rows on Right Neck Shaping (Front and Back), sc dec in edge of Row 1 of Back Right Neck Shaping and in next sc on Row 14 of Right Back, sc in next 6 sc on Row 14, sc in edge of next 4 rows on Right Placket: 58 sc. Finish off.

## Placket and Neck Edging

**Row 1:** With wrong side facing, join mint with sl st in last sc on Row 4 of Right Placket, ch 1, sc in same sc as joining, sc in next 3 sc, 2 sc in next ch-2 sp, sc in next 4 sc, 2 sc in next ch-2 sp, sc in next sc, sc in edge of Neck Edging, sc in edge of last sc made, sc in each sc of Neck Edging, working sc dec in sc before and after sc dec in each of 4 corners (skipping each sc dec), sc in edge of last sc made, sc in edge of Neck Edging, sc in each sc on Row 4 of Left Placket: 80 sc; ch 1, turn.

**Row 2 (right side):** Sc in first 15 sc, sc in edge of last sc, sc in next 52 sc, sc in edge of last sc, sc in next 15 sc: 84 sc. Finish off; weave in ends.

Sew bottom edges of Plackets to skipped sc on Row 4 of Back Armhole Shaping between Left Back and Right Back. Sew buttons onto Left Placket.

## SLEEVES (MAKE 2)

With lime, ch 23.

**Row 1 (wrong side):** Sc in 2nd ch from hook and in each rem ch across, changing to mint in last sc: 22 sc. With mint, ch 1, turn. Finish off lime.

**Row 2 (right side):** Sc in first sc and in each sc across; ch 1, turn.

**Row 3:** Rep Row 2.

**Row 4:** Work 2 sc in first sc, sc in each sc across to last sc, 2 sc in last sc, changing to lime in last sc: 24 sc. With lime, ch 1, turn. Finish off mint.

**Row 5:** With lime, sc in first sc and in each sc across, changing to white in last sc. With white, ch 1, turn. Finish off lime.

**Rows 6 and 7:** With white, rep Row 2 two times more.

**Row 8:** Work 2 sc in first sc, sc in each sc across to last sc, 2 sc in last sc: 26 sc; ch 1, turn.

**Rows 9 through 11:** With white, rep Row 2 three times more.

**Row 12:** Rep Row 8: 28 sc.

**Rows 13 through 20:** Rep Rows 9 through 12 two times more. At end of Row 16: 30 sc. At end of Row 20: 32 sc.

**Row 21:** With white, rep Row 2.

**Row 22:** Rep Row 8: 34 sc.

**Rows 23 and 24:** With white, rep Row 2 two times more.

**Row 25:** Rep Row 8: 36 sc. At end of row, do not ch 1. Finish off; weave in ends.

Set in sleeves. Sew sleeve and side seams.

# Pants with Booties

**Size:** 3 to 6 months

**Materials**

Light worsted weight yarn
    3³/₄ oz lime
    small amount white (for pompons)
    small amount mint (for pompons)

Size F (3.75 mm) crochet hook (or size required for gauge)
¹/₂" wide elastic, 17" long

**Gauge**

In pattern, 18 sts = 4"; 20 rows = 4"

## Instructions

### PANTS BACK

#### Left Leg

Starting at bottom of leg with lime, ch 13.

**Row 1 (right side):** Sc in 2nd ch from hook and in each rem ch across: 12 sc; ch 1, turn.

**Row 2:** Sc in first sc; *tr in next sc, sc in next sc; rep from * across to last sc; sc in last sc: 12 sts; ch 1, turn.

**Row 3:** Sc in first st and in each st across: 12 sc; ch 1, turn.

**Row 4:** Rep Row 2.

**Row 5:** Work 2 sc in first st, sc in each rem st across: 13 sc; ch 1, turn.

**Row 6:** Sc in first sc; *tr in next sc, sc in next sc; rep from * across: 13 sts; ch 1, turn.

**Row 7:** Rep Row 3: 13 sc.

**Row 8:** Rep Row 6.

**Row 9:** Rep Row 5: 14 sc.

**Row 10:** Rep Row 2: 14 sts.

**Rows 11 through 18:** Rep Rows 3 through 10. At end of Row 13: 15 sc. At end of Row 17: 16 sc.

**Rows 19 through 22:** Rep Rows 3 through 6. At end of Row 21: 17 sc.

**Row 23:** Rep Row 5: 18 sc.

**Rows 24 through 26:** Rep Rows 4 through 6. At end of Row 25: 19 sc. At end of Row 26, do not ch 1. Finish off; weave in ends.

#### Right Leg

Starting at bottom of leg with lime, ch 13.

**Row 1 (right side):** Sc in 2nd ch from hook and in each rem ch across: 12 sc; ch 1, turn.

**Row 2:** Sc in first sc; *sc in next sc, tr in next sc; rep from * across to last sc; sc in last sc: 12 sts; ch 1, turn.

**Row 3:** Sc in first st and in each st across: 12 sc; ch 1, turn.

**Row 4:** Rep Row 2.

**Row 5:** Sc in first st and in each st across to last st, 2 sc in last st: 13 sc; ch 1, turn.

**Row 6:** Sc in first sc; *tr in next sc, sc in next sc; rep from * across: 13 sts; ch 1, turn.

**Row 7:** Rep Row 3: 13 sc.

**Row 8:** Rep Row 6.

**Row 9:** Rep Row 5: 14 sc.

**Row 10:** Rep Row 2: 14 sts.

**Rows 11 through 18:** Rep Rows 3 through 10. At end of Row 13: 15 sc. At end of Row 17: 16 sc.

**Rows 19 through 22:** Rep Rows 3 through 6. At end of Row 21: 17 sc.

**Row 23:** Rep Row 5: 18 sc.

**Rows 24 through 26:** Rep Rows 4 through 6. At end of Row 25: 19 sc. At end of Row 26, do not finish off.

### Body

**Row 1 (right side):** Sc in first st and in each st across Row 26 on Right Leg, pick up Left leg, with right side facing, sc dec in same st as last sc on Right Leg and in first sc on Row 26 of Left Leg, sc in same st and in each st across Row 26 of Left Leg: 39 sc; ch 1, turn.

**Row 2:** Sc in first sc; *tr in next st, sc in next sc; rep from * across: 39 sts; ch 1, turn.

**Row 3:** Work 2 sc in first st, sc in each st across to last st, 2 sc in last st: 41 sc; ch 1, turn.

**Row 4:** Sc in first sc; *sc in next sc, tr in next st; rep from * across to last 2 sc; sc in last 2 sc: 41 sts; ch 1, turn.

**Row 5:** Sc in first st and in each st across: 41 sc; ch 1, turn.

**Rows 6 through 19:** Rep Rows 4 and 5 seven times more.

**Row 20:** Rep Row 4.

**Row 21:** Sc dec in first 2 sc, sc in each st across to last 2 sc, sc dec in last 2 sc: 39 sc; ch 1, turn.

**Row 22:** Rep Row 2.

**Row 23:** Rep Row 5.

**Row 24:** Sc in first 18 sc, sc dec in next 2 sc, sc in each sc across: 38 sc; ch 1, turn. Do not finish off.

### Waistband

**Row 1 (right side):** Sl st in front lp of each sc across: 38 sl sts; ch 1, turn.

**Row 2:** Sc in back lp of each sc on Row 24 of Body: 38 sc; ch 1, turn.

**Rows 3 and 4:** Sc in first sc and in each sc across; ch 1, turn.

**Rows 5 through 8:** Rep Rows 1 through 4, working sc in Row 6 in back lp of each sc on Row 4 of Waistband. At end of Row 8, do not ch 1. Finish off; weave in ends.

## PANTS FRONT

### Right Leg

Work same as Back Left Leg.

### Left Leg

Work same as Back Right Leg.

### Body

**Row 1 (right side):** Sc in first st and in each st across Row 26 on Left Leg, pick up Right leg, with right side facing, sc dec in same st as last sc on Left Leg and in first sc on Row 26 of Right Leg, sc in same st and in each st across Row 26 of Right Leg: 39 sc; ch 1, turn.

**Rows 2 through 24:** Work same as Rows 2 through 24 on Back Body.

### Waistband

Work same as Back Waistband.

### Assembly

With wrong sides facing, joining front and back together, sew side and crotch seams. Sew ends of elastic together. Fold Row 8 of Waistband back over elastic to wrong side and sew Waistband seam.

## BOOTIES (MAKE 2)

### Instep

With lime, ch 7. Place marker in first ch.

**Row 1 (right side):** Sc in 2nd ch from hook and in each rem ch across: 6 sc; ch 1, turn.

**Rows 2 through 6:** Sc in first sc and in each sc across; ch 1, turn.

**Row 7:** Sc in first sc and in each sc across. Do not turn.

### Sides

**Rnd 1 (right side):** Ch 18, being careful not to twist ch, join with sl st in free lp of marked ch (move marker to 9th ch of ch-18), ch 1, sc in same ch, sc in free lp of next 5 chs, work 6 sc evenly spaced across edge of rows, sc in each sc on Row 7 of Instep, sc in each rem ch around, join with sl st in first sc: 36 sc; ch 1, turn.

**Rnd 2:** Sc in first sc and in each sc around; join as before; ch 1, turn.

**Rnds 3 through 5:** Rep Row 2 three times more. At end of Rnd 5, do not turn.

### Sole

**Rnd 1 (right side):** Sc in same sc as joining and in next 5 sc, sc dec in next 2 sc, sc in next 4 sc, sc dec in next 2 sc, sc in next 11 sc, sc dec in next 2 sc, sc in next 2 sc, sc dec in next 2 sc, sc in next 5 sc: 32 sc; join with sl st in first sc.

**Rnd 2:** Ch 1, sc in same sc as joining and in next 5 sc, sc dec in next 2 sc, sc in next 2 sc, sc dec in next 2 sc, sc in next 11 sc, (sc dec in next 2 sc) 2 times, sc in last 5 sc: 28 sc; join as before.

**Rnd 3:** Ch 1, sc in same sc as joining and in next 4 sc, (sc dec in next 2 sc) 2 times, sc in next 10 sc, (sc dec in next 2 sc) 2 times, sc in last 5 sc: 24 sc; join. Finish off.

Sew bottom seam on Sole.

## Cuff

**Row 1:** With right side facing, join lime with sl st in free lp of marked ch on Rnd 1 of Sides, ch 1, sc in same ch, sc in free lp of next 8 chs, work 6 sc evenly spaced across edge of Instep rows, sc in free lp of next 9 chs: 24 sc; ch 1, turn.

**Row 2:** Sc in first sc and in each sc around; ch 1, turn.

**Row 3:** Sc in first sc; *ch 1, skip next sc, sc in next sc; rep from * across to last sc; sc in last sc: 13 sc and 11 ch-1 sps; ch 1, turn.

**Row 4:** Sc in each sc and in each ch-1 sp across. Finish off; weave in ends.

Sew back seam on Cuff. Sew bootie to pant leg. Weave in all ends.

### TIES (MAKE 2)

Cut two 8 foot long pieces of lime. With both pieces held together, ch 75. Finish off.

Weave ties through ch-1 sps on Row 3 of each Cuff.

### POMPONS

Make 4 pompons with white, lime and mint according to pompon instructions on page 80. Attach pompons to each end of ties.

# Romper

**Size:** 3 to 6 months

**Materials**
Light worsted weight yarn
6 oz mint
Four ⁵⁄₈" diameter buttons
Matching sewing thread
Sewing needle

**Gauge**
In pattern, 19 sts = 4"; 19 rows = 4"
22 sc rows = 4"

## Instructions

### BACK

#### Left Leg

Starting at bottom of leg, ch 13.

**Row 1 (right side):** Sc in 2nd ch from hook and in each rem ch across: 12 sc; ch 1, turn.

**Row 2:** Sc in first sc; *tr in next sc, sc in next sc; rep from * across to last sc; sc in last sc: 12 sts; ch 1, turn.

**Row 3:** Sc in first st and in each st across: 12 sc; ch 1, turn.

**Row 4:** Rep Row 2.

**Row 5:** Work 2 sc in first st, sc in each rem st across: 13 sc; ch 1, turn.

**Row 6:** Sc in first sc; *tr in next sc, sc in next sc; rep from * across: 13 sts; ch 1, turn.

**Row 7:** Rep Row 3: 13 sc.

**Row 8:** Rep Row 6.

**Row 9:** Rep Row 5: 14 sc.

**Row 10:** Rep Row 2: 14 sts.

**Rows 11 through 18:** Rep Rows 3 through 10. At end of Row 13: 15 sc. At end of Row 17: 16 sc.

**Rows 19 through 22:** Rep Rows 3 through 6. At end of Row 21: 17 sc.

**Row 23:** Rep Row 5: 18 sc.

**Rows 24 through 26:** Rep Rows 4 through 6. At end of Row 25: 19 sc. At end of Row 26, do not ch 1. Finish off; weave in ends.

### Right Leg

Starting at bottom of leg, ch 13.

**Row 1 (right side):** Sc in 2nd ch from hook and in each rem ch across: 12 sc; ch 1, turn.

**Row 2:** Sc in first sc; *sc in next sc, tr in next sc; rep from * across to last sc; sc in last sc: 12 sts; ch 1, turn.

**Row 3:** Sc in first st and in each st across: 12 sc; ch 1, turn.

**Row 4:** Rep Row 2.

**Row 5:** Sc in first st and in each st across to last sc, 2 sc in last sc: 13 sc; ch 1, turn.

**Row 6:** Sc in first sc; *tr in next sc, sc in next sc; rep from * across: 13 sts; ch 1, turn.

**Row 7:** Rep Row 3: 13 sc.

**Row 8:** Rep Row 6.

**Row 9:** Rep Row 5: 14 sc.

**Row 10:** Rep Row 2: 14 sts.

**Rows 11 through 18:** Rep Rows 3 through 10. At end of Row 13: 15 sc. At end of Row 17: 16 sc.

**Rows 19 through 22:** Rep Rows 3 through 6. At end of Row 21: 17 sc.

**Row 23:** Rep Row 5: 18 sc.

**Rows 24 through 26:** Rep Rows 4 through 6. At end of Row 25: 19 sc. At end of Row 26, do not finish off.

### Body

**Row 1 (right side):** Sc in first st and in each st across Row 26 on Right Leg, pick up Left leg, with right side facing, sc dec in same st as last sc on Right Leg and in first sc on Row 26 of Left Leg, sc in same st and in each st across Row 26 of Left Leg: 39 sc; ch 1, turn.

**Row 2:** Sc in first sc; *tr in next sc, sc in next sc; rep from * across: 39 sts; ch 1, turn.

**Row 3:** Work 2 sc in first sc, sc in each st across to last sc, 2 sc in last sc: 41 sc; ch 1, turn.

**Row 4:** Sc in first sc; *sc in next sc, tr in next sc; rep from * across to last 2 sc; sc in last 2 sc: 41 sts; ch 1, turn.

**Row 5:** Sc in first st and in each st across: 41 sc; ch 1, turn.

**Rows 6 through 18:** Rep Rows 4 and 5 six times more, then rep Row 4 once more.

**Row 19:** Rep Row 3: 43 sc.

**Row 20:** Rep Row 2: 43 sts.

**Row 21:** Rep Row 5: 43 sc.

**Rows 22 through 38:** Rep Rows 20 and 21 eight times more, then rep Row 20 once more.

**Row 39:** Sc in first 20 sts, sc dec in next 2 sts, sc in next 21 sts: 42 sc; ch 1, turn.

**Rows 40 and 41:** Sc in first sc and in each sc across; ch 1, turn.

### Armhole Shaping

**Row 1 (wrong side):** Sl st in first 3 sc, ch 1, sc in same sc and in each sc across to last 2 sc: 38 sc; ch 1, turn, leaving rem sts unworked.

**Rows 2 through 18:** Sc in first sc and in each sc across; ch 1, turn.

### Left Neck Shaping

**Row 1 (wrong side):** Sc in first 10 sc: 10 sc; ch 1, turn, leaving rem sts unworked.

**Row 2:** Sc in first sc and in each sc across. Finish off.

### Right Neck Shaping

**Row 1:** With wrong side facing, skip next 18 sc on Row 18 of Armhole Shaping, join with sl st in next sc, ch 1, sc in same sc as joining and in each rem sc across: 10 sc; ch 1, turn.

**Row 2:** Sc in first sc and in each sc across. Finish off.

## FRONT

### Right Leg

Work same as Back Left Leg.

### Left Leg

Work same as Back Right Leg.

### Body

**Row 1 (right side):** Sc in first st and in each st across Row 26 on Left Leg, pick up Right leg, with right side facing, sc dec in same st as last sc on Left Leg and in first sc on Row 26 of Right Leg, sc in same st and in each st across Row 26 of Right Leg: 39 sc; ch 1, turn.

**Rows 2 through 21:** Work same as Rows 2 through 21 on Back Body.

### Right Front

**Row 1 (wrong side):** Sc in first sc; *tr in next sc, sc in next sc; rep from * 8 times more: 19 sts; ch 1, turn, leaving rem sts unworked.

**Row 2 (right side):** Sc in first st and in each st across: 19 sc; ch 1, turn.

**Rows 3 through 18:** Rep Rows 1 and 2 eight times more.

**Rows 19 and 20:** Sc in first sc and in each sc across; ch 1, turn.

**Row 1 (wrong side):** Sl st in first 3 sc, ch 1, sc in same sc and in each sc across: 17 sc; ch 1, turn.

**Rows 2 through 11:** Sc in first sc and in each sc across; ch 1, turn. At end of Row 11, finish off.

**Row 1:** With right side facing, skip first 7 sc, join with sl st in next sc, ch 1, sc in same sc as joining and in each sc across: 10 sc; ch 1, turn.

**Rows 2 through 9:** Sc in first sc and in each sc across; ch 1, turn. At end of Row 9, do not ch 1. Finish off; weave in ends.

**Row 1:** With wrong side facing, skip next 5 sc on Row 21 of Front Body, join with sl st in next sc, ch 1, sc in same sc as joining; *tr in next sc, sc in next sc; rep from * 8 times more: 19 sts; ch 1, turn.

**Rows 2 through 20:** Rep Rows 2 through 20 on Right Front.

**Row 1 (wrong side):** Sc in first 17 sc: 17 sc; ch 1, turn, leaving rem sts unworked.

**Rows 2 through 11:** Sc in first sc and in each sc across; ch 1, turn.

**Row 1:** Sc in first 10 sc: 10 sc; ch 1, turn leaving rem sts unworked.

**Rows 2 through 9:** Sc in first sc and in each sc across; ch 1, turn. At end of Row 9, do not ch 1. Finish off; weave in ends.

**Row 1:** With wrong side facing, join with sl st in edge of first sc on Row 1 of Left Front, ch 1, sc in edge of same row, work 29 more sc evenly spaced in edge of rows on Left Front and Left Front Armhole Shaping, ending with sc in edge of Row 11 of Left Front Armhole Shaping: 30 sc; ch 1, turn.

**Row 2:** Sc in first sc and in each sc across; ch 1, turn.

**Row 3:** Sc in first 3 sc; *ch 2, skip next 2 sc, sc in next 6 sc; rep from * 2 times more; ch 2, skip next 2 sc, sc in last sc: 22 sc and 4 ch-2 sps; ch 1, turn.

**Row 4:** Sc in first sc; *2 sc in next ch-2 sp, sc in next 6 sc; rep from * 2 times more; 2 sc in next ch-2 sp, sc in last 3 sc: 30 sc; ch 1, turn.

**Row 5:** Sc in first sc and in each sc across. Finish off; weave in ends.

**Row 1:** With wrong side facing, join with sl st in edge of last sc on Row 11 of Right Front Armhole Shaping, ch 1, sc in edge of same row, work 29 more sc evenly spaced in edge of rows on Right Front Armhole Shaping and Right Front, ending with sc in edge of Row 1 of Right Front: 30 sc; ch 1, turn.

**Rows 2 through 5:** Sc in first sc and in each sc across; ch 1, turn. At end of Row 5, finish off; weave in ends.

Sew shoulder seams.

**Row 1:** With right side facing, join with sl st in top edge of Row 5 on Right Placket, ch 1, sc in edge of same row, sc in edge of next 4 rows, sc in next 6 sc on Row 11 of Right Front Armhole Shaping, sc dec in next sc of Right Front Armhole Shaping and in edge of Row 1 of Right Front Neck Shaping, sc in edge of next 9 rows on Right Neck Shaping (Front and Back), sc dec in edge of Row 1 on Right Back Neck Shaping and in next sc on Row 18 of Back Armhole Shaping, sc in next 16 sc on Row 18 of Back Armhole Shaping, sc dec in next sc on Back Armhole Shaping and in edge of Row 1 on Left Back Neck Shaping, sc in edge of next 9 rows on Left Neck Shaping (Back and Front), sc dec in edge of Row 1 on Left Front Neck Shaping and in next sc on Row 11 of Left Front Armhole Shaping, sc in next 6 sc on Row 11, sc in edge of next 5 rows of Left Placket: 60 sc; ch 1, turn.

**Row 2:** Sc in first sc and in each sc around, working sc dec in sc before and after sc dec in each of 4 corners: 52 sc. Finish off; weave in ends.

With right side facing, join with sl st in last sc on Row 5 of Right Placket, ch 1, sc in same sc as joining, sc in each sc across Row 5, sc in edge of Rows 1 and 2 of Neck Edging, sc in edge of last sc made, sc in each sc on Row 2 of Neck Edging, sc in edge of last sc made, sc in edge of Rows 2 and 1 of Neck Edging, sc in each sc on Row 5 of Left Placket: 118 sc. Finish off; weave in ends.

Sew bottom edge of Plackets to skipped sc on Row 21 of Front Body between Right Front and Left Front. Sew buttons onto Right Placket.

### SLEEVES (MAKE 2)

Starting at bottom of sleeve, ch 23.

**Row 1 (right side):** Sc in 2nd ch from hook and in each rem ch: 22 sc; ch 1, turn.

**Row 2:** Sc in first sc; *tr in next sc, sc in next sc; rep from * across to last sc; sc in last sc: 22 sts; ch 1, turn.

**Row 3:** Sc in first st and in each st across: 22 sc; ch 1, turn.

**Row 4:** Rep Row 2.

**Row 5:** 2 sc in first st, sc in each st across to last st, 2 sc in last st: 24 sc; ch 1, turn.

**Rows 6 through 8:** Sc in first sc and in each sc across; ch 1, turn.

**Row 9:** Rep Row 5: 26 sc.

**Rows 10 through 12:** Rep Row 6 three times more.

**Rows 13 through 20:** Rep Rows 9 through 12 two times more. At end of Row 20: 30 sc.

**Rows 21 through 25:** Rep Rows 5 and 6 two times more, then rep Row 5 once more. At end of Row 25: 36 sc. Finish off. Weave in ends.

Set in sleeves. Sew sleeve, side and crotch seams.

# Hat

**Size:** 3 to 6 months

### Materials

Light worsted weight yarn
  1 3/4 oz lime
  small amount white (for pompons)
  small amount mint (for pompons)
Size F (3.75 mm) crochet hook (or size required for gauge)

**3 LIGHT**

### Gauge

Rnds 1 through 8 = 3" diameter

### Special Stitch

Sc decrease (sc dec): Insert hook in first specified st and draw up a lp, insert hook in second specified st and draw up a lp; YO and draw through all 3 lps on hook: sc dec made.

## Instructions

### CROWN

Starting in center with lime ch 3; join with sl st to form a ring.

**Rnd 1 (wrong side):** Ch 1, 6 sc in ring: 6 sc; join with sl st in first sc; ch 1, turn.

**Rnd 2 (right side):** 2 sc in first sc and in each sc around: 12 sc; join as before; ch 1, turn.

**Rnd 3:** Sc in first sc, 2 sc in next sc; *sc in next sc, 2 sc in next sc; rep from * around: 18 sc; join; ch 1, turn.

**Rnd 4:** Sc in first 2 sc, 2 sc in next sc; *sc in next 2 sc, 2 sc in next sc; rep from * around: 24 sc; join; ch 1, turn.

**Rnd 5:** Sc in first 3 sc, 2 sc in next sc; *sc in next 3 sc, 2 sc in next sc; rep from * around: 30 sc; join; ch 1, turn.

**Rnd 6:** Sc in first 4 sc, 2 sc in next sc; *sc in next 4 sc, 2 sc in next sc; rep from * around: 36 sc; join; ch 1, turn.

**Rnd 7:** Sc in first 5 sc, 2 sc in next sc; *sc in next 5 sc, 2 sc in next sc; rep from * around: 42 sc; join; ch 1, turn.

**Rnd 8:** Sc in first 6 sc, 2 sc in next sc; *sc in next 6 sc, 2 sc in next sc; rep from * around: 48 sc; join; ch 1, turn.

**Rnd 9:** Sc in first 7 sc, 2 sc in next sc; *sc in next 7 sc, 2 sc in next sc; rep from * around: 54 sc; join; ch 1, turn.

**Rnd 10:** Sc in first 8 sc, 2 sc in next sc; *sc in next 8 sc, 2 sc in next sc; rep from * around: 60 sc; join; ch 1, turn.

**Rnd 11:** Sc in first 9 sc, 2 sc in next sc; *sc in next 9 sc, 2 sc in next sc; rep from * around: 66 sc; join; ch 1, turn.

**Rnd 12:** Sc in first sc and in each sc around; join; ch 1, turn.

**Rnds 13 through 19:** Rep Rnd 12 seven times more.

**Rnd 20:** Sc in back lp of first sc and in back lp of each sc around; join; ch 1, turn.

**Rnds 21 through 23:** Rep Rnd 12 three times more. At end of Rnd 23, finish off; weave in ends.

## EAR FLAPS

### Right Flap

**Row 1:** With right side facing, skip first 9 sc on Rnd 23, join lime with sl st in next sc, ch 1, sc in same sc as joining, sc in next 9 sc: 10 sc; ch 1, turn.

**Row 2:** Sc in first sc and in each sc across; ch 1, turn.

**Row 3:** Sc dec in first 2 sc, sc in each sc across to last 2 sc, sc dec in last 2 sc: 8 sc; ch 1, turn.

**Rows 4 through 8:** Rep Rows 2 and 3 two times more, then rep Row 2 once more. At end of Row 5: 6 sc. At end of Row 7: 4 sc.

**Row 9:** Sc in first 2 sc, sc dec in last 2 sc: 3 sc; ch 1, turn.

**Row 10:** Rep Row 2.

**Row 11:** Skip first sc, sc dec in last 2 sc: 1 sc. Finish off; weave in ends.

### Left Flap

**Row 1:** With right side facing, skip next 29 sc on Rnd 23, join lime with sl st in next sc, ch 1, sc in same sc as joining, sc in next 9 sc: 10 sc; ch 1, turn.

**Rows 2 through 11:** Rep Rows 2 through 11 on Left Flap.

### Edging

**Row 1:** With wrong side facing, join lime with sl st in 2nd sc on Rnd 23, ch 1, (sc, dc) in same sc as joining; *skip next sc, (sc, dc) in next sc*; rep from * to * 2 times more; ***(sc, dc) in edge of Row 1 of flap, **skip next row, (sc, dc) in edge of next row**; rep from ** to ** 3 times more on same edge of flap, (sc, dc) in sc dec and in ch-1 sp on Row 11 of flap; rep from ** to ** 5 times more on other edge of same flap***; rep from * to * 14 times more across Rnd 23; rep from *** to *** on edges of other flap; (sc, dc) in next sc on Rnd 23; rep from * to * 4 times more: 94 sts; join with sl st in first sc. Finish off; weave in ends.

## BRIM

**Row 1:** With right side facing and flaps at bottom, join lime with sl st in front lp of first sc on Rnd 19, ch 1, sc in front lp of same sc and in next 7 sc; *2 sc in front lp of next sc, sc in front lp of next 9 sc, 2 sc in front lp of next sc, sc in front lp of next 8 sc; rep from * 2 times more; 2 sc in front lp of last sc: 73 sc; ch 1, turn.

**Rows 2 through 5:** Sc in first sc and in each sc across; ch 1, turn.

**Row 6:** Sc in first sc; *tr in next sc, sc in next sc; rep from * across: 73 sts; ch 1, turn.

**Row 7:** Sc in first st and in each st across: 73 sc; ch 1, turn.

**Rows 8 through 15:** Rep Rows 6 and 7 four times more. At end of Row 15, do not ch 1. Finish off; weave in ends.

Sew back seam of Brim. Fold first 5 rows of Brim down and last 10 rows of Brim up.

## TIES

Cut a piece of lime yarn 9 feet long. Fold piece in half and draw fold through bottom of ear flap. Insert hook in fold. With both strands of yarn held together, ch 38. Finish off. Cut a piece of lime yarn 10 feet long. Fold piece in half and draw fold through bottom of other ear flap. Insert hook in fold. With both strands of yarn held together, ch 48. Finish off.

## POMPONS

Make 2 pompons with white, lime and mint according to pompon instructions on page 80. Attach pompons to free end of ties.

# Bonnet

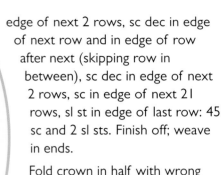

**Size:** 3 to 6 months

**Materials**
Light worsted weight yarn
   1 oz lime
   small amount white
     (for tassels)
   small amout mint (for tassels)
Size F (3.75 mm) crochet hook
   (or size required for gauge)

**Gauge**
In pattern, 19 sts = 4"; 19 rows = 4"

## Instructions

### CROWN

Starting at bottom with lime, ch 18.

**Row 1 (right side):** Sc in 2nd ch from hook and in each rem ch across: 17 sc; ch 1, turn.

**Row 2:** Sc in first sc; *tr in next sc, sc in next sc; rep from * across: 17 sts; ch 1, turn.

**Row 3:** Work 2 sc in first sc, sc in next st and in each st across to last sc, 2 sc in last sc: 19 sc; ch 1, turn.

**Row 4:** Sc in first sc; *sc in next sc, tr in next sc; rep from * across to last 2 sc; sc in last 2 sc: 19 sts; ch 1, turn.

**Row 5:** Rep Row 3: 21 sc.

**Row 6:** Rep Row 2: 21 sts.

**Row 7:** Sc in first st and in each st across: 21 sc; ch 1, turn.

**Rows 8 through 46:** Rep Rows 6 and 7 nineteen times more, then rep Row 6 once more.

**Row 47:** Sc dec in first 2 sts, sc in next st and in each st across to last 2 sts, sc dec in last 2 sts: 19 sts; ch 1, turn.

**Row 48:** Rep Row 4.

**Row 49:** Rep Row 47: 17 sts.

**Row 50:** Rep Row 2.

**Row 51:** Rep Row 7. At end of row, do not ch 1. Finish off; weave in ends.

### Back Edging

**Row 1:** With wrong side facing, join lime with sl st in edge of first sc on Row 51, sc in edge of next 21 rows; sc dec in edge of next 2 rows, sc dec in edge of next row and in edge of row after next (skipping row in between), sc dec in edge of next 2 rows, sc in edge of next 21 rows, sl st in edge of last row: 45 sc and 2 sl sts. Finish off; weave in ends.

Fold crown in half with wrong side together and short ends matching. Sew back seam along Back Edging.

### Front Edging

**Row 1:** With right side facing, join lime with sl st in edge of last sc on Row 51, ch 1, sc in edge of same row, sc in edge of next 24 rows, 2 sc in edge of next row, sc in edge of last 25 rows: 52 sc; ch 1, turn.

**Row 2:** Sc in first sc; *tr in next sc, sc in next sc; rep from * across to last sc; sc in last sc: 52 sts; ch 1, turn.

**Row 3:** Sc in first st and in each st across: 52 sc; ch 1, turn.

**Row 4:** Rep Row 2. Do not ch 1 or turn.

### Neck Edging

**Row 1:** With wrong side facing, working across bottom of crown, work 36 sc evenly spaced across edge of Front and Back Edgings, last row of crown and free lps of foundation ch: 36 sc; ch 1, turn.

**Row 2:** Sc in first sc and in each sc across. Finish off; weave in ends.

### TIES

Cut a piece of lime yarn 9 feet long. Fold piece in half and draw fold through corner of bonnet (first sc on Row 2 of Neck Edging). Insert hook in fold. With both strands of yarn held together, ch 38. Finish off. Cut a piece of lime yarn 10 feet long. Fold piece in half and draw fold through other corner of bonnet (last sc on Row 2 of Neck Edging). Insert hook in fold. With both strands of yarn held together, ch 48. Finish off.

### TASSELS

Make 2 tassels with white, lime and mint according to tassel instructions on page 80. Attach top of tassels to free end of ties.

# Booties

**Size:** 3 to 6 months

**Materials**

Light worsted weight yarn

**3 LIGHT**

    $^1/_2$ oz mint

    small amount white (for pompons)

    small amount lime (for pompons)

Size F (3.75 mm) crochet hook (or size required for gauge)

Stitch markers

**Gauge**

In sc, 19 sts = 4"; 19 rows = 4"

## Instructions

### BOOTIES (MAKE 2)

#### Instep

With mint, ch 7. Place marker in first ch.

**Row 1 (right side):** Sc in 2nd ch from hook and in each rem ch across: 6 sc; ch 1, turn.

**Rows 2 through 7:** Sc in first sc and in each sc across; ch 1, turn. At end of Row 7, do not ch 1 and do not turn.

#### Sides

**Rnd 1 (right side):** Ch 18, being careful not to twist ch, join with sl st in free lp of marked ch (move marker to 9th ch of ch-18), ch 1, sc in same ch, sc in free lp of next 5 chs, work 6 sc evenly spaced across edge of rows, sc in each sc on Row 7 of Instep, sc in each rem ch around: 36 sc; join with sl st in first sc; ch 1, turn.

**Rnds 2 through 5:** Sc in first sc and in each sc around; join as before; ch 1, turn. At end of Rnd 5, do not turn.

#### Sole

**Rnd 1 (right side):** Sc in same sc as joining and in next 5 sc, sc dec in next 2 sc, sc in next 4 sc, sc dec in next 2 sc, sc in next 11 sc, sc dec in next 2 sc, sc in next 2 sc, sc dec in next 2 sc, sc in next 5 sc: 32 sc; join with sl st in first sc.

**Rnd 2:** Ch 1, sc in same sc as joining and in next 5 sc, sc dec in next 2 sc, sc in next 2 sc, sc dec in next 2 sc, sc in next 11 sc, (sc dec in next 2 sc) 2 times, sc in last 5 sc: 28 sc; join as before.

**Rnd 3:** Ch 1, sc in same sc as joining and in next 4 sc, (sc dec in next 2 sc) 2 times, sc in next 10 sc, (sc dec in next 2 sc) 2 times, sc in last 5 sc: 24 sc; join. Finish off.

Sew bottom seam on Sole.

#### Cuff

**Row 1:** With right side facing, join mint with sl st in free lp of marked ch on Rnd 1 of Sides, ch 1, sc in same ch, sc in free lp of next 6 chs, sc dec in free lp of next ch and in edge of last row on Instep (skipping last ch on Rnd 1 of Sides), sc in edge of next 5 rows of Instep, sc dec in edge of last row on Instep and in free lp of 2nd ch on Rnd 1 of Sides (skipping first ch), sc in free lp of last 7 chs: 21 sc; ch 1, turn.

**Row 2:** Sc in first sc; *ch 1, skip next sc, sc in next sc; rep from * across: 11 sc and 10 ch-1 sps; ch 1, turn.

**Row 3:** Sc in each sc and in each ch-1 sp across: 21 sc; ch 1, turn.

**Row 4:** Sc in first sc; *tr in next sc, sc in next sc; rep from * around: 21 sts; ch 1, turn.

**Row 5:** Sc in first st and in each st across: 21 sc; ch 1, turn.

**Rows 6 and 7:** Rep Rows 4 and 5. At end of Row 7, do not ch 1. Finish off.

Sew back seam on Cuff. Weave in all ends.

### TIES (MAKE 2)

Cut two 8 foot long pieces of mint. With both pieces held together, ch 75. Finish off.

Weave tie through ch-1 sps on Row 2 of Cuff.

### POMPONS

Make 4 pompons with white, lime and mint according to pompon instructions on page 80. Attach pompons to each end of ties.

# General Directions

## Abbreviations and Symbols

Crochet patterns are written in a special shorthand which is used so that instructions don't take up too much space. They sometimes seem confusing, but once you learn them, you'll have no trouble following them.

## Abbreviations

| | |
|---|---|
| Beg | beginning |
| CL(S) | cluster(s) |
| Ch(s) | chain(s) |
| Dc | double crochet |
| Dec | decrease |
| Hdc | half double crochet |
| Inc | Increase(ing) |
| Lp(s) | loop(s) |
| Mm | millimeters |
| Oz | ounces |
| Prev | previous |
| Rem | remaining |
| Rep | repeat(ing) |
| Rnd(s) | round(s) |
| Sc | single crochet |
| Sl st | slip stitch |
| Sp(s) | space(s) |
| St(s) | stitch(es) |
| Tog | together |
| Tr | triple crochet |
| YO | yarn over hook |

## These are Standard Symbols

*An asterisk (or double asterisks**) in a pattern row, indicates a portion of instructions to be used more than once. For instance, "rep from * three times" means that after working the instructions once, you must work them again three times for a total of 4 times in all.

: The number of stitches after a colon tells you the number of stitches you will have when you have completed the row or round.

( ) Parentheses enclose instructions which are to be worked the number of times following the parentheses. For instance, "(ch 1, sc, ch1) 3 times" means that you will chain one, work one sc, and then chain one again three times for a total of six chains and three sc's.

Parentheses often set off or clarify a group of stitches to be worked into the same space of stitch. For instance, " (dc, ch 2, dc) in corner sp".

[ ] Brackets and ( ) parentheses are also used to give you additional information.

## Terms

**Join**—This means to join with a sl st unless another stitch is specified.

**Finish Off**—This means to end your piece by pulling the cut yarn end through the last loop remaining on the hook. This will prevent the work from unraveling.

**Continue in Pattern as Established**— This means to follow the pattern stitch as it has been set up, working any increases or decreases in such a way that the pattern remains the same as it was established.

**Work even**—This means that the work is continued in the pattern as established without increasing or decreasing.

## Gauge

This is probably the most important aspect of crocheting!

Gauge simply means the number of stitches per inch, and the number of rows per inch that result from a specified yarn worked with a hook in a specified size. But since everyone crochets differently—some loosely, some tightly, some in between—the measurements of individual work can vary greatly, even when the crocheters use the same pattern and the same size yarn and hook.

If you don't work to the gauge specified in the pattern, your project will never be the correct size, and you may not have enough yarn to finish your project. The hook size given in the instructions is merely a guide and should never be used without a gauge swatch.

To make a gauge swatch, crochet a swatch that is about 4" square, using the suggested hook and the number of stitches given in the pattern. Measure your swatch. If the number of stitches is fewer than those listed in the pattern, try making another swatch with a smaller hook. If the number of stitches is more than is called for in the pattern, try making another swatch with a larger hook. It is your responsibility to make sure you achieve the gauge specified in the pattern.

## Pompons

Cut a piece of cardboard 3" wide and as long as you want the diameter of your finished pompon to be. Wind the yarn around the cardboard until it is approximately ¹/2" thick in the middle (**Fig. 1**). Carefully slip the yarn off the cardboard and firmly tie an 18" length of yarn around the middle

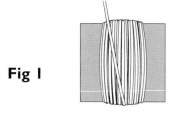

**Fig 1**

(**Fig 2**). Leave yarn ends long enough to attach the pompon. Cut the loops on both ends and trim the pompon into a smooth ball (**Fig 3**).

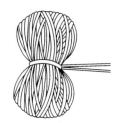

**Fig 2**

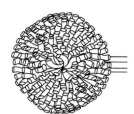

**Fig 3**

## Tassels

Cut a piece of cardboard about 6" wide and the desired length of the finished tassel. Wind the yarn around the length of the cardboard the number of times necessary to make the desired tassel. Cut a piece of yarn about 20" long and thread a double strand into a tapestry needle. Insert the needle through all strands at the top of the cardboard, pull up tightly and knot securely, leaving ends for attaching. Cut the yarn at the opposite end of the cardboard, and remove the cardboard.

Cut another strand of yarn 12" long and wrap it tightly twice around the tassel approximately ¹/2" below the top knot. Knot securely and allow excess ends to fall in as part of the tassel.

## Crochet Terminology

The patterns in this book have been written using the crochet terminology that is used in the United States. Terms which may have different equivalents in other parts of the world are listed below.

| United States | International |
| --- | --- |
| Double crochet (dc) | treble crochet (tr) |
| Double triple crochet (dtc) | triple treble crochet (ttr) |
| Gauge | tension |
| Half double crochet (hdc) | half treble crochet (htr) |
| Single crochet | double crochet |
| Skip | miss |
| Slip stitch | single crochet |
| Triple crochet | double treble crochet (dtr) |
| Yarn over (YO) | yarn forward (yfwd) |
| Yarn over (YO) | yarn around needle (yrn) |

## CROCHET HOOKS CONVERSION CHART

| U.S. | B-1 | C-2 | D-3 | E-4 | F-5 | G-6 | H-8 | I-9 | J-10 | K-10¹/2 | N | P | Q |
| --- | --- | --- | --- | --- | --- | --- | --- | --- | --- | --- | --- | --- | --- |
| Metric | 2.25 | 2.75 | 3.25 | 3.5 | 3.75 | 4 | 5 | 5.5 | 6 | 6.5 | 9 | 10 | 15 |

**Produced by The Creative Partners™, LLC. • Managing Editor: Susan Lowman • Book Design: Joyce Lerner**

Every effort has been made to ensure the accuracy of these instructions. We cannot, however, be responsible for human error or variations in your work.